'How is constitutional review to be institutionally reconciled with democracy? Dennis Dixon offers an account of the resolution offered by the Human Rights Act in Britain. While informed and critical, his analysis gives us an illuminating picture of the issues at stake and the aspects of that controversial arrangement that are worth celebrating. Even if the Act is overturned, the book will remain essential reading for anyone focused on this crucial question in democratic theory and design'.

Philip Pettit, L.S.Rockefeller University Professor of Human Values,
Princeton University; Distinguished Professor of Philosophy,
Australian National University

'At a time of increasing tensions between the judiciary and government, not just in the UK, but around the world, this book is a must read. Are judicial decisions upholding human rights anti-democratic in their genesis and character? By contrast, should governments be held to greater judicial account; is this in fact the true nature of democracy? This book approaches these and other questions in a lively and accessible manner. I recommend it to all students of constitutional democracy'.

Michelle Everson, Professor of Law, Birkbeck College,
University of London

'In a radical departure from traditional norms of the common law, the Human Rights Act 1998 empowered judges to assess the proportionality of legislation which democratically elected politicians have put in place. In an innovative and refreshing approach to the subject, the author explores the implications of this change in the constitutional balance between Parliament and Courts. Drawing heavily of analytical tools borrowed from republican political thought, he makes an invaluable contribution to the contemporary debate'.

Jonathan Fisher QC, Member,
Commission on a Bill of Rights for the UK, 2011–2012

Democracy and the Human Rights Act

This book discusses the extent to which the UK Human Rights Act successfully balances protection of rights and democracy. It is generally accepted that the Act prevents government from violating fundamental rights, but the extent to which the Act can legitimately be overridden as a result of public opinion and participation is less clear.

The work considers the Act's effect on this popular element of the British Constitution. It uses analytical tools from republican political theory to explore the claim that the Act achieved a reconciliation between the protection of rights and democracy. In particular, it employs republican analysis of domination to consider how the Human Rights Act could operate so that public opinion invigilates legislative responses to judicial decisions. The key question is whether judicial decisions under the Human Rights Act serve to 'remove, reduce or replace' opportunities for the electorate to control judicial decision-making, remembering always that the electorate is seldom engaged in politics, but should it choose to, its ability to do so is at the heart of democracy. The study also examines the difficulty of isolating national constitutional forms where bills of rights are internationalised as with the European Convention on Human Rights.

The book will be a valuable resource for students and academics researching constitutional legal theory and comparative constitutional law. While the focus is on the UK HRA, broader theoretical issues of constitutional review will have significant international interest and relevance to domestic debates on a British Bill of Rights.

Dennis Dixon is a Legal Adviser to the Law Officers' Department of the States of Jersey, and tutor at the Institute of Law, Jersey.

Routledge Research in Constitutional Law
Series Editor: David Marrani

This series features thought-provoking and original scholarship on constitutional law and theory. Books explore key topics, themes and questions in the field with a particular emphasis on comparative studies. Where relevant, titles will engage with political and social theory, philosophy and history in order to offer a rounded analysis of constitutions and constitutional law.

Available titles in this series include:

Freedom of Speech
Importing European and US constitutional models in transitional democracies
Uladzislau Belavusau

Colonial and Post-colonial Constitutionalism in the Commonwealth
Peace, Order and Good Government
Hakeem O. Yusuf

Dynamics in the French Constitution
Decoding French Republican Ideas
David Marrani

Constitutionalism in the Global Realm
A Sociological Approach
Poul F. Kjaer

The Legal Philosophy and Influence of Jeremy Bentham
Essays on 'Of the Limits of the Penal Branch of Jurisprudence'
Edited by Guillaume Tusseau

The Internet and Constitutional Law
The protection of fundamental rights and constitutional adjudication in Europe
Edited by Oreste Pollicino and Graziella Romeo

The Accountability Gap in EU law
Marios Costa

Equal Citizenship, Civil Rights, and the Constitution
The Original Sense of the Privileges or Immunities Clause
Christopher R. Green

Democracy and the Human Rights Act

Republican Analysis of Citizen Power

Dennis Dixon

Routledge
Taylor & Francis Group
LONDON AND NEW YORK

First published 2017 by Routledge

2 Park Square, Milton Park, Abingdon, Oxfordshire OX14 4RN
52 Vanderbilt Avenue, New York, NY 10017

Routledge is an imprint of the Taylor & Francis Group, an informa business

First issued in paperback 2018

British Library Cataloguing in Publication Data
A catalogue record for this book is available from the British Library

Library of Congress Cataloging in Publication Data
Names: Dixon, Dennis, author.
Title: Democracy and the Human Rights Act : republican analysis of citizen power / Dennis Dixon.
Description: Abingdon, Oxon ; New York, NY : Routledge, 2017. | Series: Routledge research in constitutional law | Includes bibliographical references and index.
Identifiers: LCCN 2016050973 | ISBN 978-1-138-24276-0 (hardback)
Subjects: LCSH: Human rights—Great Britain. | Human rights—Political aspects—Great Britain. | Great Britain. Human Rights Act 1998.
Classification: LCC KD4080 .D59 2017 | DDC 342.4108/5—dc23LC record available at https://lccn.loc.gov/2016050973

ISBN: 978-1-138-24276-0 (hbk)
ISBN: 978-0-367-19660-8 (pbk)

Typeset in Galliard
by FiSH Books Ltd, Enfield

To Maria, Carmen and Oliver.

Contents

Preface

This book started life as a PhD on the Human Rights Act undertaken part-time at Birkbeck College from early in 2009. At the time the possibility of change to the Human Rights Act was a distant prospect. By the time I completed by viva in May 2016, the Act itself was imminently under threat. Completing the PhD and, even more so, the revisions for this book has been to some extent a race to complete before history moved on.

It was not entirely a race for relevance. The book focuses on the Human Rights Act, but the essential ideas are of broader application to the perennial problem of the counter-majoritarian problem, particularly in the context of 'weak-form' constitutionally review. It is unlikely that reform of the Human Rights Act will lead to a British Bill of Rights where judges could strike down primary legislation, and even less likely that they would have this power without even a 'notwithstanding clause' to allow Parliament to override such decisions. This being so, the book should retain relevance whatever the future of the Human Rights Act.

The basic idea developed in the course of the PhD is that the balance of rights and democracy must view democracy through the eyes of the citizens. This means citizens who seldom participate, but expect to have their way when they participate in great numbers. The thesis started with the republican theory of Philip Pettit, whose analysis of 'domination' well illustrates the importance and practical nature of popular power in a democracy. Later I accumulated other inspirations such as Robert Dahl, David Beetham and Anthony Downs, whose ideas were synthesised into what I believe is a realistic view of democracy. Directed towards the problem of the counter-majoritarian effect and the Human Rights Act, the conclusion is essentially that legislative override will amount to a 'legitimate breach' when the demand for such override can genuinely be traced back to public opinion. Whether a political culture can arise where this possibility can exist in balance with a general observance of constitutional review remains to be seen. As with all reforms, it would be a matter of experiment.

In reaching this point, I would in particular like to thank Adam Geary, my supervisor, for his patience and suggestions; my 'upgrade viva examiners' (Costas Douzinas and Bill Bowring) for pointing me towards David

Beetham's work; Claire De Than for her assistance on the international effectiveness of the European Convention on Human Rights (ECHR) obligations; and Dr Arif Ahmed for vetting Chapter 3 for philosophical blunders. Most of all I would like to thank my wife, Maria, for her patience. Along the way we have gained two children, moved house three times and moved countries once, and without her support I could not have finished it.

1 Introduction

Lord Justice Laws, speaking judicially, said of the Human Rights Act: 'Its structure, as has more than once been observed, reveals an elegant balance between respect for Parliament's legislative supremacy and the legal security of the Convention rights' (*International Transport Roth Gmbh v Secretary of State for the Home Department* [2002] EWCA Civ 158; [2003] QB 728 [71]).

The Human Rights Act brought constitutional review to the United Kingdom, which is to say made it possible for courts to review primary legislation for compliance with published constitutional or human rights. As the above quote from Laws LJ suggests, it did so by maintaining the supremacy of democracy. Introducing the legislation, the Lord Chancellor, Lord Irvine, described the then Human Rights Bill as being 'carefully drafted and designed to respect our traditional understanding of the separation of powers' (HL Debates, 1997a: col. 1228). The Government White Paper preceding the Act stressed the importance in a democracy of maintaining the supremacy of the 'elected, accountable and representative' House of Commons (White Paper, 1997: [2.13]). Lord Scarman, one of the longest standing proponents of introducing constitutional review to Britain, argued that '[t]he quality of the Bill is that it recognises that in a democracy, the democratically elected assembly – for us, that is Parliament – must be sovereign' (HL Debate, 1997a: col. 1256).

Despite many such claims and plaudits, the Human Rights Act remains a matter of political controversy and public debate in the United Kingdom. Whereas the Canadian equivalent, the Charter of Rights and Freedoms, had within its first twenty years reached a politically unassailable position in national political culture (Manfredi, 2001: pp. 187–188), the Human Rights Act's very existence in the United Kingdom remains one of active political controversy. The Conservative Party (2015) manifesto for the 2015 election promised reform of constitutional review in terms of introducing a 'British Bill of Rights' in place of the Human Rights Act. In the course of the EU Referendum debate, the then Home Secretary, Theresa May, argued not for 'Brexit' from European Union but from the European Convention on Human Rights ('ECHR' or 'the Convention') (BBC Online, 2016). The prospects of such action appeared to recede in the aftermath of the referendum vote to leave the European Union, but since then the new Justice Secretary has placed the creation of a British Bill of Rights in place of the Human Rights Act on the agenda, although with no plan to denounce the ECHR itself (Elgot, 2016; Wilkinson, 2016). Whatever might happen in the near future, the nature of constitutional review in Britain is a live subject for political debate.

However, whilst the immediate subject matter of this book may be in danger of being abolished, the fundamental issue addressed in the book will remain. There appears to be no intention to abolish constitutional review in the United Kingdom. The intention appears to be to create a British Bill of Rights. Similarly, there appears to be no intention to denounce the European Convention, but instead to sever the interpretative link between that Convention and British human rights adjudication. If a British Bill of Rights were to be enacted, there appears to be no suggestion that it will give domestic judges greater power than exists under the present Human Rights Act. The central issue of whether the Human Rights Act achieved the 'elegant balance' asserted by Lord Justice Laws centres on the importance of judges having no power to set aside Acts of Parliament, but being limited in terms of direct consequences to an interpretative power. As such the issue of whether the Human Rights Act achieved the putative 'elegant balance' will remain of importance whether because the Act itself remains, or the body of the Act forms the basis of a British Bill of Rights, or as a case study for the possibly intractable question of whether an effective bill of rights can co-exist with an effective power to ignore judicial decisions made under it.

The elegant balance

This 'elegant balance' hypothesis can be stated simply. The Human Rights Act operates as a bill of rights in that it sets out a list of fundamental rights by incorporating rights protected by the European Convention. The courts interpret the meaning of these rights, and decide whether any derogations are justified in any particular case. The power of the courts is subject to limitations where primary legislation was concerned. When faced with primary legislation that conflicts with the requirements of the Act, the courts cannot set aside the offending statute. The courts can either (a) under section 3(1) of the Act seek an alternative rights-compatible interpretation of the statute concerned, or (b) issue a declaration of incompatibility under section 4, if such an interpretation is impossible. If a declaration of incompatibility is issued, then there is a fast-track procedure for introducing remedial legislation, which requires affirmative resolutions on the part of both Houses of Parliament rather than the full procedure for passing Acts of Parliament. Parliament is entitled to ignore declarations of incompatibility, and can overturn purposive interpretations. Parliament is free to exercise its sovereignty as regards individual decisions of the courts. The Human Rights Act does not dictate what the law must or must not be – as, for example, is the case when the US Supreme Court strikes down an Act of Congress. Instead, the Act directs the minds of the government and legislature to the human rights issues, and ensures that there is a fully reasoned human rights analysis on which legislators can focus. The Human Rights Act focuses Parliamentary attention on rights issues not just through litigation: section 19 requires that a Minister presenting a Bill to Parliament should either make a 'statement of compatibility', or make a formal request that Parliament should proceed despite possible incompatibility.

The Human Rights Act thus incorporated procedures that bring human rights issues to the fore. It requires ministers to seek legal advice on whether their proposals were human rights-compatible; and at the other end of the process, litigation would give ministers and legislators a reasoned judgment on how incompatible legislation offended human rights. And, of course, behind the workings of the Human Rights Act in the United Kingdom stands the Convention at the international level. Lord Bingham in the Human Rights Bill debate stressed that the Bill would provide a mechanism to reduce the need for British cases to be brought to Strasbourg, and for British case law to influence that of the European Court of Human Rights ('ECtHR' or 'Strasbourg') (HL Debates, 1997a: col. 1245). However, the Act was structured so as to also keep the Convention to an extent at arm's length. The decisions of the ECtHR lack direct authority in the United Kingdom. As a matter of domestic law, the case law of Strasbourg is something for domestic courts to 'take into account'. The ECtHR's decisions do not pass into domestic law – as a matter of the legislative response to such decisions, Parliament's freedom (such as it is) to ignore international law obligations was unchanged.

The reconciliation or balance sought in the Human Rights Act addressed a fundamental tension in modern constitutional thought that arises whenever a system of constitutional review is created to protect fundamental rights. It is, as Bickel (1962, p. 16) explained: '[t]he root difficulty is that judicial review is a counter-majoritarian force in our system', yet 'democracies do live by the idea, central to the process of gaining the consent of the governed, that the majority has the ultimate power to displace the decision makers and to reject any part of their policy', (p. 27). However, the counter-majoritarian effect is not a side-effect of constitutional review but a goal. It is precisely the fear that democratic process may violate human rights that forms the principal justification offered for creating systems of constitutional, although an extensive study has suggested that legislators' motives are often less noble, including a desire to guarantee the continuation of their policies following anticipated electoral defeats (Ginsberg and Versteeg, 2013, p. 587).

For this reason, the subject of constitutional review inherently exists in the context of a debate on achieving, as Baroness Hale said, 'a fair balance, between the universal values of freedom and equality embodied in the Convention, and the particular choices made by the democratically elected

Parliaments of the member states' (Hale, 2011: p. 21). There are of course those in the debate whose views are inherently hostile to compromising one or other of those principles. There is the argument that Parliament should be unfettered, which is often based on a faith that 'Parliament may possess power to enact evil laws, but can be trusted not to do so' (Goldsworthy, 2000; p. 704). And there are fears that Parliamentary Sovereignty may be the route to enacting oppressive regimes, as was the case with apartheid legislation in South Africa (Goldsworthy, 1999: pp. 260–261). Sir Stephen Sedley (2015; pp. 273–275), writing recently, put forward the examples of Nazi Germany and apartheid South Africa as to why the rule of law requires restraints on the range of decisions that might be taken by a legislature, a point also made by Danny Friedman (2016: pp. 384–385). The Human Rights Act is structured so as to neither wholly accept nor wholly reject faith in Parliament nor fear of what it might do. The Act was drafted keeping in mind competing worries about 'majority tyranny' (Ely, 1980: pp. 7–8), and 'the counter-majoritarian effect' (Bickel, 1962: p. 16). Faith in Parliament is not so strong as to leave primary legislation outside of judicial scrutiny, but nor is that faith so weak as to deny Parliament the final word speaking in its ordinary way through statutes. The balance struck is somewhat in-between, but the question is: 'where?' Janet Hiebert (2015: pp. 57–58) has argued that a lack of debate on how the two sides of the balance should be reconciled has led to unprincipled opportunism: 'a willingness to invoke whichever one perspective best serves the argument at hand'.

Republicanism and democracy

It is, of course, possible to deny the utility of such an investigation. Firstly, it might be argued that there is no genuinely democratic side to the constitution worth investigating. Secondly, it might be argued that democracy inherently includes rights protection, so everything is on the same side of the metaphorical balance.

We shall see that, for many, a realistic view of democracy is one of power concentrating in elites who rule a largely passive electorate – this elitist (or Schumpeterian) version seeing democracy largely in terms of enforcing governance (Schumpeter, 2011: pp. 284–296; Arora and Awasthy, 2007; p. 107; Sunstein, 1988: p. 1556). If this view is correct, then any weaknesses in democratic control of government and legislation – weaknesses in what Dicey (2008: pp. 8–9) described as the link between public opinion and legislative change – would be intractable. This would doubtless affect concern for the 'democratic' side of the rights/democracy balance. For example, Richard Clayton and Aileen Kavanagh have separately questioned how strong democratic concerns should be in the debate on constitutional review matters given that the link between public opinion and legislation is often weak or even non-existent (Clayton, 2004; p. 40; Kavanagh, 2009: p. 376; see also Fredman, 2001: pp. 199–200). Against this, John Hart Ely

(1980: p. 67) notably argued that the cure for too little democracy ought to be *more* not *less* democracy. But if the elitist (Schumpeterian) approach is correct and Ely's ideal solution of 'more democracy' is not in practice available, then the counter-majoritarian objection to constitutional review would be irrelevant. All that would have changed was the nature of the decision makers, not the electorate's control over the state, which, *ex hypothesi*, would remain illusory.

The second way of undermining the very utility of the investigation is the opposite of that described in the last paragraph: instead of narrowing our understanding of democracy so that the electorate's concerns are sidelined, we could expand our understanding so as to internalise rights protection within our concept of democracy. This is essentially the 'rights-based' concept of democracy particularly associated with Professor Jowell (2003: p. 597) – the argument that there are substantive values which are component parts of democracy. We shall return to this in the next chapter.

However, it should be stressed that neither of the above arguments address the counter-majoritarian difficulty. The democracy-based objection to constitutional review cannot be seen as a philosophical debate around the true nature of democracy, but must be seen from the perspective of citizens and their position in the state. If a citizen objects that judges are overruling the concerns of the public in matters of importance, then it is no answer to say that, probably understood, democracy allows for, or requires, such a judicial power to exist. Citizens are interested in where power lies, in their relationship to it, and whether the resulting system will work well or badly. Abstract arguments over whether '[our] notion of 'democracy' … is no longer synonymous with 'majority rule' (Jowell, 2006: p. 575), or whether the rule of law requires substantive rights protections (Sedley, 2015: pp. 273–275; Bingham, 2010: pp. 66–84), collapse the distinction between the benefits of constitutional review and the citizen's power in the state. Anthony Downs (1957: p. 150), concluding his original economic theory of democracy, argued: 'The way every government actually makes decisions depends upon the nature of the fundamental power relation between the governors and the governed in its society'. The 'governed', are entitled to know their position in this fundamental relationship – and should be fully informed when making constitutive choices (Bingham, 2010: p. 170). An analysis of the impact of a system of constitutional review on democracy is thus the analysis of how far, within the relevant constitutional forms and practice, the effect of constitutional review is within the reach of public opinion.

Republican theory

The twin claims of the 'elegant balance' is that the Human Rights Act gives the judiciary a power to interfere with legislative and executive decisions by reason of protecting fundamental rights, but that such power is subject through Parliamentary Sovereignty to a still-dominant force in the shape of democratic decision-making. The reality of the political power to restrain judicial power of interference, and the electorate's relationship with that power, require close and realistic analysis. This book will take as its principal theoretical framework Philip Pettit's (2008; 2009, pp. 42–49; 2012, pp. 26–74) systematisation of power relationships, identifying where relationships of domination exist or do not exist. It is an approach which can be used, without being laden in predetermining value judgments, to reveal the 'fundamental power relation between the governors and the governed'.

Applying Pettit's analysis, we will argue that democracy in any system of government, depends on the following proposition: any individual must be able to think rightly that, 'If a majority of fellow citizens can be convinced that X is right, then we-over-time can achieve X'. If such a majority in public opinion can be formed, then there is no veto-holding power that must be convinced, nor any external force that must be overcome. This does not mean that there are no influences external to public opinion that affect decision-making calculations, but such influences either (a) work by affecting public opinion by contributing to electors' reasoning, what Pettit describes as a 'co-reasoning' role, (b) are always subject to correction if the external influence promotes ideas unacceptable to public opinion, what Pettit describes as a power of 'counter-control' (Pettit, 2008: pp. 116–118), or (c) are part of the facts of life that government needs to address, as opposed to an attempt to influence government.

At the heart of a citizen's political freedom is the freedom to choose laws and policies insofar as this is consistent with his or her political equality with other citizens. This freedom of undominated choice amounts to the ability to think and think rightly, 'I can do that' (Pettit, 2008: pp. 110–111), which in a representative democracy amounts to a less egotistical, 'if a majority of fellow citizens come to share my opinion, we-over-time can do that'. It would be impossible for a citizen to think that and be right where constitutional review is determinative as to what must or must not be done. Constitutional review might make the citizen's 'we-can-do-that' hypothesis become contingent on judicial support ('we-can-do-that, but we must also gain judicial permission'), or might even become wholly independent of achieving majority support ('we-can-do-that, and need only to convince the judges'). In such cases the freedom to choose would be subject to domination external to a body of equal citizens. The judges will exercise what Pettit calls 'alien control'.

Democratic theory

Having set out the tools of analysis for power relationships, it will be necessary to apply those tools in due course to the British constitution as affected by the Human Rights Act. To do so first, the generalised republican analysis of non-domination must be brought within an understanding of democracy itself. What will be set out is an approach which identifies the different levels of decision-making and deliberation within a democracy, and then draws from Robert Dahl's theory of 'polyarchy' and David Beetham's 'democratic audit' to create a practical analysis congruent with Pettit's analysis of domination.

The republican ideal is that there should be a system of popular control which is 'properly individualised, unconditioned and effective' (Pettit, 2012: p. 279; see also p. 302). However, Pettit set out a 'dual-aspect' theory of democracy in that the citizens are free to choose systems which fall short of a democratic ideal. In every choice as to voting system, terms of office, use of referenda, use of bills of rights, there are issues of democracy, efficiency, and stability. The expression of individual opinion within a system of government and legislation is by participating in the political system as constituted. The key form of participation is the act of voting, whether voting for representatives or directly for laws. Without public voting any actual citizen participation in public debate is not systematically connected to legislative change. A system of democracy is a system for participation – where electors may decide how to vote and seek to influence the voting decisions of others. Democracy is, as David Beetham's democratic audit demonstrates, a matter of formal constitutional structures and social qualities – 'the quality and vitality of a country's democracy will be revealed in the character of its civil society as well as its political institutions' (Beetham, 1999: p. 166). The theory of 'polyarchy' expounded by Robert Dahl is instructive. Any system of democracy with a representative element (which means any imaginable, workable system) will give immediate power to elected politicians and officials. Unless the electorate, meaning all electors as individuals, can participate in decision-making on a position of equality, the system will tend towards a 'closed-hegemony'; but, insofar as the system permits such participation, it can be called a 'polyarchy'. Democracy is never obtained. Instead, a polyarchy, by being open to the public exercising their participatory rights to displace the power of politicians and officials, will tend towards democracy (Dahl, 1956, pp. 63–89; 1971a; 1971b; 1989: pp. 225–264; 2000).

A constitution will represent choices as to how public opinion should control government and legislation. A constitution may incorporate direct democracy recognising public opinion in the terms of majority votes for specific outcomes. A constitution may cause public opinion to be mediated entirely through elected representatives – in which case democracy might be limited to the proposition that 'specific policies will rarely violate highly ranked, intense, stable, and relatively broad preferences of the greater number for a longer period than about the interval between elections' (Dahl and Lindblom 1953; p. 314). Control by the public means control over the choices that the elected representatives make. The practical extent of popular control in such a system will depend significantly on how far the electorate avail themselves of the opportunity to participate. Pettit (2012; pp. 230, 268–269) admitted that public opinion operates often as a 'reserve' power, not obviously actively inhibiting politicians and administrators in their day-to-day choices.

How far a system operates as a democracy thus depends on (1) the decisions as to how to constitute the system of government, and (2) the habits of participation by the electorate within the system. The creation and maintenance of a system of constitutional review is a decision by the constituting power (which ought to be the electorate, directly or indirectly) to introduce and maintain a counter-majoritarian element into the constitution. In doing this, the electorate needs to make an informed choice as to the nature of that counter-majoritarian element. As Lord Bingham said of any future introduction of a judicial power to overturn primary legislation, such a reform 'should be only made if the British people, properly informed, choose to make it' (Bingham, 2010: p. 170). It cannot be right to wilfully create constitutional forms that misrepresent reality. If Lord Lester is right to dismiss the practical significance of retaining Parliamentary Sovereignty (Lester, 1998: p. 668), then the retention of Parliamentary Sovereignty may misdirect citizens as to the nature of the constitution. The nature of judicial power and its impact on the electorate's ability to make its opinions a controlling force in the constituted power needs to be understood without any red herrings or constitutional smoke and mirrors.

We will place the debate into a realistic description of the electorate's role in a democracy, and in the British constitution in particular.

Approach of this thesis

At the heart of the 'elegant balance' is the effect of the Human Rights Act on the relationship between 'public opinion' and 'legislation'. Dicey analysed the link between public opinion and legislation in terms how the two might fail to connect (Dicey, 2008: pp. 8–9):

> There are ... three different reasons why we cannot assert of all countries, or of any country at all times, that laws are there the result of public opinion. [(1)] No 'opinion', in the proper sense of that word, with regard to the change of the law may exist; [(2)] the opinion which does direct the development of the law may not be 'public opinion'; and [(3)] lastly, there may be lacking any legislative organ adapted for carrying out the changes of the law demanded by public opinion.

Public opinion cannot rule if the public has no opinions as to what should or should not be the law; nor can it rule if there is a force separate from public opinion that has greater power; and, finally, public opinion requires a system so it can either make laws directly or control those who have that immediate power.

By 'public opinion' we mean the opinion of 'the mass of the people' as opposed to a monarch or the aristocracy or any elite (Dicey, 2008; p. 9). As Bagehot (2007: pp. 171–172) said, there should be no privileged say for the opinions of the 'too clever by half' people who live in 'Bohemia'. Public opinion is an egalitarian concept in that it denies any special weight to the opinions of any groupings. Opinions may be held strongly or loosely; they represent close considered or emotional responses; Mr Jones may be certain what is right but not really care, yet Mrs Smith may think the subject vital and be wracked with doubts. However opinions are held, their holders' votes are the same – no power can decide whose opinions are more important. As Dicey (2008: pp. 121–122) noted, opinions may be particular or highly generalised: the link between legislation and public opinion may be 'the spirit of the time' or 'the spirit of an age' rather than specific public opinions on specific subjects. Dicey (2008: p. 330) ended his lectures on public opinion by quoting the essayist Mark Pattison:

> Deeper than opinions lies the sentiment which predetermines opinion. What it is important for us to know with respect to our own age or any age is, not its peculiar opinions, but the complex elements of that moral feeling and character in which, as in their congenial soil, opinions grow.

What Dicey called 'peculiar opinions' may come and go. They may even for a time contradict the spirit of the age, but will be overwhelmed by those deeper moral feelings unless such sentiments themselves shift – as happened over the course of the nineteenth century 'legislative quiescence' shifted to 'individualism', and 'individualism' to 'collectivism' (Dicey, 2008: pp. 45–50).

Public opinion in a broad sense can exist independently of any system for translating such opinion into legislative action. Public opinion is nothing more than the aggregate of all opinions held by every member of the public: there is no need for a country to be democratic for the public to have views on what the government should do. But public opinion, as we are considering it, requires the formation and expression of opinion by the public, if only in the privacy of the voting booth. There is no meaningful public opinion if the public's opinions are kept private.

Having recognised that the extent public opinion shapes legislative change is affected by both the opportunities for the electorate's participation and their willingness to take those opportunities, we must note Dicey's second factor by which public opinion may cease to direct legislation – the possible effect of external forces on legislation (Dicey, 2008: pp. 8–9). Dicey (2008: p. 264 fn. 12) argued that public opinion will be thwarted if 'Parliament is guided ... by the power which powerful bodies may bring to bear upon its action', so we must ask whether there are any forces more powerful than a participating electorate.

Here lies what we shall argue is the key issue for a genuine reconciliation between human rights protection and democratic control. The establishment of a system of constitutional review must operate as a force acting on legislative opinion, and that it must at times act external to public opinion on the particular issues concerned. Those are basic requirements for it to create the counter-majoritarian effect which is inherent to systems of constitutional review. However, for the democratic balance, it will be argued that two further conditions are necessary.

Firstly, it will be necessary that the force that constitutional review exerts on legislative opinion must be traceable to public opinion in terms of a constitutive choice. It is not enough to appeal generally to constitutional review being supported by 'political costs' without tracing the source of those costs. In a democracy, the most decisive costs should be those levied by the citizens against their politicians. As long as we can hypothesise that the electorate support the concept of constitutional review as part of their system of government and legislation, we can hypothesise that politicians will act on the working presumption that non-compliance is likely to give rise to political costs come the next election. Politicians will face an electorate that generally believes in having a system of constitutional review for the purpose of restraining politicians. Politicians will face electors who seldom become fully engaged with politics or explanations by politicians. A breach of human or constitutional rights would act as what Downs (1957: pp. 141–142) called an ideological 'shortcut', meaning the way many electors identity misconduct and make their voting choices. A system of constitutional review on this view is a structure put in place to police their representatives, with compliance underpinned by the strength of public favour in favour of the integrity of the structure.

Secondly, within the system as constituted, it must be possible to legitimately breach the system of constitutional review without it representing an existential crisis for the system. The constitutional review structure put in place by the electorate must create a strong argument for compliance as against electorates, but this structure should not apply to the electorate. For the 'elegant balance', the logic of the constitutive choice is that politicians should expect to be held accountable for non-compliance. However, it does not follow that a general support for the Human Rights Act by the electorate cannot co-exist with occasions where politicians are held to account for choosing to *comply* with judicial decisions under the Act. The concept of a balance between rights and democracy presupposes that politicians cannot present compliance with the Human Rights Act and/or decisions under the Act as a complete and unanswerable justification for their action and inaction. If Parliamentary Sovereignty's retention has democratic substance, the legal freedom of non-compliance must carry with it the possibility for political accountability for choosing to comply with Human Rights Act decisions. And, which is the essence of what we call a theory of 'legitimate breach', in doing so the existence and continue useful operation of the Act should not be called into question. With the Human Rights Act, the potential for 'legitimate breach' does not exist simply at the level of classic British constitutional theory (i.e. any law can be overridden by a subsequent statute), but also because the Act itself contemplates that its own requirements can be breached deliberately by Parliament and yet still retain its integrity and continue to review executive and legislative action. How far the Act (or any type of 'weak-form' constitutional review) achieves such a compromise in practice is the subject of this thesis, concentrating always on the electorate's power in the constitution.

Chapter overview

Chapter 2 will review the literature principally on the Human Rights Act. The Act combines counter-majoritarian attempts to protect rights from action by the elected legislature and government, with an aspiration to uphold democracy by giving the last word to Parliament when it passes primary legislation. The chapter will consider the significance of the judiciary not having the power to set aside primary legislation, including discussion in the recent case of *R (Nicklinson) v Ministry of Justice* [2014] UKSC 38; [2014] 3 WLR 200. Legislative compliance with human rights decisions is often attributed to the 'political costs' which must be paid for choices to legislate non-compliantly (*R v Secretary of State for the Home Department, ex parte Simms* [2000] 2 AC 115, 131). The nature of those costs is largely unexamined. It will be important for the relationship between constitutional review and democracy whether such 'political costs' are exacted by the electorate at the ballot box, or whether they come from another source, or, for that matter, whether such costs are more presumed rather than real.

The democratic mandate of the Act is only complete insofar as it refers to ongoing decisions to maintain the Act and respect constitutional review decisions, which leads directly to consideration of whether the Human Rights Act upholds democracy by creating a 'dialogue' between the judiciary and legislators. In respect of judicial deference to decision makers, and its relevance to the Act's impact on democracy, the rival 'separation of powers', 'institutional competence' and 'justificatory' approaches will be considered. The review will consider arguments for reconciling constitutional review and democracy at a conceptual level, such as 'legislative rights review', the improvement of democracy through the promotion of rights necessary to democracy.

Chapter 3 sets out the theoretical framework of domination offered by Philip Pettit. It will be argued that the republican theories of government and of personal freedom must be kept separate. Republican government requires the electorate to be free from domination by any external party or internal elite when its view of the 'common good' is translated into legislative action. The principal of equality requires a majoritarian hypothesis, and freedom as a citizen requires the ability to think rightly, 'If I can convince a majority of my fellow of citizens of X, then we-over-time can do X'. Domination is described in terms of Pettit's theory of 'alien control'. Alien control exists whenever an external power can interfere with freedom of choice. Such interference is not necessarily an imposition of a single choice, but the 'removal, replacement or reduction' of any ability to choose. Choice may be reduced through 'manipulation' and 'misrepresentation', so the transparency of decision-making must be emphasised. If an external agency (such as the judiciary) can forbid X, or appear to forbid X, or attach a penalty to achieving X, then that agency will exert alien control.

Chapter 4 considers the nature of democracy. It starts with the mechanics of democracy in terms of (i) public deliberation, (ii) public voting, (iii) select group deliberation (e.g. an elected Parliament), and (iv) expert deliberation (e.g. a specialist commission). Schumpeter's view of democracy as competition by politicians for votes is correct in describing the system of public voting on which democracy turns. However, democracy must be seen as a system to link public opinion with legislative action, whilst permitting administration to continue in the absence of meaningful participation. Under Pettit's dual-aspect theory of democracy, the electorate have a free choice as to how to constitute their system of government, which should allow the right of equal participation without assuming the reality of participation. Robert Dahl's theory of polyarchy and David Beetham's 'democratic audit' will be considered. In particular, the extent to which a system operates democratically will be set by the willingness and ability of electors to participate, and not just formally available opportunities.

Chapter 5 will set out the different ways in which the counter-majoritarian effect of constitutional review is defined in respect of particular 'bills of rights' or other such constitutional or human rights instruments. These will be analysed in terms of (1) entrenchment, (2) enforcement, (3) scope, (4) rules on interpreting scope, (5) judicial approach to interpreting scope (6) rules on application and justification, (7) judicial approach to application and justification, and (8) internationalisation. Any counter-majoritarian effect significantly derives from having used the bill of rights to link the rights in the first place. It follows that bills of rights operate as rights protection pacts, a dynamic which creates what we shall call the 'structural argument' against the viability of simultaneously supporting a particular human rights instrument and supporting non-compliance in respect of individual judicial decisions.

Chapter 6 sets out the classic constitution, using Anthony King's 'canonical sextet' of Dicey, Jennings, Bagehot, Amery, Laski and Low. The effect of the Human Rights Act should be understood by reference to the classic constitution as it was understood by the contemporary views of those leading theorists, as opposed to applying revisionist views on Dicey's theories. Parliamentary Sovereignty means the right to make or unmake any law whatsoever, and the rule of law means that Acts of Parliament are implemented (Dicey, 1982: p. 3). Acts of Parliament could suspend the application of any law, or even make the Parliament the judge in the implementation of a law. The effect of Parliamentary Sovereignty was that accountability for failure could not be avoided by blaming a lack of authority. Government, in Bagehot's (2007, pp. 98–99) terms was 'come-at-able' for this reason. The dominance of the executive over Parliament is a long term feature of the constitution, Bagehot's 'efficient secret' that allows for a government to be elected, govern and be held to account at the next election. The real 'elective dictatorship' problem is not the government's dominance over the legislature, but the lack of time for Parliamentary or even ministerial oversight of many decisions with an ostensible democratic imprint.

Chapter 7 will present a positive case for how the Human Rights Act could operate so as to create a rights/democracy balance. The form of the Act is entirely compatible with citizens' right to freely participate to persuade fellow citizens to achieve a majority for a policy and thus ensure its long term success. The Act does not allow judges to be determinative of issues. The Act will help citizens identify areas where the law is working oppressively, and place such issues onto the legislative agenda. In many cases where declarations of incompatibility were made, the need for remedial legislation has been freely accepted, although the issues might never have been given time absent the Human Rights Act. The approach set out by Baroness Hale in respect of assisted suicide in *Nicklinson* provides an example of how the Act may in areas of controversy serve to bring issues into real debate.

Chapter 8 will argue that the government, legislators and leading proponents of the Act have frequently acted as if compliance with Human Rights Act decisions is mandatory. Considering Jennings's criteria for a constitutional convention, it will be seen that the most obvious reason for compliance is provided by the internationalisation of the Human Rights Act, i.e. when violations of the Act will also be violations of the Convention. This will not apply where British judges take a more expansive approach than the ECtHR, particularly on questions of proportionality where Strasbourg gives states a margin of appreciation broader than is necessary for a local, national court. The question arises as to whether the reason for compliance is the inherent (structural) impossibility of meaningfully (a) wanting the Human Rights Act to exist, and (b) also wishing to set the Act aside in particular cases. For the democracy side of the elegant balance to be achieved, it will be necessary for the electorate to hold politicians to account for choosing to comply with the Act. This is difficult if legislators can convincingly present themselves as having no choice but to comply, and with the public having a lack of information as to the consequences of non-compliance. This will be particularly so where Human Rights Act obligations are simultaneously international obligations under the Convention.

Chapter 9 will suggest that the first condition for legitimate non-compliance is a common understanding that the Human Rights Act was structured not to uphold 'ceremonial forms' or 'façades', but to preserve the ability of the electorate to require legislative action even where the courts finds incompatibility. In particular, it will be necessary to respect the ability of electors through public deliberation and voting to collectively define their own 'common good'. If the electorate's general position is favourable to compliance with the Act, such events of specific public participation requiring non-compliant action will be rare in practice. However, democracy requires the opportunity to participate – it is not contradicted by establishing a system to restrain politicians in the absence of such participation.

Chapter 10 will set out the conclusions, centring on the requirements for what will be termed a theory of 'legitimate breach'. That theory will centre on the right of the citizens to define the common good, and the Human Rights Act as giving judges the opportunity to frame judgments so as to promote public deliberation on the common good rather than *de facto* dictating where the common good lies.

2 Literature review

Introduction

The aim of this chapter is to summarise important debates in the literature on the effect of the Human Rights Act on democracy. It will start by framing the issues in respect of what is commonly called the 'counter-majoritarian problem', and the search for ways to reconcile the power inevitably given to judges under constitutional review with democracy. It will be argued that the literature has assumed that compliance with the Act is underpinned by a need for politicians to avoid the 'political costs' (*Simms* 131) or 'political consequences' (Masterman, 2011: pp. 58–59) for non-compliance, but this dynamic has not been adequately explored.

Other approaches that have sought to bridge the gap between judicial power and democratic process through the interaction between courts and politicians include the 'legislative-rights review', 'constitutional dialogue' and 'passive virtues' approaches. However, such approaches fail to sufficiently explore the reasons for Parliament's actual compliance with judicial decisions under the Act. Such reconciliations have tended either to internalise rights protection within democracy (e.g. rights-based democracy, see Jowell (2003)), or, have tended to gloss, ignore or justify the counter-majoritarian effect of the Human Rights Act, whilst demonstrating genuine democratic positives that can come from systems of constitutional review (e.g. legislative-rights review, see Hiebert (2015)).

Also of importance from our perspective is that the literature is overwhelmingly institution-centred (Tierney, 2013: p. 2185). Even amongst sceptics, we find clear concern for the freedom of legislators (Tomkins, 2005: pp. 136–139), and concern for legislatures (Nicol, 2006b), but the heart and soul of democracy, the relationship between the governed and governors is not developed. Hiebert (2013: p. 2268) notes the curious lack of questioning in the literature of 'how to assess the justification of Parliament's dissenting rulings' in human rights matters, but the electorate itself is missing. In a literature that talks much of 'political costs', 'political consequences', politics is seldom traced back to the people. Waldron's (2005: p. 445) discussion of the 'complex and delicate interplay' between public opinion, elections and legislatures is a rare exception in the context of constitutional review. This is perhaps unsurprising in academic legal literature, but without an awareness of the omission that literature must be inherently unsatisfactory.

Counter-majoritarian effect

Any system of constitutional review must necessarily be in part counter-majoritarian (Bickel, 1962: p. 16). Even where a system of constitutional review does not give judges the last word (subject to the possibility of constitutional amendment), the aim is still for judicial decisions to have a restraining effect on the ordinary political process.

Creating a counter-majoritarian problem is typically justified by invoking a problem with majoritarianism. Writing in the context of the Human Rights Act, Aileen Kavanagh (2009: pp. 344–352) lists three weaknesses for democratic decision-making when it impinges on important matters of liberty: (1) 'responsiveness to popular views and electoral orientation', i.e. politicians may sacrifice what is right for what will win votes; (2) 'responsiveness to majoritarian concerns', i.e. a bias towards majority interest may 'create a risk that minority interests will be marginalized or overridden'; and (3) 'responsiveness to short-term interests', i.e. important principles may be sacrificed to the long term detriment in order to deal with short-term problems. None of these problems identified by Kavanagh is due to a failure of the democratic process to represent public opinion – much the opposite. What is sought from constitutional review is a 'corrective mechanism enforced by the courts', and this mechanism is sought for reasons which are avowedly counter-majoritarian: 'the institutional structure of the courts is such that the courts are better placed to resist popular opinion and the hostility of powerful groups in some circumstances' (Kavanagh, 2009: p. 351; see also Kyritsis, 2012: p. 321). It is the majority that creates the risk to the minority; and the grant of power to the judiciary by way of constitutional review under the Human Rights Act is a remedy.

John Hart Ely (1980: pp. 7–8) summarised thus the problem of rights protection and democracy pulling in different directions: 'The task of constitutional law has been and remains that of devising a way or ways of protecting minorities from majority tyranny that is not a flagrant contradiction of the principle of majority rule'.

Bickel (1962: p. 27) himself gave a similar summary of the problem of reconciling constitutional review with democracy:

> [D]emocracies do live by the idea, central to the process of gaining the consent of the governed, that the majority has the ultimate power to displace the decision-makers and to reject any part of their policy. With that idea, judicial review must achieve some measure of consonance.

The Human Rights Act was drafted with a view to achieving more than just avoiding a 'flagrant contradiction' or 'some measure of consonance'. It was to create an 'elegant balance' between rights protection and democracy, or at least between rights protection and Parliamentary Sovereignty – what Alison Young (2011: p. 797) described as 'a justifiable middle ground between a constitutional and a parliamentary model of human rights protections'.

Basic structure of the Human Rights Act

The Human Rights Act is a non-entrenched form of constitutional review as against primary legislation. It can have a strong interpretative effect on primary legislation, but cannot override the express requirements of Parliament. It is however a supreme form of law as against executive and administrative action, including secondary legislation insofar as incompatibility is not expressly required by statute.

The Act is thus a 'weak-form' of constitutional review, to use Tushnet's (2003a: pp. 2782–2786) division of constitutional review into weak- and strong-forms, depending on whether judicial decisions can be overridden without constitutional amendment. The Act is neither constitutionally entrenched nor enforceable against ordinary primary legislation; it does not dictate what the law must or must not be.

Aspiration to uphold democracy

The aim of introducing a form of constitutional review that did not undermine democracy was made clear from the start. For example, the White Paper (1997: [2.13]) which preceded the Human Rights Act emphasised the government's concern for democratic decision-making, and how it met this concern by upholding Parliamentary Sovereignty. This is in keeping with the view that Parliamentary Sovereignty is the constitutional embodiment of popular sovereignty (Dicey, 1982: pp. 26–29, 285; Weill, 2003). It was not, as Lord Lester (1998: p. 668) would subsequently suggest, a matter of respecting the sovereignty of Parliament as a matter of 'dogma' only. Such sentiments as Lord Lester's are not difficult to find. Lord Cooke (1998: p. 49), similarly, argued at the time that it was only 'the façade of Parliamentary Sovereignty' that 'the United Kingdom Bill is at pains to maintain'; and Professor Jowell (2003: pp. 596–597) talked of the need for 'judges at this stage to pay occasional lip service to the continuing superior constitutional status of Parliament'.

However, the statements of the Act's principal founding fathers make it clear that for them the retention of Parliamentary Sovereignty was aimed at achieving a substantive and desired end. When closing his speech presenting the Human Rights Bill to the House of Lords, Lord Irvine was unequivocal that the Bill would 'deliver a modern reconciliation of the inevitable tension between the democratic right of the majority to exercise political power and the democratic need of individuals and minorities to have their human rights secured' (HL Debate, 1997a: col. 1234). He subsequently reiterated this writing in 2003, rejecting the idea that the Human Rights Act's respect for Parliamentary Sovereignty was a matter of political expediency – replying to Laws LJ's suggestion that the Act meant that Britain stood 'at an intermediate stage between parliamentary supremacy and constitutional supremacy' (*Roth* [71]). Lord Irvine (2003: pp. 310–311) argued that the Act represented an attempt at a permanent settlement between the competing concerns (although speaking of Parliamentary Sovereignty as if it were an end in itself):

> The present arrangements ... represent our reconciliation of effective rights protection with parliamentary sovereignty. The balancing of these is central to the Act. It retains Parliament's legal right to enact legislation which is incompatible with the Convention. *But it dramatically reduces its political capacity to do so.* It does this by introducing, through the declaration of incompatibility, a limited form of constitutional review, which serves as *a political and perhaps moral disincentive to legislate incompatibly.*
>
> [Emphasis added]

A balance, of course, has two sides. There is rights protection; and there is the upholding of democratic principles. It is the latter that is our focus. Our question is to consider what is actually meant when Lord Irvine says that the HRA 'dramatically reduces [Parliament's] political capacity' to pass certain laws, and to consider the nature of the 'political and perhaps moral disincentives' to do so.

The obvious summary of how the Human Rights Act upholds democratic principles is simply that any decision can be overruled by Parliament in primary legislation. Lord Irvine argued that the Act 'maximises the protection of human rights without trespassing on parliamentary sovereignty' (HL Debate, 1997a: col. 1229). Lord Scarman, speaking in the House of Lords debates on the Human Rights Bill, addressed the same point in terms of democracy (HL Debate, 1997a: col. 1256): 'If we are to be a democracy, the people must have the last word ... [t]he Bill has stood up for parliamentary sovereignty'. This view was echoed by Lord Scott, speaking judicially, when he argued that a declaration of incompatibility against an Act of Parliament 'provides, of course, ammunition to those who disapprove of the Act and desire to agitate for its amendment or repeal' (*A v Secretary State for the Home Department* [2004] UKHL 56; [2005] 2 AC 68 [145], ('*Belmarsh*')). The results of constitutionally reviewing statutes under Human Rights Act fed into rather than directed the legislative process.

The importance of Parliament's final word was stressed by Baroness Hale when supporting an immediate declaration of incompatibility in the recent case of *Nicklinson* [300] on assisted suicide. The courts could issue a declaration and:

> Parliament is then free to cure that incompatibility … or to do nothing. It may do nothing, either because it does not share our view that the present law is incompatible, or because, as a sovereign Parliament, it considers an incompatible law preferable to any alternative.

These are calm assessments of the legal position. Lord Kerr, similarly supporting the making of a declaration of incompatibility, concluded his decision by noting that '[t]he ethos of the Human Rights Act is to direct remedies to the true source of the incompatibility' (*Nicklinson*, [365]).

Strikingly, in all the talk of the constitutional issues around issuing a declaration of incompatibility, there is no reference in *Nicklinson* from Baroness Hale or Lord Kerr as to any expectation that a declaration of incompatibility ought to lead to any legislation. There is no discussion of any 'political and perhaps moral disincentive to legislate incompatibly' (Irvine 2003: pp. 310–311), with Hale and Kerr writing as if a declaration of incompatibility is only as good as the persuasiveness of the reasons given for making it. There is much said in terms of what Parliament's role as a matter of strict law, and how it related to the what could properly be decided by the Supreme Court in Nicklinson (see in particular Neuberger at [117] and [127]; Mance at [191]; Wilson at [205]; and Sumption, Hughes, Clarke and Reed in the minority at [230]–[234], [267], [293]–[294], [296]–[297]). *Nicklinson* thus provides detailed consideration of the interaction between Parliament and the judiciary. The result was arguably an attempt to stimulate parliamentary debate, without the majority prejudging the issues. However, none of the nine justices meaningfully considered the issue of how the making of a declaration of incompatibility was likely to affect Parliament's approach – it was as if the courts were simply presenting the arguments in favour of legislative change.

Herein lies the tension within the literature on the Human Rights Act. There are of course those who believe the Act to be inadequate in protecting rights due to the absence of a power to strike down legislation (e.g. HL Debate, 1997a (per Lord Lester): col. 535; Fordham, 2011: pp. 2–3), but the adequacy of rights protection is not the focus of this thesis. The question to be explored is whether the Human Rights Act's putative 'elegant balance' upholds democracy, whether the Act answers the worries about the democracy side of the 'elegant balance', or whether a practical assertion of democracy's supremacy over constitutional review would create an existential crises for the Act. Does the omission of a power to strike down primary legislation mean that the Act gives rise, in Conor Gearty's (2006: p. 96) words, to 'courteous requests for a conversation, not pronouncements of truth from on high'? Or was Lord Borrie (supporting the Human Rights Bill) correct when speaking in the debates on the Human Rights Bill that (HL Debate, 1997a: col. 1275):

> [T]he political reality will be that ... in the field of human rights Parliament will carry out the will of the courts ... [T]he intention of the Bill surely is that government and Parliament will faithfully implement any declaratory judgment made by the High Court[?]

However, those behind the Bill did not see Parliament's role as a mere conduit for judicial pronouncements. Lord Irvine, as we have seen, envisaged the Human Rights Act working through a 'political and perhaps moral disincentive' for legislators to choose to legislate incompatibly (Irvine, 2003: pp. 310–311). It is to this crucial idea of political disincentives, or 'political costs', that we turn now.

Political costs

Decisions on incompatibility with human rights take many forms. Most obvious is a formal declaration of incompatibility, but the decision may also be in the form of striking down executive action or replacing a natural but incompatible meaning of a statute with a purposive compatible interpretation. The question is how far such decisions are determinative of the issues addressed.

An empirical answer is that such judicial decisions under the Human Rights Act have overwhelmingly been reflected in subsequent legislative choices. Incompatible activity concerns just two issues: prisoner voting and political advertising. Prisoner voting gives rise to the only declaration of incompatibility not to be acted on (*Smith v Scott* [2007] CSIH 9; Crawford, 2013: p. 86). The same issue prevented a statement of incompatibility in respect of the House of Lords Reform Bill 2012, which for other reasons was not passed (House of Commons, 2012: [272]–[278]). The issue of the blanket ban against television political advertising led to the Communications Act 2003 being passed without a statement of compatibility. This was not really a case of defying human rights jurisprudence, but rather hoping that risky legislation would be held to be compatible. It was so held,[1] but for which the legislation would have been brought into line with adverse decisions (HL Debate, 2003a: cols. 658–659; DCMS, 2002: [12]).

However, precedent in terms of political behaviour does not of itself show the existence of a rule. Chintan Chandrachud considered Parliament's compliance with the Human Rights Act by applying Ivor Jennings's criteria for constitutional conventions: the existence of a precedent, belief on the part of political actors that they are bound by the precedent, and a reason for the rule (Chandrachud, 2014; p. 639; Jennings, 1938; pp. 129–131). Chandrachud argued that Parliament would most likely comply, but that 'sufficient precedent is not yet available and political actors' beliefs on the

1 *R (Animal Defenders International) v Secretary of State for Culture Media and Sport* [2008] UKHL 15; [2008] 1 AC 1312; *Animal Defenders International v United Kingdom* (2013) 57 EHRR 21.

binding nature of this expectation are not firmly developed'. We shall return in Chapter 8 ('Legislative acceptance of obligation to comply') to empirical evidence of a sense of duty felt by legislators to comply with Human Rights Act and ECtHR decisions, such as the compliance under protest with the decision in *R (F and Thompson) v Secretary of State for the Home Department* [2010] UKSC 17; [2011] 1 AC 331 (see HL Debate, 2012: col. 886). However, such empirical evidence cannot show with accuracy any limits to that sense of duty.

If we knew why politicians accepted a duty to comply, despite the Human Rights Act expressly not creating one, we would be better able to estimate the limits of compliance. The legal literature lacks detailed analysis of how the third part of Ivor Jennings's analysis of constitutional conventions relates to a sense of duty to comply: a convention must have a reason. Such a reason may often be found in non-compliance leading to illegality, as Dicey (2008: pp. 296–300) stressed. Alternatively, as Jennings argued: 'the creation of a convention must be due to the reason of the thing, because it accords with the prevailing political philosophy' (Jennings, 1938: p. 131). In Canada, the power to add a 'notwithstanding clause' to override constitutional review decisions under the Charter of Rights and Freedoms ('the Charter') goes unused. This is said to be largely rooted in public suspicion of notwithstanding clauses following their early misuse by Quebec by attaching such clauses indiscriminately to all legislation for five years, creating an unacceptable political cost on its use, and subsequently to 'Bill 178' where Quebec used a notwithstanding clause to impose discriminatory legislation on the public use of English language (Manfredi, 2001: pp. 186–188). The Canadian explanation roots compliance in the electorate at large, although lacking empirical studies the question must be asked whether the belief in the political cost is rooted more in the assumptions of politicians and commentators than in actual public opinion. A recent study into the atrophication of constitutional powers has suggested that, if powers are allowed to go unused or are generally believed to not to have been used, their use may come to be seen as illegitimate (Vermeule, 2012). That study, as we shall argue in Chapter 8 ('Atrophication and constitutional review') did not fully consider the possible existence of reasons for the constitutional conventions. As described by Vermeule (2012: pp. 421, 443–444), atrophication would mean that illegitimacy became unchallengeable in political deliberation.

If politicians are happy to assert their opinion that a particular judicial finding of incompatibility is wrong, and the electorate see this as a wholly respectable approach, then the Human Rights Act has a greatly different position in the process of government than it would if politicians tremble at the perceived enormity of overturning a human rights decision. As of now, it appears the latter is true: the Act's original White Paper's (1997: [2.10]) prediction that '[a] declaration ... will almost certainly prompt the government and Parliament to change the law' has been vindicated (Masterman, 2011: pp. 58–59).

But why has Parliament complied? It is the 'political cost' that is invoked by the much cited dicta of Lord Hoffmann in *Simms* as underpinning human rights compliance in the British system (*Simms* 131): 'The principle of legality means that Parliament must squarely confront what it is doing and accept the political cost. Fundamental rights cannot be overridden by general or ambiguous words'.

The idea of the 'political cost' or (see Masterman, 2011: pp. 58–59) 'the political consequences' as the reasons for Parliament behaving as if bound to comply begs the question: how great are those costs for the power-holding politicians? Similarly, David Feldman has argued that Parliament is under a 'heavy responsibility' to act compatibly with the Human Rights Act (Feldman, 2002: p. 324; Irvine, 2003: pp. 310–311; see also Waldron, 2006: p. 1392); but to whom is this responsibility owed?

If correct, the nature of the political costs would be the immediate reason for any constitutional convention, and the terms of that convention would be determined by the nature of the costs. If those costs represented the 'prevailing political philosophy' (Jennings, 1938: p. 131), then the stability of the convention will depend on whether that philosophy is an inherent part of the system, something that would be revolutionary to change and would be likely to spark effective popular resistance; or a temporary trend. As Dicey noted, from a late Victorian perspective, forms of government are subject to fashions like other aspects of human behaviour (Dicey, 1899: p. 71).

Simms was an early case witnessing the rebirth of the doctrine that courts will not 'assume without the clearest language that Parliament intended to destroy common law rights of Her Majesty's subjects' (*Rendall v Blair* (1890) 45 Ch.D 139, 155), a principle described in 1996 by Roderick Munday (1996: p. 33) as being '(possibly) defunct'. Although *Simms* related to common law rights, the idea translates into context of overriding constitutional review under bills of rights (Ahmed and Perry, 2014: pp. 515–521, 525). Tom Hickman (2005: pp. 326–330) correctly saw the approach of 'common law dialogue' explained in *Simms* translated into the Human Rights Act. Roger Masterman (2009: p. 126) has made a similar point as regards Victoria's Charter of Human Rights and Responsibilities, and Paul Craig (2014: p. 387) noted that the approach had been carried by Laws LJ into the context of constitutional statutes as early as 2002 (*Thoburn* [62]–[64]). Indeed, Lord Hoffmann's dicta in *Simms* was cited by the Secretary of State for Justice in a Commons debate on compliance with the *Hirst* decision on prisoner voting (HC Debate, 2012: col. 745).

The dicta of Lord Hoffmann in *Simms* notably separate 'squarely confronting' from 'political cost'. Taking the 'squarely confronting' idea in isolation, it would say nothing more than that Parliament should know what the effect of the statute was, and that the particular Act in question did not give clear authority for the rules in question. The approach brings the policy-making from the executive and administrative level of decision-making directly to the legislature – Parliament would be directly posed the question of whether it wanted section 47 of the Prison Act 1952 to be used to restrict visits by journalists. But, again, what is the 'political cost'? On its own, a requirement to 'squarely confront' avoids the 'risk that the full implications of their unqualified meaning may have passed unnoticed in the democratic process' (Jowell, 2004: p. 248); but this does not of itself guarantee that a political cost attaches to an oppressive measure, only that glosses and euphemisms cannot be used to avoid a cost that might be attached to the plain truth.

The idea of a 'political cost' acting as an (incomplete) hindrance to amending or overriding a bill of rights is key to understanding the existence, extent or absence of any domination incurred by the electorate and/or their representatives under a system of constitutional review. The problem is that, although we may have it on 'good authority' (Loveland, 2007: p. 263) that the principle of legality requires the approach stated by Lord Hoffman in *Simms*, authority cannot tell us the nature (if any) of such 'political cost' in any particular case. Indeed one finds citation after citation of *Simms* and 'political cost' without the dynamic being elaborated. We may readily find such elaboration in other contexts; in terms of free-trade litigation, the political cost is the risk of domestic unpopularity for a government that complies with free-trade decisions (Hudec, 2002: p. 213). In the human rights context, by contrast, the political cost said to underpin compliance with constitutional review decisions is potentially external to the electorate.

In the journal *Public Law*, there were fourteen uses of the expression 'political cost' between 1998 and July 2014, including direct quotes of *Simms* (Steyn, 2009: p. 232; Steyn, 2002: p. 480; O'Neill, 2002: p. 737; Knight, 2011: p. 106; Masterman, 2009: p. 126; Jowell, 2004: p. 248; Loveland, 2000: p. 210; Hickman, 2005: p. 326; Barber and Young, 2003: pp. 114, 125; Tushnet, 2007: p. 606; Malkani, 2011: p. 572; Craig, 2014: p. 387; Horne and Walker, 2014: pp. 286–287; Ip, 2012: p. 83). Only in Tushnet's review of a book by David Dyzenhaus do we find anything approaching a theory on what the 'political costs' might be – Dyzenhaus arguing that to legislate incompatibly with human rights 'comes with a political cost', namely (Tushnet, 2007: p. 606): 'The people to whom the government is accountable will be able to judge whether they want a government that is not committed to the rule of law ...'

Horne and Walker (2014: pp. 286–287) touch on another possible nature of 'political costs', but not restricted to the human rights context as such. The requirement of having to continually justify the re-enactment of legislation will have political costs where that legislation is unpalatable. These approaches beg an important question: other than the time and monetary costs of going through the exercise of justification, what would the costs (political or otherwise) be if voters approved of the measure and did not in fact find it unpalatable? This is an important question that typically goes unaddressed in the literature.

Christopher Crawford's (2013) detailed analysis of the response to declarations of incompatibility attributes compliance with the decision in

Belmarsh on anti-terrorist detention orders thus: 'the political pressure to do anything else was just too great'. Yet the narrative presented by Crawford (2013: pp. 63–69) involves many predictions of a constitutional crisis, but in terms of evidence, the only primary source produced is one quote from a backbench opposition MP, Rupert Baldry, expressing not a threat of constitutional upheaval but instead the opinion that the judges' decision was a 'legal judgment' not an 'ethical moral or philosophical one'. In respect of the controversy over *F and Thompson* on the reporting requirements for sex offenders, Crawford suggests that it was ultimately a desire to avoid 'direct conflict with the highest court in the nation', and the prospect of inevitable defeat in the ECtHR that underpinned compliance (Crawford, 2013: p. 84). The 'costs' threatened by such problems do not necessarily involve public opinion.

Danny Nicol's at times polemical analysis of how multinational businesses find that human rights instruments support their interests, and how the demands of such businesses help to entrench those same instruments, argues that transnational regimes such as the European Union, the World Trade Organization and the ECHR may become an indissoluble package (Nicol, 2010: p. 8):

> Furthermore, membership of these regimes forms a package deal in which individual elements cannot be 'unpicked' from the whole, and this constitutes an entrenching device. Whilst states retain their theoretical ability to change course, the World Bank has pointed out that they need to calculate the costs and benefits of withdrawal, including the threat of international censure.

Whilst the concerns of international capitalism are too remote from the subject matter of many of the keenest human rights debates (e.g. the retention of DNA evidence, prisoner voting, and anti-terrorist laws), the idea of international obligations as a 'package deal' is important, particularly insofar as the Human Rights Act's obligations are largely concurrent with international obligations under the Convention. We shall return to this when outlining the idea of bills of rights as 'rights protection pacts' in Chapter 5 ('The linking of issues').

The literature does include the suggestion that political costs may be underpinned by majoritarian democracy, notwithstanding that constitutional review is counter-majoritarian. The political costs may derive from a 'constitutional culture' which may or may not operate in tandem with the formal difficulty of making a legal amendment, and such a culture rather than the hurdles for amending a constitution amendment may be the true operative reason for a lack of constitutional amendments (Sinnott-Armstrong, 2003: p. 387).

Democratic mandate

An important argument in the literature is that of the 'democratic mandate', crystallised by Lord Bingham (*Belmarsh* [42]):

> The effect [of the Human Rights Act] is not, of course, to override the sovereign legislative authority of the Queen in Parliament, since if primary legislation is declared to be incompatible the validity of the legislation is unaffected (section 4(6)) and the remedy lies with the appropriate minister (section 10), who is answerable to Parliament. The 1998 Act gives the courts a very specific, wholly democratic, mandate. As Professor Jowell has put it[:]
>
> > 'The courts are charged by Parliament with delineating the boundaries of a rights-based democracy' ('Judicial Deference: servility, civility or institutional capacity?' [2003] PL 592, 597)'.
>
> See also Clayton, 'Judicial deference and "democratic dialogue": the legitimacy of judicial intervention under the Human Rights Act 1998' [2004] *PL* 33.

The citations of this passage abound (e.g. Knight, 2011: p. 98; Goodwin, 2012: p. 465; Starmer, 2007: p. 124; Steyn, 2006: pp. 249–250; Steyn, 2005a: p. 350; Klug and Starmer, 2005: p. 727; Lester, 2005: p. 254; Arden, 2005: p. 622; Bowen, 2016: p. 363). But it must be stressed that there are two intimately related ideas to the 'democratic mandate' in Bingham's quote: (1) the democratic origin of the judicial power in the Act of Parliament, and (2) the ongoing nature of Parliament's power as to giving the remedy, which is underlined by the citation of Richard Clayton's article. The first part on its own leads to a democratic origin, but without democratic control. The fact that the Human Rights Act was passed by Parliament is all the mandate the courts require to interpret and apply the Act, and thus quite different to judicial legislation in the guise of common law development (Bowen, 2016: pp. 362–363). But this does not, from the perspective of a citizen, determine whether the state of constitutional affairs created by the Act's passing will be more or less democratic. The origin of a law does not determine its effect on the power relationships between the governors and the governed.

Dialogic theory

The question of reconciliation of rights and democracy within the processes of the Human Rights Act is, in the literature, dealt with frequently under the heading of 'dialogue'.

The idea of constitutional dialogue between courts, executive and legislature was first championed by Hogg and Bushell in respect of the Canadian Charter. The idea was that the courts should not have a monopoly in defining rights, but rather that rulings and legislative responses will interact, leading to a rights-compatible solution: 'The effect of the Charter is rarely to block a legislative objective, but rather to influence the design of implementing legislation' (Hogg and Bushell, 1997: p. 75). Replying to criticism that dialogue invariably meant legislative obedience to court orders (Manfredi and Kelly, 1999), Hogg and Bushell (now Thornton) (1999: p. 536) ended by asserting that, because 'the legislature nearly always has a range of choice, it is difficult to maintain that the legislature is not exercising any of that choice when it implements the court's decision'. Geraldine Van Bueren (2002: pp. 464–466) has taken a similar approach in seeing a choice of how to comply as sufficient to satisfy democratic concerns. Nevertheless, in the important context of the effect of human rights jurisprudence, governmental choices as to how to respond to Human Rights Act rulings 'were, in reality, severely curtailed' (Wray, 2013: p. 845; *R (on the application of Aguilar Quila) v Secretary of State for the Home* Department [2011] UKSC 45; [2012] AC 621). Despite the ability of the legislature to override Canadian Charter jurisprudence being at the heart of the dialogic theory (Hogg and Bushell, 1997: p. 79), Hogg and Bushell shied away from suggesting that this power ought to be used actively.

Dialogic theory has had its critics and initial Canadian judicial enthusiasm has waned (Hickman, 2005: pp. 306–307). But it has attracted significant academic interest in the United Kingdom (Klug, 2001: pp. 370–372; Clayton, 2004; Nicol, 2006b; Yap, 2012). The British judiciary showed initial scepticism (Clayton, 2004: p. 47), although, in *Nicklinson* ([117] and [204]), Lords Neuberger and Wilson took a more positive view of 'dialogue' or 'collaboration' between the courts and Parliament.

Clayton (2004: p. 43) had noted that democratic dialogue suggested a willingness of the legislature to give 'in your face' replies when disagreeing with human rights decisions. It was Crawford's argument, reviewing legislative responses to declarations of incompatibility, that there is no real dialogue when the legislature behaves as if under an obligation to comply (Crawford, 2013: pp. 83–84). Unless subject to a real prospect of legislative correction, the democratic mandate to carry out constitutional review will not give democratic credentials to legislative outcomes. Judicial decisions may affect legislative outcomes, but any accountability to the public for the state of the country's legislation will lie with lawmakers not judges (Yap, 2012: p. 544):

> Judicial supremacists may argue that the courts have a democratic mandate either conferred by their constitution or their human rights instrument to interpret rights but this argument, while true, in no way refutes the critique that judges are less accountable to the public than lawmakers ....

Such accountability is difficult if legislative responses are taken as automatic obligations.

Nicol (2006b: p. 750) has been bolder in his approach to dialogue:

> [C]ourts need to reconfigure themselves as ideological partisans who will lay down fearless challenges to legislators in defence of constitutional liberties. For its part, Parliament is entitled to reply with its view of how rights conflicts be resolved.

Nicol asserts the political nature of the decisions that often arise under the proportionality test. He argues that courts and elected bodies are essentially doing the same task from different perspectives, and that there is no necessary reason to favour the preferences of judges (Nicol, 2006b: pp. 733 and 750).

Despite 'dialogic' theories only being briefly mentioned in *Nicklinson*, the decision itself is a good example of the potential for such dialogue. The result in *Nicklinson* was that the assisted suicide issue was passed back to Parliament, with a threat of a declaration of incompatibility if the courts decide that the matter had been dealt with inadequately. In not giving a declaration of incompatibility, the UK Supreme Court was perhaps following what Alexander Bickel described in the American context as the 'passive virtues' i.e. courts should avoid deciding matters of public controversy until the time is right for acceptance of judicial intervention (Bickel, 1962: pp. 143–156; Hickman, 2005: pp. 317–321). An example of 'ripeness' in the Human Rights Act occurred when the Supreme Court avoided issuing a declaration of incompatibility in the context of prisoner voting, where Baroness Hale, having noted public opposition to prisoner voting, added: 'In such circumstances, it is incumbent upon the courts to tread delicately' (*R (on the application of Chester) v Secretary of State for Justice* [2013] UKSC 63; [2014] 1 AC 271 [86]–[87]). But, unlike in the United States, in the context of weak-form constitutional review such as that created by the Human Rights Act, judicial self-restraint is not at the heart of the theory of constitutional dialogue. Of greater importance is that the legislature has the power to restrain a judiciary that does not restrain itself.

Ultimately, this gets the literature no further than when we were considering political costs. We return to the nature of Parliament's role in overturning or ignoring judicial decisions, and received no real insights as to when this can properly be done, i.e. (1) 'always', as the Act permits it, (2) 'never', as any such action harms the integrity of the Act, or (3) anywhere in between.

The passive virtues

It is useful to say a little more about the 'passive virtues' mentioned above. From the perspective of court decisions, the passive virtues are about holding off making a definitive ruling. The effect of such an approach, seen from the perspective of the political process, cannot be understood by cutting directly to such time (if any) that the judges make a definitive ruling. The effect on the political process must also be viewed from the perspective of stimulating deliberation prior to any such ruling.

Use of the passive virtues may improve the democratic process. Building on American literature (Stephenson, 2008: pp. 11–17), Po-Jen Yap (2013: pp. 798–799) argued:

> The judicial enforcement of constitutional norms through subconstitutional doctrines allows the courts to play an active role in advancing human rights concerns but it also preserves a degree of legislative flexibility that better accommodates the political branches' primary role in governance than quasi-immutable substantive constitutional prescriptions do. When the judiciary crafts subconstitutional norms that are substantive in nature, these doctrines impose additional enactment costs on the legislature if it seeks to reverse the judicial decisions in question; after deliberation and careful consideration, 'the better-informed government decision-makers will only be willing to act when their true interest in the policy is sufficiently strong'.

It should be said that this is more subtle that the use of 'enactment costs' to deter certain courses of action, although a delaying power will defeat proposals if promptness is essential (Dicey, 1982: p. xlii). The aim is to ensure that decisions are thought through well, as there is no loss to government in abandoning ideas where on closer scrutiny it turns out that their interest in the policy is insufficiently strong – and no loss to the democracy if the electorate's interest in the policy (if any) is similarly weak. This dialogic approach, as Po-Jen Yap (2013: pp. 791–792) points out, is a close relation to the American theory of 'resistance norms'. In the American literature, 'resistance norms' are 'constitutional rules that make governmental action more difficult, but do not categorically exclude it', and are contrasted with 'invalidation norms' of striking down statutes (Young, 2002: p. 1652). This has obvious parallels to the *Simms* approach which we saw earlier (Hickman, 2005; pp. 326–330; Roach, 2001; pp. 483–486, 486). However, the dialogic approach that Yap outlines differs greatly in that its aspiration is to improve the reasoning process, and the 'enactment cost' is exacted to ensure that the political branches of state carry through the process – it is not a 'political cost' imposed for taking the final choice.

Such an approach suggests a reconciliation with democracy. 'Constitutional review' may be welcomed by a parliament for pointing out its errors in overlooking or underestimating the rights issues relevant to particular legislation (Young, 2009: p. 138; Kavanagh, 2009; p. 363). The courts in constitutional review proceedings interfere with the executive and legislative actions, but the decision and ultimate reasoning processes belong to the democratic element (or, at least, the political element) of the constitution. As we shall see in

Chapter 7 (Improved contestation), declarations of incompatibility have often been the spur to non-controversial law changes.

However, it must be noted that dialogic theory is essentially inter-institutional. This accords with a common feature of constitutional debate noted in the introduction: the literature seldom incorporates the people into its discussion of how the constitution works (Tierney, 2013: p. 2185).

Deference and the scope of counter-majoritarianism

One of the most difficult issues in Human Rights Act literature is that of 'judicial deference', which is essentially what Baroness Hale described as 'the weight to be accorded the views of the various public authorities involved in making the decision which is alleged to have infringed convention rights' (*Belfast City Council v Miss Behaving Ltd* [2007] UKHL 19; [2007] 1 WLR 1420 [32]). Issues of justification are structured by the proportionality test, which confronts the court with questions where judges will ask themselves if and how far they know best. The test is comprised of (1) legitimate aim, (2) rational link between means and ends, (3) least intrusive means, and (4) fair balance of rights of individual and interests of society, (*R v Oakes* [1986] 1 SCR 103, 139; *Huang v Secretary of State for the Home Department* [2007] UKHL 11; [2007] 2 AC 167 [19]). In Canada, as of 1998, in every case where a measure passed the 'least intrusive means', a finding of proportionality followed (Trakman, Cole-Hamilton and Gratien, 1998: pp. 100–101). The willingness of the court to assert that there is or may be a viable and less intrusive way to achieve the policy goal, will thus typically be determinative of issues of justification (Edwards, 2002: p. 872). If legislation has attempted to 'balance the interests of society with those of individuals and groups' (Clayton, 2001: p. 514), then, as Simon Brown LJ recognised (*Roth* [54]), holding a measure to be 'unfair' means passing judgment on the 'means used to achieve social goals', for which a measure of deference is required.

Zero deference would point to 'a single lawful solution' (Nicol, 2006b: p. 734); but, complete deference would, as Lord Hoffmann noted in the context of security threats, defeat the purpose of a tribunal existing (*Secretary of State for the Home Department v Rehman* [2001] UKHL 47; [2003] 1 AC 153 [54]; Edwards, 2002: p. 872). The greatest activism is for judges to abdicate interpreting or applying a law altogether (Frantz, 1963: pp. 741–742; see also Jowell, 2003: p. 597). It follows that the courts must adjudicate, although the well-known difficulties in rationally adjudicating problems of policy management and resource allocation is noted in the literature by citations of Lon Fuller's analysis of the limits of adjudication and polycentricity (Edwards, 2002: p. 859; *Nicklinson* [232]; Fuller, 1978: pp. 394–404).

There was a debate subsequent to the enactment of the Human Rights Act between champions of (i) the 'institutional competence model' championed by Lord Steyn (2005a: pp. 360–361 ; 2005b, p. 352) and Professor

Jowell (2003: pp. 598–601), (ii) the 'separation of powers model' championed by Lord Hoffmann (2002),[2] and (iii) a 'justificatory model', e.g. Rivers (2006: pp. 202–206; 2014), Fredman (2013: pp. 293, 300–311). Of these models, the institutional competence approach was about expertise rather than democratic concerns. A difficulty with such an approach is that perhaps the most important institutional capacity of legislators is their representativeness (Laski, 1951: p. 37), a point more easily processed in the next model. The 'separation of powers model' was explicitly concerned with the constitutional importance of laws being made by those who were democratically accountable (e.g. *Rehman* [62]), but solely concerned the limits of where constitutional review adjudication could properly come to positive decision and thus create a counter-majoritarian effect. The theory said nothing about resolving conflicts between the legislature/government/public opinion and judicial decisions where that effect arose.

It is the justification approach that has the potential to create a political response that promotes democratic considerations. The 'justificatory model' tries not to rule on whether something is or is not justified, but on the adequacy of the justification as evidenced. Here we see again the 'passive virtues', Bickel's theory of 'ripeness', whereby judges avoid purporting to finally resolve issues of political controversy when possible (Bickel, 1962: pp. 143–156), although the passive virtues are lost when an ultimate decision on the merits is made, and until then the courts are no less invigilating by virtue of limiting their interference. Hence, Fredman (2013: pp. 306–308) suggests that the correct judicial response in prisoner voting is not a ruling that prisoners must be allowed to vote, but rather that present justifications are (in her view) inadequate. Such a proceduralist approach is open to the possibility of accepting as proportionate the considered judgement of the legislature whilst striking down an identical measure if done by lesser forms of legislation and executive action (*Huang* [17]). As long as judges hold off a final resolution, counter-majoritarianism is ostensibly reduced – although with every adverse decision the reality will tend to narrow the theoretical gap between judicial findings of 'unjustified (on the evidence)' and 'never to be accepted as justified'. The approach is further complicated in that the passing of primary legislation does not presuppose significant debate in Parliament, nor does a lack of debate in Parliament presuppose an absence of informed deliberation ahead of Parliament voting (Laski, 1951: p. 31). The difficulty of courts commenting on the degree of practical scrutiny given to legislation is shown by Lord Sumption's rebuttal of the suggestion that the ban on prisoner voting had been continued without legislative debate (*Chester* [132], [136]); the legislation represented the consensus of detailed debate outside the legislative chamber.

2 See also Edwards (2002, p. 861), as to the considerable case-law support at the time for Lord Hoffmann's position.

Recently, it has been the justificatory model that has often come recently to the fore. Lord Sumption has argued that, where the Human Rights Act requires adjudication, the question is not one of constitutional propriety, but one of 'what evidential weight is to be placed on the executive's judgment'. This is in turn affected by the court's sense of its competence to contradict the executive, particularly where the correctness of the measure requires the prediction of future events, and rationality may be the only possible standard of review (*R (Carlile) v Home Secretary* [2014] UKSC 60; [2014] 3 WLR 1404 [30]–[32]). Nevertheless, an exacting approach to considering the evidence for a measure was seen in *Aguilar Quila*, where the immigration restrictions on spouses of those marrying under 21 were declared to be unjustified discrimination for want of 'robust evidence' that this was a proportionate way to tackle the issue of forced marriages. This has been criticised extra-judicially by Lady Justice Arden (2013: pp. 508–511) in that a 'requirement for robust evidence may preclude action where legislative action is inevitably experimental in nature, and there is "understandably a dearth of hard numbers"'. The speculative nature of the consequences of legislation may be seen in one case as a reason for the judges to show restraint, but in a different case as a reason to condemn infringing rights due to uncertain gain.

European Convention interplay

The relationship between constitutional review under the Human Rights Act and before the ECtHR is crucial to understanding the counter-majoritarian effect. We are not interested here in questions of inter-judicial dialogue when the British courts make a decision knowing it is more restrictive of rights than the most proximate Strasbourg authority (*Al-Khawaja v United Kingdom* (2009) 49 EHRR 1; *R v Horncastle* [2009] UKSC 14; [2010] 2 AC 373; *Horncastle v United Kingdom* [2014] ECHR 1394; Bjorge, 2011). It is rather the extent to which the international duty of compliance with the ECHR underpins compliance with the Human Rights Act.

It was argued as long ago as 1968 that 'the realities of international politics predicate that Parliament will either have to pass the necessary incorporating legislation or alternatively refrain from passing any legislation which would lead the United Kingdom into conflict with the international norms by which she is bound'. On this view, it was not a 'meaningful statement' to analyse the effect of the Convention in terms of Parliamentary Sovereignty (Gilmour, 1968: pp. 62, 72; Bates, 2010: p. 242). In the modern literature. Francesca Klug, an early British champion of constitutional dialogue (Klug, 2001: pp. 370–372), was quick to stress that overriding the HRA is made impractical by the oversight of the ECtHR (Mulholland, 2006). Opinions nevertheless divide amongst the Act's supporters on whether internationalisation requires strict compliance. Lord Irvine argued that departing from the ECHR was a state matter with no definite result (Irvine, 2012: pp. 245–246), whilst Philip Sales (2012: p. 262) responded that 'there is no doubt that the Council of Europe ... will stand behind judgments of the ECtHR and require them to be implemented'. In 2011, the Conservative Attorney General argued in parliamentary debates on prisoner voting that compliance with the ECtHR's *Hirst* decision was an unavoidable legal duty, and Parliament would behave 'tyrannically' to do otherwise (HC Debate, 2011b: col. 512).

Where a treaty is incorporated into national law, it may be argued that national constitutional forms are rendered academic in the face of external legal obligations (Sand, 2007: p. 288). International governance may create a high level of constitutional entrenchment, either rendering the power of national legislatures and electorates empty, or at least materially weakening them (Nicol, 2010: pp. 7–11).

However, the authority of the Convention over the United Kingdom is not relevant where the United Kingdom courts find a violation of the Human Rights Act in a case where the ECtHR would see the matter as lying within the contracting states' margin of appreciation. In *Nicklinson* [74], Lord Neuberger (and a majority of the Supreme Court agreed), took the view that, as regards issues of justification, the fact the Strasbourg Court confers a 'margin of appreciation' on states does not preclude national courts being more assertive: '[T]he terms of the Human Rights Act ... and the principle of subsidiarity ... require UK judges ultimately to form their own view as to whether or not there is an infringement of [a] Convention right for domestic purposes'.

The result will be domestic decisions, possibly the ban on assisted suicide, where a law has been held to be unjustified by the United Kingdom courts, but with the ECtHR holding that there was no Convention obligation (*Nicklinson v United Kingdom* [2015] ECHR 709).

This distinction is important and was implicitly made by Baroness Blackstone when considering the ban on political advertising under the Communications Bill 2003. She explained that a loss in the domestic courts under the Human Rights Act would cause the government 'to reconsider its position', but 'there is no question but that we would amend the ban in accordance with any judgment of the European Court of Human Rights in Strasbourg that ruled against the UK legislation' (HL Debate, 2003a: col. 659). Hence, compliance with Human Rights Act decisions would only be certain if supported by international obligations under the Convention.

Overcoming the zero-sum game

The central problem with theories to reconcile constitutional review with democracy is that power over legislation appears to be a zero-sum game. If a judicial decision under the Human Rights Act has a counter-majoritarian effect in causing an otherwise popular law to be changed, it is difficult to deny a counter-majoritarian restriction to democracy. This is what Bickel

(1962, p. 16) described as the inevitability of a counter-majoritarian effect in constitutional review. What is gained in rights protection is lost in democratic choice. Instead of accepting this inevitability, the literature includes theories that, if not wholly refuting the pervasiveness of counter-majoritarian difficulties, at least reduce the zero-sum nature of the problem by bringing constitutional review into harmony with democracy.

Legislative-rights review

The theory of legislative-rights review is that where the legislature has the final say on the implementation of constitutional review decisions, it is possible to resist 'judicial hegemony' without rejecting the bill of rights. In such contexts, the legislature should reject 'the assumption that respecting rights is only, or primarily, a judicial responsibility' and take a direct responsibility' (Hiebert, 2005b: pp. 240–245).

This approach has recently risen to the fore in British literature with the work of Murray Hunt, Hayley Hooper and Yowell (2012, 2015), firstly in their report 'Parliaments and Human Rights: Redressing the democratic deficit', and subsequently in their anthology of same name. That anthology included contributions from many of leading legal academics on human rights such as Murray Hunt, Janet Hiebert, David Feldman, Aileen Kavanagh, David Dyzenhuas and Sandra Fredman. As Dyzenhaus (2015: pp. 428–429) has highlighted, noted sceptics of judicial power in human rights matters, such as Jeremy Waldron and Richard Bellamy appear to have taken the position that all that matters is 'the last word'. As the Human Rights Act gives Parliament the last word, and creates mechanisms to deliberate on rights issues, their concerns about judicial supremacy are assuaged (Waldron, 2009: pp. 23–24; Bellamy, 2011: pp. 99–102, 110–111). In the debate between 'legal constitutionalists' and 'political constitutionalists', Dyzenhaus concludes that the latter 'no longer object to bills of rights, as long as legislatures have the last word – indeed, think that such bills with court-produced legal effects can be productive'. Hunt (2015: pp. 6–10) similarly asserts that the 'political constitutionalist' argument against constitutional review is over, with the debate being more about the details of how it should be achieved. Hence, we see the question of democracy and human rights turn from one of balance to one where the role of an elected legislature is seen in terms of 'legislative-rights review'.

Hunt (2015, p. 14) argues that instead of arguments as to the 'last word', debate should concentrate on facilitating Parliament's role in relation to human rights (see also Hiebert, 2015). The theme which runs through the work, as it did with the original presentation from which the volume grew (Hunt, Hooper, Yowell, 2012), is very much one of the allocation of responsibility between legislature and judiciary to maximise the pre-determined end of human rights protection. It is stressed that the involvement of an elected legislature confers 'legitimacy' and increases 'effectiveness' on human rights protection. In the United Kingdom constitutional context, the role of the Joint Committee on Human Rights (JCHR) is of pivotal importance in supplying the raw material of human rights analysis for legislators to properly bring the executive to account (Feldman, 2015; Kavanagh, 2015; Yowell, 2015). Within the legislative-rights review literature, Hiebert (2013: pp. 2268–2274) has broadly suggested that justification will be key to parliamentary dissent against Human Rights Act decisions. The tantalising possibility of a substantive discussion of justification issues in terms of overruling constitutional review decisions was perhaps thwarted by the nature of the sole test case for actual parliamentary dissent (*Hirst* and prisoner voting). In the relevant debates, Parliament did not actually consider the justifications for denying prisoners the vote. Instead, Hiebert's (2013: p. 2273) discussion of 'institutional procedures or normative criteria to govern use of [the dissenting] power' rapidly turned to formal hurdles such as supermajorities or burdens of proof. Despite denying that 'parliamentary dissent will necessarily represent a reasoned or reasonable judgment about rights' (p. 2268), Hiebert returned ultimately the idea of 'dissenting rulings' being given by an institutionally sceptical Parliament whose default institutional role is the maximisation of rights.

There is in this part of the literature an implicit teleological assumption that the constitution serves a rights-maximising end, something which elides the counter-majoritarian problem. It is as David Kinley (2015: p. 32) argues that:

> Like the motto of the Musketeers, the arms of our government are 'all for one and one for all' being the inseparable and intersecting constituents of our democratic system. No one part of the whole, therefore, can lay legitimate proprietary claim to be the, or even the principal, seat of democratic process, and nor, in this process, can any one branch answer 'We do' to the 'Who decides?' question …

As such, Waldron and Bellamy as arch political constitutionalists can be satisfied that the answer to 'who decides' can be said to be 'Parliament', see above; and legal constitutionalists can be satisfied that the answers will almost certainly be those given by law. Whereas Alison Young (2011: p. 797) had looked for 'a justifiable middle ground between a constitutional and a parliamentary model of human rights protections', legislative-rights review casts both models as being on the same ground.

But to an electorate who might disagree with the outcome of 'legislative-rights review' as much as they would had the same come from 'constitutional review', the counter-majoritarian problems remains as pervasive as Bickel argued. Politicians have been given a role in the process, but democracy-based concerns remain.

A link with the 'justification' theory of judicial deference is obvious. As Dyzenhaus (2015: pp. 425–426) points out:

> [P]arliamentarians offer political justifications to the electorate for their laws, ... [and] they offer legal justifications in terms of the values set out in the bill of rights. That is a kind of political justification. But it is more than a justification of why one policy is better than another since it is also a justification of why the policy is consistent with the legally protected rights of those it affects. Moreover, it is a justification not only to citizens but also to the courts, a feature inherent in the structure of a bill of rights that permits rights to be limited.

This is what is meant by a 'Democratic Culture of Justification': the fact of constitutional review generating simultaneously a (successful or failed) legal justification to the courts, and a political justification to the electorate. It is inherent to much constitutional review litigation that the state will be asked to justify its laws and actions in the court. Whatever might be the theory of judicial approach to matters of deference, the fact of justifying and any failures to justify will add value to the democratic process (Dyzenhaus, 2015: p. 440). As will be seen in Chapter 7 (Improved contestation) there is considerable evidence of Human Rights Act litigation bringing unjustifiable laws, or the unintended consequences of legislation, to public and legislative notice.

But whilst Dyzenhuas (2015: p. 440) accepts Manfredi's criticism that judges will be drawn into deciding whether justifications offered were 'good' or 'good enough', there is no discussion as to what follows should the electorate believe that, viewed from their perspective, a constitutional review decision would lead to an unjustifiable law. This gap is, perhaps, inevitable in the assumption that the legislative process is focused on achieving human rights compliance, even when the issue is – as it overwhelmingly will be (Kinley, 2015: p. 30) – the justification of non-compliance with headline rights such as free speech or family life.

Internalising the democracy/rights balance

The literature includes further arguments that seek to reconcile rights protection and democracy by arguing for an inherent compatibility between the two concepts. Jeffrey Jowell has argued that (Jowell, 2003: p. 597):

> It is important to note that the conception of democracy which the ECHR advances fundamentally differs from that which has hitherto prevailed in the United Kingdom. ... No longer can we equate 'democratic principle' with 'majority approval'. Nor can we any longer arrogate the monopoly of legitimacy to those decisions endorsed by the electorate. The new expectations have at their heart the protection of a limited but significant catalogue of rights even against overwhelming popular will.

In the same article, Jowell (2003: p. 597) argued that '[t]he courts are charged by Parliament with delineating the boundaries of a rights-based democracy', a position adopted by Lord Steyn (2005a: p. 360) and Lord Bingham (*Belmarsh* [42]). However, that expression 'rights-based democracy' contains a certain ambiguity as to whether the rights-basis of democracy operates as an externally imposed constraint on democracy, or as a limit which is integral to democracy. It is the latter which Jowell suggested. This is the 'fat conception of democracy', a 'morally overlain account', in contrast to a 'thin' concept, which separates out majority rule from how such rule is exercised, much as HLA Hart argued that the nature of law ought not to be conflated with a moral assessment of laws (Allan, 2006: pp. 533–536). James Allan (2006: pp. 535–536) cites the British constitutional lawyer Trevor Allan (2000: pp. 23–24) as a leading exponent of the 'fat' conception of democracy.

Lord Bingham (*Belmarsh* [42]) also framed the point in terms of the 'rule of law' as 'a cardinal feature of the modern democratic state'. This leads to a further argument to internalise rights protection into democracy by way of taking a 'substantive' conception of the rule of law. (Hunt, 2015: pp. 6–8). The 'argument' as to the substantive theory of the rule of law 'is over as far as political actors and international institutions are concerned', listing the UN General Assembly, the European Commission, the Council of Europe amongst others. Constitutional choices, implicitly, ought to fall into line – an approach that overlooks the electorate's power to choose a constitution to their meet its needs, which cannot include a duty to comply with the internationally popular theory.

Kavanagh's three reconciling factors

Aileen Kavanagh (2009: pp. 401–402) presented three factors that justify or reduce any erosion of democratic decision-making caused by constitutional review. Firstly, the reasons why we restrict democracy are congruent with the reasons why we value participation, or democracy, in the first place. This argument for the compatibility of democracy and judicial supremacy was also put by Rabinder Singh on the basis that 'both concepts are based on the same understanding of the dignity of human beings' (Palmer, 1998: p. 409, citing Singh, 1997: p. 45).

Secondly, constitutional review may operate as 'an added channel for participation'. To be able to challenge the outcome of democratic process by means of court proceedings is a form of participation, enabling groups such as mental patients, criminals, prisoners, asylum seeks and immigrants to question the justification of measures, (Kavanagh, 2009: pp. 341–342; Young, 2009: p. 135; Wray 2013: p. 860). It enables them to bring to attention the existence of violations of absolute rights *(R (on the application of Limbuela) v Secretary of State for the Home Department* [2005] UKHL 66; [2006] 1 AC 396); and it enables them to demand that violations of conditional rights should be justified before an impartial tribunal. At the heart of this argument is a shift away from the vote-centred procedural conception of democracy.

This is an ongoing process. Even the achievements of human rights principles in one generation may be subject to human rights scrutiny in the next. Kavanagh's stress on advances on mental health issues under the Human Rights Act is interesting in that the relevant statute, the Mental Health Act 1983, had itself been inspired by human rights principles (Grubb, 1986, p. 153).

A question inevitably arises whether this form of participation is separate from or designed to feed into the democratic process, *R (Countryside Alliance) v Attorney General* [2007] UKHL 52; [2008] 1 AC 719 [45]: 'The democratic process is liable to be subverted if, on a question of moral and political judgment, opponents of the Act achieve through the courts what they could not achieve in Parliament'.

Constitutional review can at best provide a supplemental route into the ordinary political process. But the 'added channel of participation' does not work if the channel is in fact a more effective alternative to the political process.

Thirdly, Kavanagh argues that constitutional review may serve as 'enhanced protection for what we might call "democratic right"'. It can be argued with considerable truth that some rights are necessary to the existence of political freedom: there can be no democracy if the people cannot freely express their views on political matters. Jowell (2003: p. 598) noted that for 'a rights-based democracy … free expression is an integral element – whatever the indications of majority opinion'. Hence, the High Court of Australia implied a constitutional freedom of political communication into the Australian constitution (*Nationwide News Pty Ltd v Wills* (1992) 177 CLR 1; and *Australian Capital Television Pty Ltd v Commonwealth of Australia* (1992) 177 CLR 106), although the court has since reined back on this approach (*McGinty v Western Australia* (1996) 134 ALR 289). The idea of a 'democratic right' need not be confined to the obvious territory of free speech. However, other principles required for or supportive of democracy have not necessarily been recognised in human rights jurisprudence. Democracy requires an informed and educated populace so as to understand, deliberate and choose (Beetham, 1999: p. 167). It has accordingly been argued that the right to freedom of expression requires a right to freedom of information (Mba, 2009). This proposition has not been ruled out by the ECtHR (*Gillberg v Sweden* [2012] ECHR 569 [86]), although the present state of Strasbourg jurisprudence is unfavourable (*Kennedy v Charity Commission* [2014] UKSC 20; [2015] 1 AC 455).

It is true that democracy is not just about formal structures, but the ability (legal, practical, intellectual) to participate in those opportunities. As Robert Dahl (2000: p. 38) put it: '[T]he political institutions of actual democracy all imply as necessary to them certain rights and opportunities'. Nevertheless there are limits to how far fundamental freedoms can be analysed in these terms as a justification for judicial intervention. Whilst John Hart Ely (1980: pp. 73–75, 98) argued that much of the US Supreme Court activism of the Warren Court represented judicial intervention to support democracy, he also stressed that many of the most important rights, such as freedom for slavery, cannot be satisfactorily conceptualised as a function of political participation.

Conclusion

What has been seen is that major theories and approaches have fallen short of properly addressing the co-existence of rights protection and popular control within the constitution. There is considerable literature on how the elected branches of the constitution may be harnessed to promote rights protection (e.g. Murray, Hooper and Yowell, 2012 and 2015) – but that is not quite the same thing. There is considerable and excellent literature on the institutional relationship between Parliamentary Sovereignty and the Human Rights Act (e.g. Young, 2009) – but that again is not quite the same thing.

The most important point to take from the literature review applies to 'political costs'. The arguments as to 'dialogue', the 'passive virtues' or the more theoretical reconciliations of constitutional review and democracy are unsatisfactory in terms of analysing the 'democracy' side of the elegant balance. They present cogent reasons why, notwithstanding any limits created on democracy, there may be utility in terms of rights protection and the quality of decision-making processes. However, such approaches do not of themselves explain the extent to which democracy will have been limited. The 'political costs' argument recognises that there must one or more reasons why politicians have almost invariably complied with Human Rights Act decisions, so it may properly be hypothesised that legislators believe that there are costs attached to non-compliance. The literature is, however, weak on the point of what those costs are.

It is important to know that the electorate's acceptance of the results of constitutional review represents informed consent. It may realistically be suggested that to some degree 'human rights is politics by other means' (Douzinas; 2000: p. 95), a means by which certain political ends are advanced or otherwise privileged (Ginsberg and Versteeg, 2013; p. 587), then in our examination of the democracy side of the 'elegant balance', we shall need to know how far the electorate is able to control the results of such 'political' activity. In other words, how far is the electorate exacting any political costs?

3 Theoretical framework

Introduction

This chapter sets out the proposed use of republican theory to provide a theoretical framework to analyse the effect of the Human Rights Act on democracy in the British Constitution. We are in essence considering the claim made that the Human Rights Act provides an 'elegant balance' between protecting rights and maintaining Parliamentary Sovereignty; and thus that it reconciles judicial protection of fundamental rights and democracy. In terms of constitutional theory, we are considering the continued validity of two claims that Dicey made as regards relationships of domination within the British Constitution: firstly the claim that '[t]he sovereignty of Parliament is, from a legal point of view, the dominant characteristic of our institutions' (Dicey, 1982: p. xxxvi), and, secondly, the claim that the relationship between public opinion and legislative change is such that the electorate is the 'political sovereign' within the Constitution (Dicey, 1982: pp. 26–29, 285). An analysis of domination will demonstrate how far the British Constitution can be said to be a 'controlled constitution' (*Jackson v Attorney General* [2005] UKHL 56; [2006] 1 AC 262 [102]) by reason of the role given to the courts under the Human Rights Act.

In order to systematically approach the question of where power lies within a constitutional system, we shall employ republican insights into the concept of 'domination', the idea at the heart of republican theory (Pettit, 2008; Skinner, 2008). We shall set out and justify the use of Philip Pettit's analysis of 'domination' in terms of concepts such as 'alien control' (the ability to 'reduce, replace, or remove' the choices of others), 'non-alien control', 'counter-control' and 'co-reasoning' (Pettit, 2008; 2009: pp. 42–49; 2012: pp. 26–74). By concentrating on these tools of analysis, we shall seek to avoid a criticism that Trevor Allan (2006: p. 173) made of Tomkins's *Our Republican Constitution*, that Pettit's work appeared to favour bills of rights and methods for restraining populism – which suggests that a republican framework would inherently internalise and validate the rights/democracy balance rather than be a useful tool of analysis.

Republicanism and domination

The defining characteristic of republicanism is that of freedom as defined in terms of 'non-domination', in contrast to the liberal approach of defining freedom in terms of non-interference. The basic republican approach to individual liberty is that offered by Pettit (1997: p. 52):

> There are three aspects to any relationship of domination. Putting the aspects starkly, and without yet adding glosses, someone has dominating power over another, someone dominates or subjugates another, to the extent that:
>
> 1. they have the capacity to interfere
> 2. on an arbitrary basis
> 3. in certain choices that the other is in a position to make.

Taken to the extreme of the master/slave relationship, we see the epitome of dominating power. A slave, as Quentin Skinner (2008: pp. 92, 96–97) explains, may live under a liberal master free from disagreeable interference, but will not be free because that freedom is at all times precarious, dependent on the master's good will. To illustrate, we can use perhaps the warmest master-slave relationship in recorded Roman history, that between Cicero and his secretary and confidante, Tiro. Let us suppose that Cicero's rival, Crassus, had made an offer to buy Tiro. Tiro might put many arguments against the sale. He could appeal to the years of good service. He might talk of the genuine affection that Cicero had always expressed. He could argue that Cicero would not find a better secretary, and that, if sold, he would have to use to use his talents against Cicero and tell his new master all of Cicero's secrets. But the one argument that could not be brought by a slave against his sale was that the master was not within his rights. However much of a shock it might be for a slave in Tiro's position to suffer the full force of the master-slave relationship, there is no sense in which he can deny Cicero's entitlement to do what he wants. The lack of freedom comes from the nature of the power relationship, not the exercise of the power.

This relationship of absolute power is also seen in the argument put in Oskar Schindler's mouth in the film Schindler's List (Zaillian, 1990: p. 64; see also Keneally, 2007: pp. 240–241):

> They don't fear us because we have the power to kill, they fear us because we have the power to kill arbitrarily. A man commits a crime, he should know better. We have him killed, we feel pretty good about it. Or we kill him ourselves and we feel even better. That's not power, though, that's justice. That's different than power. Power is when we have every justification to kill – and we don't. That's power …
>
> That's what the emperors had. A man stole something, he's brought

> in before the emperor, he throws himself down on the floor, he begs for mercy, he knows he's going to die ... and the emperor pardons him. This worthless man. He lets him go ... That's power ... That's power.

It is an extreme example, but it serves to illustrate the relationship of power that is an essential part of the republican analysis. It looks not just at the individuals who suffer interference in their freedom, but at the cause of the interference and its motives. If we imagine a world where the principles of legality are achieved in full (Fuller, 1969: pp. 33–41), the law is clear as to the requirements of justice, and whoever is the agent executing that law exercises no personal power – they carry out a sentence which was preordained by the criminal's own actions. In contrast we have the emperor who may do as he pleases, who may carry out the requirements of the formal law, exceed them or waive them. That is a relationship of power between the individual who is emperor and the individual before him.

What follows from the concept of 'freedom as non-domination' is that there must be a will to interfere behind the dominating force, targeted at the individual or individuals suffering the interference. This is what Pettit (2012: pp. 35–49) describes as the distinction between 'vitiating' and 'invasive hindrances'. A 'vitiating hindrance' is an impersonal force; an 'invasive hindrance' is an act of deliberate power. It does not mean that the power is maliciously targeted – Pettit gives the example of a trade union whose strike of necessity means that the individual cannot read his usual newspaper. This would be an act of power designed to cause inconvenience – there is no point in striking unless it is to interfere with the ultimate receipt of the employer's goods and services – and it is therefore invasive; it contrasts with 'the vitiating sort of constraint you impose on me when you have no choice' (Pettit, 2012: p. 40).

The contrast can be illustrated with the 'locked room' scenario that has been put forward by a liberal theorist to argue against the republican distinction as being relevant to the existence or absence of freedom (Kramer, 2008: p. 41). An individual ('A') is able to lock another ('B') into a room. It may be that A will do so absent-mindedly, or deliberately. We have an accidentally locked-door scenario of 'vitiating hindrance', and a deliberately locked-door scenario of 'invasive interference'. But prima facie B's loss of liberty is independent of A's motive or lack thereof – he is either locked in or he is free. But, let us suppose that these do not represent one-off scenarios, but alternative scenarios for a general state of affairs to which B may be subject. Whilst the immediate effect on B of A locking the door will be the same, the two scenarios are fundamentally different. 'To be free, on the republican view, is to be free from arbitrary power' (Laborde and Maynor, 2008: p. 2); and there are crucial differences between B living with the risk of being accidentally locked in, and being subject to the deliberate power of A to lock him in. If B is subject to the deliberate power of A to confine him, then B has every reason to conduct himself so as to dissuade A from exercising that power – the dominated person must respect the logic of their position in their dealings with the dominator, which may involve anything from servile flattery to prudent self-censorship (Skinner, 2008: pp. 93–94). By contrast if the risk of B being locked in is due to reasons of A's absentmindedness, then flattery and self-censorship will get B nowhere: it is just an accident, and the limit of A's interference is to confine B on random occasions. But the dominating-A is not only able to pick and choose when to interfere and why, but the deliberate nature of the exercise of the power means that A may threaten B's freedom by saying 'do X, or I use my power over you'.

However, it does not follow that an individual will necessarily prefer to be subject to vitiating as opposed to invasive hindrances. 'B' might prefer to live subject to a dominating-A if the reality of an absentminded A was interference on a scale that destroyed his quality of life. As regards an individual's relationship with the state, matters such as cold, hunger and lawlessness are often vitiating hindrances to personal choice; but if a non-invasive state fails to prevent life being 'nasty, brutish and short', an invasive state may seem attractive.

To be genuinely free from interference, there needs to be a 'disabling effect' which means something that acts as a sufficient restraint on the potentially dominating agent, as opposed to the confidence that someone with the power to interfere will choose to leave well alone (Pettit, 2008: pp. 123–125). As we shall see, the disabling effect may derive from the potentially dominated individual's own power to strike back – but it may be that an individual's protection from interference derives from an ability for dominated-B to call for assistance from third parties to prevent dominating-A from doing his worst. In this third-party protection from interference, we have the bare bones of what Laborde and Maynor (2008: p. 3) describe as 'the powerful ideal of freedom under the rule of law'. If B is protected by C from domination by A, but C is free to choose to protect B not, then B's freedom to choose is still subject to the will of another. In contrast, if the protection comes from a predictable force such as the law, then B ceases to be subject to anyone's will.

Such is republican theory viewed from the perspective of an individual facing interference. But it naturally begs the question as to the content of the laws that will restrain interference and thwart the existence of a relationship of domination. Even if B can say, 'A does not dominate me as I know that the law tells him not to interfere, and that law is enforced', this is subject to the question of whether that the law which protects B today will continue to exist. We naturally move from the republican approach to individual freedom, to questions of the republican theory of government.

The republican theory of government

An obvious tension within the republican theory of government is between the concepts that laws should be made for the common good, and that laws should be made by the people. For James Harrington, the individual is free although controlled by law if such laws are 'framed by every private man unto no other end (or they may think themselves) than to protect the liberty of everyman' (Skinner, 2008: p. 87). We have not just the concepts of popular self-government and that the government's legitimate end is the good of the people, but freedom also requires that the people in exercising their role in the government must be motivated by the common rather than personal or factional good. A democratic system populated by entirely non-civically minded factions will fail to be republican. Laws in such a state would still be made by 'every private man', but for ends other than 'to protect the liberty of everyman'. This leads some republican theorists to conclude that it is the orientation towards the 'common good' that is paramount. MNS Sellers (2003: p. 1) strips out the role of the people in making the laws from the core republic governmental doctrine: '[T]he republican doctrine that laws and the state should always serve the common good or res publica of a nation's people or citizens'. On this view, it is not that republicanism requires democracy, but rather it is empirically true that a successful republic has always required a form of democracy (Sellers, 2003: p. 33).

A better approach is to separate the power of the people over the state, and the power of the state over the people. It is not every issue of the common good that is reducible to 'freedom as non-domination' from the individual's perspective. It is a poor metric for issues such as the effect of planning control on local amenities, devising transport networks, or existing citizens' interests in immigration policy.

There are thus two different aspects of an individual's relationship with the state, which can be subject to a republican analysis: (1) the individual as the *subject* of state power, and (2) the individual as a *citizen* with a share of power of the state. The former represents the rights protection part of the Human Rights Act's 'elegant balance', and the latter represents the democracy side. The citizens are interested in their position and vulnerability as subject, but also in broader issues of the common good which are less reducible to a rights-centred analysis. Republicanism is thus a 'fat' concept – but unless broken down to its 'freedom as subject'/'power as citizen' components, it becomes as James Allan (2006) presents the 'fat' concept of democracy: incapable of analysing the tensions between individual freedom and freedom of political participation. As explained in Chapter 2 ('Internalising the democracy/rights balance'), by internalising the two concepts of 'liberty' and 'democracy' that are on either side of the balance that the Human Rights Act tries to strike, republicanism in this 'fat' sense would serve to finesse issues rather than help to analyse them. Our interest is in what Downs (1957: p. 150) described as 'the power relation between the governors and the governed' in terms of how that power relationship gives 'the governed' power in respect of decision-making. Both liberty and democracy can be analysed in terms of 'freedom as non-domination', and this thesis concerns the latter. Any state that aspires to democracy will have legislators and officials who take decisions on a day-to-day basis with little public involvement – as we shall see in Chapter 4, such a system works democratically insofar as the electorate can choose to participate and by doing so make their opinions the dominant force.

In a republican constitution, the state is not something that happens to its people, it is something constituted by its people. As John Maynor argues, it is not sustainable for a constitution built on the principle of non-denomination to seek to track political values which are separated from what the citizens actually value (Maynor, 2003: p. 115). Skinner (2008: p. 87), building on Harrington, argued that 'provided that we ourselves make the laws, then we may be said to be living as free men in a free state'. But this does not wholly explain how individuals remain free by virtue of being a citizens when they are subject to laws which they vehemently oppose and resent. We do not necessarily value democracy and the opportunity for political participation for the same reasons as we value the freedoms and opportunities that may be curtailed to promote the common good. Individuals will not necessarily be happy at the restraint of their liberty and opportunities simply because it has resulted from a perfect process of democratic deliberation. Nevertheless, Philip Pettit (1997: p. 81) argues that republican theory 'does not countenance any temporal or causal gulf between civic institutions and the freedom of citizens', meaning that if no section of society enjoys a dominant position within the political constitution then that will be constitutive of freedom as non-domination within society. Pettit is arguing that in applying the principle of non-domination to political institutions, freedom as non-domination will automatically be promoted (Pettit, 1997: p. 80).

Pettit's contention is that a republican state will have a formally republican constitution with citizens acting in a republican manner, i.e. pursuing as best they can their idea of the common good. Pettit (1997: p. 84) argues:

> Freedom as non-domination promises, no exemption from arbitrary interference, but exemption from *intentional interference on an arbitrary basis*: specifically, exemption from a capacity on the part of others for arbitrary interference. It is consistent, unlike freedom as non-interference, with a high level of non-arbitrary interference of the sort that a suitable system of law might impose. What it sets itself against is not interference as such – in particular, not interference of that non-arbitrary kind – but only the sort of interference that occurs under such a lack of checking and constraint that, for all the victim can tell, it may be guided by hostile, unshared interests and hostile, unshared ideas.
>
> [Emphasis added]

Hence, individuals will not suffer arbitrary interference if they know that the laws and policies result from a political process controlled by citizens interested in the common good.

In our ideal republican state, individuals, who as subjects of the law feel aggrieved, will know that the law derives not from spite or self-interest, but from a genuine desire to do what is right. The individuals as citizens had been entitled to vote and contest, and those who outvoted them were open to argument and will remain so. The interference ought not to be arbitrary because, a) it was based on the common good, and, b) it does not represent the view of the common good of any arbitrarily chosen group, but the view (or at least the majority view) of those whose good comprises the commonality. The latter point, which is key to why democracy is inevitably necessary for republican government as opposed to being empirically correlated, is summed up by Philip Pettit (1997: p. 56): 'What is required for non-arbitrary state power … is that the power be exercised in a way that tracks, not the power-holder's personal welfare or world view, but rather the welfare and world view of the public'.

Unless the citizens are directly and equally involved as electors then it follows that there is a power-holding group whose world view takes precedence. This is unless we implausibly imagine that such a group can view the world perfectly through the eyes of those who are excluded.

Such is the ideal of republican government, but here is the place to recognise that it is an unobtainable ideal. Any democratic system represents a division of labour (Dahl and Lindblom, 1953: p. 42; Kyritsis, 2012: p. 323) between its ordinary citizens, elected politicians and unelected officials. Ordinary citizens will very often either not have an opinion on a subject or not care enough to use their participatory opportunities to express their opinion – and logically the extent of their interest and indifference should be reflected in how a constitution establishes the division of labour. Ordinary citizens tend to value the right to participate highly, but seldom become highly engaged. As Robert Dahl (2000: p. 39) argues, most citizens find political participation neither urgent nor rewarding. If electors participate by voting, they will often be unreflective or tribal in their loyalties. A constitution will organise both how the electorate can participate through voting, and how legislative decisions are made in the absence of meaningful popular participation. The result is that the power of the electorate is likely to operate as a 'reserve' power (Pettit, 2012: pp. 230, 268–269), with politicians either unaware of citizens' opinions or estimating them as sufficiently weakly held so as not to trouble them. Politicians and administrators may thus go about their business uninhibited unless and until enough electors participate so that politicians become concerned about the citizens bringing to bear the logic of their dominant power at elections. However, when we consider Pettit's theory of alien control later in this chapter, and in keeping with Skinner's exposition of the position of a well-treated slave, we shall see that holding a power to invigilate (even if not actively used) will in principle amount to being in a dominant position. Republican theory is not, therefore, irrelevant because the electorate typically falls short of ideal levels of participation. The question is whether, when the electorate participates, its choices will be dominant? Will each elector's choice only be limited by the extent the choice is shared by fellow electors (i.e. non-alien control, as the control comes from the electorate itself as a body of equals)? Or will such choices be subject to alien control (i.e. domination from a separate force, such as an external power or an internal elite)?

The 'elegant balance' of the Human Rights Act would, if it preserves democracy, ensure that constitutional review in the United Kingdom is not something done to the people by way of judicial action, but something capable of control through the mechanism of preserved Parliamentary Sovereignty. The 'legislative rights review' approach to the relationship between human rights and democracy, outlined in Chapter 2 ('Legislative rights review'), ostensibly does this by making the achievement of rights a part of the political process. However, the limits of the theory that we noted can be highlighted in terms of the above republican principles. The 'legislative rights review' theory for reconciling constitutional review and democracy takes, arguably, a 'liberal' view of a citizen's freedom. Citizens' political freedom is not, in a liberal view, affected by hindering them from achieving ends with which they do not desire, but it is promoted by facilitating their participation towards desired ends. As a reconciliation of rights and democracy, the 'legislative rights review' thesis assumes a desire to promote human rights, but does not consider where the citizens strongly favour derogations contrary to rights jurisprudence. The assumption, perhaps true of the politically liberal, is that this scenario either does not arise or is unimportant.

Republican freedom vs republican participation

From a republican perspective there is a tension in that, if republican governmental process should maximise freedom as non-domination, a republican critique of the laws and policies created by that process ought simultaneously to be a critique of the processes of government. The fault may be in the electorate failing to dominate government. Alternatively, the fault may be in the electorate being factional, where participation is not undertaken to the end of Harrington's 'liberty of everyman' (Skinner, 2008: p. 87), but instead to promote group interest without regard for the rest of the country. In such circumstances constitutional review may promote republican freedom by being 'the means by which current arrangements are tested for democratic arbitrariness' (Bohman, 2008: p. 210). There is a direct equivalent to what James Allan (2006: p. 536) calls a fat, 'morally overlain account' of democracy: in such an approach, a moral analysis of legislative and policy output will be a sufficient critique of a state's democratic credentials. The difficulty is that, if such tests for democratic arbitrariness are carried out so as to censor laws and policy, the resulting process may look profoundly unrepublican when viewed from the perspective of the citizen's political freedom, i.e. the electorate's domination over government. The result would be a very limited form of republicanism, as Adam Tomkins (2005: pp. 42–46) argued when responding to the republican case for the judicial interventionism of the US

Supreme Court put forward by Cass Sunstein (1988: pp. 1552–1553, 1580) and Frank Michelman (1988: pp. 1494–1499). Despite reviewing decades of considerable expansion in the reach of judicial power in the United States, Sunstein and Michelman found only three US Supreme Court decisions to be unrepublican (*Bowers v Hardwick* (1986) 478 US 186; *Buckley v Valeo* (1976) 424 US 1; *Washington v Davis* (1976) 426 US 229).

In a system of strong-form constitutional review, the test for 'democratic arbitrariness' is inevitably carried out and applied independently of the electorate in order to determine whether participation for particular ends should be allowed. The result would follow what John Maynor describes as an essentially Rawlsian liberal approach. Citizens should confine their political participation to acting within a 'political identity that embraces the political principles of justice'. These may or may not overlap with individual citizens' own 'religious, moral or philosophical comprehensive doctrine' (Maynor, 2003: p. 95). If this means that a citizen cannot participate so as to promote what they actually believe, then so be it. Similarly, if this means that citizens must translate their opinions into less subjective terms with which they do not actually agree or care much for, then so be it – although this may court accusations of intellectual dishonesty (Toynbee, 2015). On this view, Maynor (2003: p. 95) explains, a reasonable citizen will have 'a political identity that embraces the political principles of justice, a non-political identity that affirms some religious moral, or philosophical comprehensive doctrine'. This view of Rawlsian thought is shared, more approvingly by Martha Nussbaum (2005: p. 205), who argues that religious doctrines must be excluded from public debate unless they are 'congruent with the principles of justice that shape the basic structure of society … [and] must include Rawls's principles of justice, even if originally they did not do so'. Beliefs based on moral reasoning (as opposed to intuition or religion) must be heard ahead of 'avowed interests' (van der Rijt, 2012: p. 117). Views, however strongly held, that are held for religious or intuitive reasons must be kept 'non-political', and left out of deliberation and voting considerations except insofar as they overlap with a non-religious and admissible political identity. The same applies to opinions rooted in self-interest.

Whilst such an approach may maximise 'freedom as non-domination' viewed from the perspective of the quality of the laws, it would create significant problems viewed from the context of republican government. Firstly, there would be an approach to the common good that seeks independence from how the individuals who make up the commonality view their own good. Secondly, it is unnatural to demand a recapitulation of every aspect of every question into a moral or political theory. The point at which a level of crime makes life nasty and brutish for those in a neighbourhood is one of human experience and not abstract theory. Hence, Pettit's view that criminal justice laws, whilst being best designed by experts, should not be determined by expert opinion. Instead Pettit suggested a penal policy board to recommend criminal justice laws on a principled basis to the legislature, but with the board having no power to screen out proposals by the legislature (Pettit, 2001–02; 2004: p. 55). José Luis Marti (2009: p. 139) argued that this was an example of 'weakly-democratic republicanism', but there is nothing unusual in 'expert deliberation' feeding into and informing the processes of legislation in a democracy. Thirdly, and importantly, the effect of such a hurdle is to exclude a significant proportion of citizens from the political process as surely as any literacy or property test. Access to the political process would be dependent either on an ability to frame one's own views in the required terms, or on finding an intercessor ready, willing and able to do so. Jack Straw, when Home Secretary, saw the language of the Convention becoming the language needed to win arguments, illustrating how deeply embedded he anticipated a human rights culture would become (Parekh, 2000: [7.16]). Factors such as 'time', 'money' and 'learned capacity' always bring advantages in political participation (Beetham, 1993: p. 64) but requiring the language of human rights to be spoken for effective participation in political debate excludes those without the language skills. Like speakers of a second language, they will be confined by what their limited language skills enable them to say, not by what they would like to say. Fourthly, and similarly, the approach would require people not to express their views, but to translate them as best they can into a permissible discourse. Regardless of proficiency in the language of human rights, they may find that their ideas simply do not translate. As John Maynor (2003: pp. 90–116) argues, an approach that seeks to respond only to the reasoned, political beliefs as opposed to ones rooted in tradition or religion, is untenable in the long term (Maynor, 2003: p. 115):

> [I]f the republican state and others are to track individuals' interest, individuals must be asked to register their interests as they are, comprehensive or not. A citizen that registers what its political interests are, especially if these political interests vary greatly from its members' comprehensive beliefs, cannot sustain non-domination.

In order to participate, people may find themselves needing to formulate an abstract, reasoned, moral view, which may in many cases only approximate to their own actual belief should that be harder to render in a publically acceptable form. Such publicly professed beliefs will part company from the actual beliefs, a state of affairs that cannot hold good forever.

Fifthly, the difficulty of screening out putatively arbitrary viewpoints is summed up by Frederick Schauer's (1999: p. 17) self-satirising confession that, 'It is a source of continuing astonishment for me that such a small percentage of even my soundest opinions command widespread assent'. Unless like Schauer we acknowledge that the majority of people face similar frustrations, and that we can provoke similar frustration on the part of others, we can lead ourselves to write off the existence of a popular majority against our opinions or candidates. One person's biased media misleading voters is often another person's factual journalism; or else we impute to the press more power over public opinion than it in fact has (Gilligan, 2008; Collins 2014).

We must therefore be wary of embedding the republican theory of freedom into the republican theory of government. The result, to cite Richard Epstein's (1988: p. 1642) criticism of the republican approach of Cass Sunstein (1988) and Frank Michelman (1988), would give 'skilled academics a comparative advantage' over others. It would give a special position for those who are qualified to conduct Bohman's (2008: p. 210) tests for 'democratic arbitrariness', or are capable of presenting their views in a manner best calculated to pass such tests. Inevitably, this means an elite filtering the opinions of the populace, a role above and beyond the inevitable advantage that the eloquent will have in broadcasting their views. If the ability to expound republican theory became a filter for effective political participation, republicanism would turn its back on political equality between citizens.

In short, if a constitution allows any elite to screen out genuinely held opinions, the result may be as Bagehot (2007: pp. 134–135) states: '[T]he most dull government is a free government on matters its ruling classes will not hear'. As Bagehot argues, a healthy legislature is one that confronts the people with the entirety of public opinion. A legislature that pre-screens opinions will not serve that function.

In saying that we track the 'world-view of the public' (Pettit, 1997: p. 56), we do not mean some form of 'collective will', the existence of which Philip Pettit (2004: p. 60 fn. 9) dismisses as metaphysical: 'The core difficulty with the notion of collective will is that it presupposes collective agency, and that the existence conditions for a collective agent are too demanding for a large-scale populace or electorate to satisfy'.

Nor is it right to think in terms of the hypothetical consent of those who object to the law. The only vague sense in which an individual might be said to give consent to many of the laws is in this crude sense of 'if they do not like the law, then they know where they can go'. It is difficult to deem the consent of citizens in this way. Most citizens will not have chosen where to live and alternative choices will be restricted by an array of personal, social, legal and political factors (Pettit, 2009: p. 52). Few would follow the example of Joseph Conrad's *Nostromo* and move to Costaguana because of political objections to his home country's constitution. However, individuals in a republican state cannot reject a law's application to them without claiming an unequal position, i.e. either that the law should apply to everyone but themselves, or that they should have a veto on laws. A citizen cannot claim anything more than equality with other citizens (Pettit, 2009: p. 53): '[A]ll members must share equally in this collective control. An equal share in collective control will give each member the highest possible level of control over the law, consistently with no one being given less than that level'.

In the republican state, the law derives from a process where citizens are full and equal participants. Individuals' political freedom *as citizens* is unaffected by merely failing to achieve their goal of finding a majority for their views (Berlin, 1969: p. 122; cited Pettit, 2012: p. 41). This is because their political freedom is to try to persuade their fellow citizens, and for the results of all such persuasion (i.e. all political debate and discussion) to be measured through electoral processes. A citizen should be able to say, even in defeat: 'I can still do that if I and other supporters can convince a majority of my fellow citizens'. Inherently, there can be no guarantee of persuading other citizens. The republican state will both tend to reduce the risk of oppressive interference in the freedom of the individual as *subject* by virtue of laws being controlled by individuals *citizens* orientated to the common good; and it will continuously offer citizens the prospect of further deliberation and possible changes to those citizens who found themselves in the losing minority. It is therefore not simply a case of saying, 'if you do not like this law, then you know where you can go', but rather that individuals who wish to assert a position of superiority over their fellow citizens ought to reconsider their position in the republic. Pettit (2012: p. 280) understandably links a constitution's ability to treat the people as equal to the people's own willingness 'to live on equal terms with others'.

It follows that David Miller (1995: p. 447) is correct to argue that republicanism does not allow the state to regulate 'what sort of demand may be put forward in the political forum'. A state doing this would dominate individuals in their capacity as *citizens*, even if we accept that such regulation would tend to produce laws promoting non-domination of the same citizens viewed from the perspective of their position as *subjects*. However much those policing for 'democratic arbitrariness' (Bohman, 2008: p. 210) may see themselves as acting in a non-arbitrary way, any decision that one view may be promoted in the political processes established by the state's constitution – but another view is excluded – will be essentially arbitrary. Such a decision would derive from and entrench the power of those who happen to be in a position to carry out the policing, or who had been in a position to create the constitution. It offends the basic principle of equality as citizens to disqualify fellow citizens from advancing genuinely held views. Equality is in outvoting opposing opinions, not in telling opponents to keep their opinions in the private sphere.

The framework approach

What concerns us is the ability of citizens as equals to control government. Collectively, citizens should be able to limit the freedom of choice of those in government who make law and policy. A useful starting point is Pettit's own analysis of how an electorate may exercise control over government, such control being categorised as 'virtual', 'inhibitory' or 'interventional' (Pettit, 2004: p. 62):

> [T]hree forms of control are likely to be enjoyed by ordinary people so far as there are contestatory institutions available for them to make their voice heard. They will have ***virtual control*** over government laws and decrees even in the absence of any intervention, because the fact that they do not contest those decisions will be partly responsible for the shape the decisions assume. They will have ***inhibitory control*** over government so far as the authorities are wary of activating any protest or appeal against their actions. And of course they will have ***interventional control*** so far as they actually do contest decisions of government and have an effect upon them.
>
> [Emphasis added]

Taken at its simplest – the level of 'interventional control' – there are two sides to freedom as a citizen: (a) the electorate must be able to make undominated choices when participating, and (b) such choices must in turn control government.

'Inhibitory control' is less structured, but presupposes certain thought processes working in tandem: (a) for 'control', there must be public opinion on an issue that is liable to turn into protest and, ultimately, into interventional control; and (b) to be 'inhibited', the government must accurately understand (i) what the majority or plurality opinion is on the issue, and (ii) whether that opinion will turn to protest and intervention. In a despotism, inhibitory control works by estimating the threat of rebellion; in a democracy, it works by estimating loss of votes (Anson, 1909: pp. 240–241). It can thus be seen that 'inhibitory control' – which, as we shall see, is a crucial part of democracy – requires a commonality of understanding between citizens and legislators. There is no inhibitory control if legislators misunderstand public opinion, and fail to see where the risks of protest and interventional control lie. To use language familiar from the literature review: the political costs that an electorate threaten to impose on legislators should be the same as the political cost feared by legislators. A lack of common understanding will undo inhibitory control.

'Virtual control' may apply in the absence of any ascertainable borders for interventional or inhibitory control. The point that Pettit makes is that, even in a world where elites might not have immediate concerns about the ordinary citizens asserting themselves, such elites only peaceably enjoy power because they have done nothing to provoke ordinary citizens into action. As Ivor Jennings (1966: p. 211) explained, an absence of revolution does not necessarily mean the rulers are dominant, nor that the people are docile. It may mean that the state simply has not been run yet in a fashion intolerable to the people: 'If the people of this country want to overthrow capitalism, the public school system, the House of Lords or the monarchy, they have the power in their hands. If they have not done so, the explanation is that they have not wanted to do so'.

The shape of a constitution is not dictated by what 'is given by a conciliatory upper class' (Jennings, 1966: pp. 209–211), but by what ordinary people have wanted enough to demand. Virtual control is like the control of the non-voters, who, as Jennings explains (1966: p. 67) really decide elections: 'Had they voted for the one party or the other, that would have won'.

In terms of constitutional review and popular power: (a) popular control is virtual insofar as decisions may lead to a response but happen to fall within the range of popular tolerance; (b) popular control should not be inhibitory as against the judiciary, because judges ought not to be influenced by popular opinion – but it may be inhibitory in respect of politicians having control of legislative override; and (c) popular control will be interventional when it successfully requires that judicial decisions should be overridden. In contrast, subject to any legislative or constitutional override, judicial power may (i) possess virtual control for as long as the political branches stay well within the bill of rights; (ii) possess inhibitory control insofar as the political branches wish to avoid adverse findings; and (iii) possess interventional control when adverse decisions are taken by the judiciary.

The basic overview of Pettit's (2009: p. 41) approach is summarised as follows:

> I interfere with you in a given choice between options x, y and z, if I treat you in any of the following ways:
>
> - I manipulate your capacity to choose deliberatively, say by overloading you with information, subjecting you to powerful rhetoric …
> - With or without your awareness, I remove one of the options from the domain of your deliberative choice, putting a block in the way of its selection.
> - With or without your awareness, I replace one of the options by a burdened counterpart, establishing a penalty that will attend its choice.
> - I deceive you into thinking that you lack deliberative capacity or, more plausibly, that an option has been removed or replaced, whether by me or another agency.

From which we must note an important point: popular control of government must by definition restrict the deliberative choices of decision-makers. Furthermore, if the electorate is sufficiently engaged in pressing its preference so as to exercise inhibitory or interventional control, then some of the effective deliberation will have taken place at the level of the electorate.

Three axioms and four theorems

Pettit's formulation of how choice may suffer interference has developed over various accounts whilst developing his analysis, and applying it in different contexts. For example, recently Pettit (2012: p. 54) saw that reduction of choice by way of 'manipulation' and 'deception' were different degrees within the common head of 'misrepresentation'. However, in the first rendering of the theory in 'Three Axioms: Four Theorems', 'reduction' of choice existed as a separate head to make a mnemonically satisfying 'reduction, removal, replacement', where 'reduction' may be in the actual 'ability to choose' (Pettit, 2008: p. 107), or be caused by an ostensible rather than a genuine removal or replacement of an option (pp. 110–111). That 'manipulation' may reduce the ability to choose is acknowledged but as a concept it is less developed than in later analysis. This increased focus on 'manipulation' may have been caused by Pettit (2012: pp. 26–74) recently applying his approach to domination to the governmental context.

Despite the later refinements, we start with Pettit's (2008) earlier analysis of republican freedom in 'Three Axioms, Four Theorems', noting relevant refinements as we progress.

The axioms

First axiom: the reality of personal choice (Pettit, 2008: pp. 104–105):

> [I]n every case there is an aspect under which each option presents itself to us such that … I can think, and think rightly: this is within my power of choice; this is something I can do …

An analysis of domination starts with the existence of choice. If I wish to travel from London to Cornwall, the choice of air, rail or road is mine. I can choose according to my resources, taste and priorities. The 'reality of personal choice' means just that: whatever risks, whatever experiments I wish to undertake, they are my choice.

Second axiom: possibility of alien control (Pettit, 2008: pp. 106–107) takes three forms, 'reduction', 'removal' or 'replacement':

> [C]ontrol exercised by A may be alien or alienating in any one of three broadly different ways. It may impact on B's ability to make a deliberative choice so that the assumption of personal choice is undermined on a general front. Or it may impact on the specific options that fall within the domain of B's choice, in which case there are two possibilities. The control may simply remove one or another option from the set of options faced by B, reducing the total options available, or may seem to remove it. Or it may replace one or another option by a significantly changed option, or seem to replace it by a significantly changed option …

To return to the London–Cornwall travel scenario, let us suppose I wish to fly, which we will call 'option-x'. If Jones books the last seats in order to prevent me flying, then option-x has been *removed* by invasive interference.[1] If Jones warns me (falsely) that the flight is cancelled half of the time, then my power to choose option-x has been *reduced* through misrepresentation/manipulation. If Jones through some influence arranges that I may take only hand-luggage, then option-x has been *replaced* with option-x*, where I can travel, but something important to travel has been changed.

A shift that has taken place in Pettit's analysis of domination from his original neat, mnemonic of 'reduction, removal and replacement' given above, to his more recent preference for 'removal, replacement or misrepresentation' (Pettit, 2012: p. 46). Misrepresentation has become an umbrella term for two closely related forms of hindrance: deception and manipulation. If we are told with sufficient authority that option-x is unavailable, then it ceases to be something that we can think of doing, even though we would be right to think that we could. In Chapter 8 ('Legislative acceptance of obligation to comply'), we shall see this later in terms of explanations given by ministers for complying with the Human Rights Act.

However, misrepresentation need not be invasive: it may be vitiating. Something may be said with authority and genuine conviction, yet misrepresent reality. Of course, our ability to choose is limited by us seeing the world through the lens of what Dicey (2008: pp. 121–122, 330) described as the spirit of the age, or what could be called its ideology. In the age of laissez-faire, collectivist ideas will appear frighteningly alien; and in the age of collectivism, laissez-faire may seem unthinkably reactionary. Anyone's ability to consider any option is dependent on the chooser's perception of the facts and risks around the option – and that perception is unlikely to come from a fully developed understanding of the subject matter, but more usually from employing currently accepted principles – or at least choosing from such a range of principles as are currently fashionable (Downs, 1957: pp. 141–142). The facts and risks may be a matter of dispute. Risks may be a mixture of objective actuarial statistics, and subjective responses to what worries us most (Sunstein, 2005: pp. 129–148). Pettit in his original analysis used 'misrepresentation' to encompass both controlled and uncontrolled interference, but subsequently the natural focus fell on the controlled (i.e. invasive) forms of misrepresentation in deception and manipulation.

In the context of government and constitutional review, strong-form constitutional review *removes* certain choices in that neither inhibitory nor interventional control exerted by the electorate may cause legislators to pass certain laws. By giving the final say to a legislature, weak-form constitutional review such as the Human Rights Act does not remove a choice, but this still leaves a potential for choice to be *reduced* or *replaced*. It may at different times be best analysed in terms of the social or political costs of making

1 Had Jones merely booked the last seats because he simply wanted to travel, the interference would be vitiating, just part of the normal ups and downs of life.

'choice x', where 'pure' choice x is replaced with encumbered choice x*, with '*' representing the costs seen as attached to the choice. What is required is a representation of the choice to legislate incompatibly that is commonly understood by both electors and legislators who support the Act. A common understanding is required unless inhibitory control by the citizens of politicians is lost through misunderstanding and misrepresentation.

Third axiom: positionality of alien control (Pettit, 2008: pp. 108–109):

> The third axiom, which is quite independent of the other two, asserts that if someone in B's position comes to be able to control what A does, then to that extent A's control over B diminishes, perhaps even disappears.

This is what Pettit calls, 'the case of counter-control'. This concept of 'counter-control' holds that it is not the probability of interference, or something such as 'a shift of attitudes or habits' on the part of the interferer, that liberate an individual from domination (Pettit, 2008: p. 123). This is an important concept for this thesis: the elegant balance of the Human Rights Act depends on the override of judicial decisions being within the system, for this is the means by which Parliament is accountable to the electorate and may remove options for interference from the judiciary.

To give an example from the British Constitution without anticipating analysis of how the Human Rights Act works in practice: to say that the Queen's consent is required for an Act to be law is legally true, but to say that she possesses the power of counter-control in respect of laws sent to her for consent would be entirely false (*Barclay v Secretary of State for Justice* [2008] EWCA Civ 1319; [2009] 2 WLR. 1205 [117]–[127]). Nothing changes in law between 1801, when George III caused the resignation of Pitt the Younger by refusing to countenance a Catholic Emancipation Bill (Pitt, 1801), and the 1860s when Bagehot (2007: p. 57) could rightly conclude that '[I]t is a fiction of the past to ascribe to [the Queen] legislative power'. There had, in between, been a radical change in 'the mode of exercising that rule' (Bagehot, 2007: p. 284).

Pettit (2008: pp. 123–125) noted that 'domination' is only relieved by the presence of a 'disabling effect'. The forbearance of a dominator does not qualify as such a feature, even if that forbearance was based on the possible dominator's own sense of propriety or competence – as, for example, in the 'separation of powers' or 'institutional competence' models for judicial deference in matters of justification. It is not mere conventional propriety that keeps the royal power in check, nor just as Dicey (1982: pp. 295–305) described, the legal impossibility of the monarch using her prerogative to maintain a ministry in that such a government would soon run out of money without Parliament's support. The legal impossibility of governing completely without Parliament does not of itself explain the absence of an occasional use of a veto power, or the sort of personal involvement in policy seen under George III. The explanation is more in what Dicey (1982: p. 301) calls 'the maintenance of political morality'. Regardless of strict legality, certain actions will provoke a reaction. 'The power of legislative veto would predictability lead to a trial of strength that could only end unfavourably for the monarch concerned, save in a "quite exceptional" situation' (Amery, 1964: pp. 6–7; Amery, 1952: p. 59). In contrast to the earlier example of Cicero considering selling Tiro, his slave, the public response to a royal veto would be that its very use was illegitimate and the predictable response to that royal action by the populace would be more powerful than anything that monarch would have to defend herself.

For the Queen to veto legislation would be a challenge to the established political order notwithstanding the theoretical legality. To quote Pettit (2012: p. 138) on political legitimacy:

> The legitimacy of a social order is often thought to correlate with the political obligation of citizens. Such political obligation … is not the pro tanto obligation to obey the laws but the pro tanto conditional obligation, if you oppose the laws, to oppose them within the system.

The British Constitution may in theory allow the Queen to veto legislation, but she would be acting outside the system as universally understood. Even if she prevailed against the predictable opposition, the old system will have been overthrown.

The four theorems

First theorem: alien control may materialise with interference (Pettit, 2008: p. 110):

> Interference involves control so far as it serves the desires of the interferer, A, by changing the probabilities associated with the different options before the interferee, B. And that control will be alien so far as the interference practiced undermines B's ability, with one or another option, to think, or think rightly: I can just do that …

We begin to get the firmer picture of what is meant by 'alien control': it is that the decision as regards a particular course of action is being reduced, restricted or replaced by a guiding mind that is not your own.

Hence, in the human rights context, strong-form constitutional review may place alien control over the electorate in (a) the constituting power that enacted the constitution, insofar as the interpretation and effect of the bill of rights is determined by the instrument itself, and (b) the judiciary, insofar as the interpretation and effect represents judicial choice. In weak-form constitutional review, the constituting power may be the same (or nearly the same) as the ordinary legislature – the ordinary legislature either being the constituting power or being able to exercise power of comparative strength. In the case of the United Kingdom, the constituting power is in form exercised identically to the ordinary legislative power when constitutional Acts of Parliament are passed (Dicey, 1982: p. 78; Weyland, 2002: pp. 6–7). Ostensibly at least, and particularly if we assume there is no gap between the opinion of legislators and the opinion of the electorate, there can be no alien control exerted by weak-form constitutional review: any control exercised by judges is on the sufferance of the same democratic process that established the system of constitutional review.

Second theorem: alien control may materialise without interference (Pettit, 2008: pp. 111–114). Pettit argues that 'invigilation is a form of control'. If A has the ability to interfere, but does not because B is making the 'right' choice, B is still subject to alien control. It is a return to the difference between liberal and republican freedom: from a liberal perspective there is no loss of freedom for citizens in being unable to do what they would not choose; from a republican perspective there is still a relationship of domination.

Similarly, a relationship of domination exists if A is biding his or her time, or is currently uninterested in whether B chooses x, y or z. Pettit (2008: p. 112) argues that such invigilation amounts to control:

> By being there ready to interfere if necessary, though not interfering as a matter of fact, A is bound to raise the probability of B's x-ing in the case at hand.

The point is that, whether B realises it, his choices are affected by whether A gives permission. Pettit (2009: p. 44) has subsequently drawn a clearer division between 'invigilation' and 'inhibition or intimidation'. 'Invigilation' means that A monitors the activity of B with a view to interfering if A chooses option-x rather than option-y. It is impossible for B to think rightly that he is free to choose option-y, because whether known or unbeknown to him option-y will be prevented by A or else substituted immediately with option-y* as soon as B indicates a desire to choose option-y.

Whereas 'inhibition or intimidation' means essentially invigilation where the invigilator has shown his power and thus causes B to 'self-censor or self-ingratiate', which means either abandoning the idea of choosing option-y, or fawning and toadying in the hope of obtaining A's permission to take option-y. Pettit (2009: pp. 44–45) adds that it is possible to inhibit and intimidate without actually having the invigilatory power by successfully pretending to have the power, which he describes as 'intimidation … without invigilation', although of course the distinction between power and the perception of power is illusive.

The purpose of constitutional review is precisely to invigilate legislative, executive and administrative action, with the effect determined by the entrenchment and enforcement provisions of the bill of rights concerned. Insofar as there is a weak-form of constitutional review, as the Human Rights

Act is, the effect of invigilation will be determined by how far compliance is seen as a duty or a choice. Compliance is sometimes talked of as a legal obligation (HL Debate, 2012: cc. 875–876, 884–886). At other times the response to Human Rights Act decisions has been presented as an open choice for the legislature no different to any other (*Belmarsh* [145]). Individual or institutional choice can be inhibited or intimidated by such a contested invigilatory power. Indeed, as we considered earlier as regards the monarch's legal power of legislative veto, the use of a contested power can be seen as a contest of power, a contest which may be constitutive of the invigilatory power if conceded by the party suffering the interference. But to say this is merely to apply the 'truism' that 'obedience to law must be enforced by opinion of some sort' (Dicey, 2008: p. 4). In respect of the power of government, Dicey quotes David Hume's dictum that 'force is always on the side of the governed, the governors have nothing to support them but opinion' (Dicey, 2008: p. 3). However much this may seem may seem optimistic as between government and people, it is plainly true as between the governed and the judiciary in a weak-form system of constitutional review. But the interaction between the comparative force of government, judiciary and the governed will not be reducible to simple statements of relative theoretical power, as the interaction between them is not obvious. Does the judiciary invigilate the politicians only, or does it also invigilate the effectiveness of citizens' choices for political participation? Is the judiciary taken by the electors to have such an invigilatory power, notwithstanding that the particular bill of rights, such as the Human Rights Act, denies them that power? Does the judiciary invigilate the government on behalf of the people, or does it also act in co-operation with the government to invigilate choices that might be pressed by a 'tyrannical' majority through electoral participation? In the constitutional context, the invigilated group's opinion of the invigilating power is thus a matter of great importance as to the nature and existence of the power itself. Lacking its own force, the ability of the judiciary to interfere with legislative choices of others, and thus to invigilate, is very much dependent on the opinion of those it invigilates. For that reason, it is important that the potentially 'invigilated' body should have a tolerably clear view of the power relationships that are meant to exist so that it can decide whether it is or is not appropriate to exercise counter-control in a particular case.

It is worth noting a parallel with the 'legislative rights review' approach considered in Chapter 2 ('Legislative acceptance of obligation to comply'). In that approach it is assumed that judicial hegemony is avoided because judiciary and legislature are working to the same end of upholding rights. Bringing legislative choices into harmony with constitutional review jurisprudence undoubtedly means there will be less judicial disapproval so less judicial interference. Importantly, the second theorem shows that an alignment of preferences between the 'dominator' and the 'invigilated' does not mean that the invigilated person is free. Whilst from a perspective of liberal freedom this means that the participatory freedom of those well-disposed to the bill of rights jurisprudence is effectively upheld, it does not of itself mean that the judiciary lack a position of domination. They have less cause to exercise such counter-majoritarian power as they have – but that is a different matter.

Third theorem: non-alien control may materialise without interference (Pettit, 2008: pp. 114–115). It is possible to create a relationship where the probability of taking a course of action will be most likely affected by what another person says they can do. But it does not affect the 'I can do that' hypothesis if the other person is playing a 'reasoning role', assisting not directing:

> [People] can lend each one another their reason, as it were, playing the role of advisors or collaborators, and helping one another to get clear on the options available in any choice and on the pros and cons of the alternatives. They can act in relation to one another as an amicus curiae …

Let us suppose a litigant has employed senior and junior counsel. A procedural matter arises. The litigant will do as advised, and such matters are typically left to junior counsel. The junior counsel has doubts. The position is this: a) if the junior seeks the advice of the senior counsel, that counsel will effectively invigilate the decision – viewed as independent agents, the counsel with the highest rank exerts alien control over the junior. However, suppose b) the senior counsel is unavailable, and the junior seeks advice from senior members of chambers, such advice will provided as 'co-reasoning' – advice even from the most distinguished retired judge is still just advice, and the humble junior is free to reject it. Importantly, should the client receive bad advice, a reasonable client knowing all the facts would understand that the junior is not responsible for relaying the views of senior counsel in the case but would be less than impressed if the junior sought to evade responsibility because he had chosen to accept the 'wisdom' of a third party, however distinguished.

In the constitutional sense, we may see this 'co-reasoning' as being a more positive view of what could otherwise be described as 'counter-control' under the 'third axiom'. We gain assistance, we do not lose power – nor do we shift responsibility. The reality of choice should carry with it the reality of responsibility, and accountability.

Fourth theorem: non-alien control may materialise with interference (Pettit, 2008: pp. 116–118), if the person subject to interference always retains the ability to counter the interference. The obvious case is where B gives a permission to A to interfere, but can revoke that permission. Pettit argues that it is enough that:

> [B] will be able to think, and think rightly: … I over-time can do that sort of thing; or I-over-time, re-inforced by my deputy or proxy, can do that sort of thing.

There is a potential tension around the issue of the probability of interference. We saw in the 'first theorem' that A exercises alien control by altering the probability of B choosing x or y. We saw in the 'second theorem' that the probability of A interfering does not alter the reality of domination: A invigilates B, so B's choices are taken with A's permission. We saw in the 'third theorem' that altering the probability does not mean alien control exists where A persuades B, as the operative will is still that of B. Finally, in the 'fourth theorem', we saw that A does not dominate B, if B has the power to counter-control A. The potential tension is this: unless a system of co-reasoning is one of 'pure co-reasoning' (i.e. no effect on the probability of a decision being taken outside A's ability to persuade B), then A's interference will typically interfere with the probability of B's decisions. If A is a trusted adviser, B will often lack the time or the confidence to overrule A. The same is true in government. Legislators, ministers, administrators, and citizens frequently rely on experts, and it is thus usually probable that experts will be followed due to a dynamic which is not wholly explicable by the merits of their conclusions on a case by case basis. Nevertheless, if we look at the 'second' and 'fourth theorem' together, it follows that B's power to counter-control is no less a power that can dominate A's interference by virtue of a low probability that it will be used in any given case. Understood from this direction, in the face of a power of counter-control, A's power to interfere will be one of alien control only if it changes the nature of (or perceived nature) of the decision facing B should he or she consider exercising a right of counter-control. If B's decision (should B take an interest) remains one on the merits – for example, an absentee landlord unexpectedly getting involved and giving instructions to the agent who is used to deciding everything – then B invigilates A's interference, and thus dominates A's choices to interfere.

In any constitution, the judiciary will often interfere with the meaning of legislation in the process of interpretation. Where there is a dispute about the meaning of a statute or judicial precedent, the act of interpretation will create new law. Even outside those cases where greater or lesser violence is given to the ordinary meanings of statutes in the name of fundamental rights (*R v Special Commissioner, ex parte Morgan Grenfell & Co Ltd* [2002] UKHL 21; [2003] 1 AC 563), the meaning given to statutes by the courts will often differ from the expectations and desires of those who supported the law, whether as legislators or as concerned electors. Judicial decisions will give a meaning to the statutes and thus present the political branches with the choice of reversing that decision. Lord Hoffmann (2002: [8]) explained:

> Normally ..., the House will decide what the law is according to what it thinks is a fair and sensible conclusion ... Such a judgment is bound to carry a certain moral authority and usually it is not politically easy to reverse it by legislation. The only department of government which seems to have no inhibitions in this respect is the Inland Revenue. But in other areas, judicial decisions are fairly immovable. This is of course

> particularly true in the case of construction of the Human Rights Act. It is bound to be extremely difficult for a government to secure the passage of legislation which the courts have said would be in conflict with human rights.

One might query whether the ordinary acceptance of judicial interpretations is uniquely dependent on the moral authority of the judiciary. Dicey (2008: p. 263) argued that judicial opinion was a cross-current of opinion, whose prestige may influence public opinion, but that would not of itself explain the degree of unlikelihood of legislative overrule that Lord Hoffmann asserts. There are questions of the extent of disagreement with judicial interpretations versus resources (e.g. limited Parliamentary time) required to reverse judicial interpretation. Such interpretation operates as a 'resistance norm' rather than as an 'invalidation norm' – see Chapter 2 ('The passive virtues'), above. Also, the judicial contribution to the meaning and application of a statute may be benign or at least unobjectionable. The example of the Inland Revenue is instructive: adverse tax decisions will typically require immediate counter-control when an avoidance scheme creates a damaging gap in the tax code requiring immediate attention. But the impact of the judiciary on the meaning of the statute is a matter of co-reasoning (and thus not a matter of alien control) insofar as legislative counter-control is a fact of the system. MPs are free to think about the decision, and free to do something if they want, as Lord Renton stressed in the Human Rights Bill debates (HL Debates, 1997a: col. 1298). Insofar as MPs may decide it is not worth the effort, they still have control of the judicial power. They may 'undo the permission' given to the interferer on an issue-by-issue basis. It is not a choice between either a rule of obedience to the co-reasoner, or terminating the co-reasoning relationship.

We return to a reoccurring theme in the literature review to see how the questions of 'counter-control' and 'co-reasoning' are central to our investigation in the Human Rights Act. What is the nature of the costs (political or otherwise) said to underpin human rights decisions? Are political costs to be exacted by the electorate, or by another force? Or is it a matter of 'enactment costs' which slow down the decision-making process, but only alter the result insofar as they alter the decision-makers' thinking about the merits? If there is a 'resistance norm' under the Human Rights Act, does it represent inertia in respect of changes of law, or a force of opinion opposing certain policies?

Conclusion

Pettit argued that 'republican theory can be cast as a research programme for constitutional and legal design' (Pettit, 2009: p. 59). It is the intention of this thesis to take the principles discussed above, in particular the detailed analysis of 'domination' or 'alien control' to consider whether the Human Rights Act can operate so that the electorate may continue to exercise virtual, inhibitory or interventional control over government on matters where the participatory choices of citizens would infringe the results of constitutional review.

Pettit's analysis centres on the idea of choice. In terms of the theory of government, this means the extent to which the electorate can choose the laws and policies that govern them; or the extent to which their choices are controlled by either external agents or internal elites. It is not that the electorate are a driving or even material force in all or most legislative decisions, but rather that they can exercise an invigilatory power over such choices. The probability that the electorate's invigilatory power will be used is not relevant in itself to it holding a position of domination over the results of constitutional review. The electorate's power is often a 'reserve power' (Pettit, 2012: pp. 230, 268–269). It can often be found in the sense of 'virtual control', which simply means that a decision is legitimised in that it did not rouse popular disapproval (Pettit, 2004: p. 62), as Jennings (1966: pp. 209–211) argued in respect of the post-1832 British Constitution: a quiet populace is not necessarily a dominated populace. The power may be brought out from 'reserve' and into public debate. Public opinion can operate by way of 'inhibitory control', when politicians respond to or anticipate public opinion by avoiding vote-losing action. Both virtual and inhibitory control require the possibility of 'interventional control' – such as when elections involve clear choices or when matters of controversy are put to a referendum. It should be possible to say, and say rightly, 'If I can convince a majority of my fellow citizens that X is right, then we-over-time can do X'. This majority 'we can do that' hypothesis is necessary for political equality: there ought to be no groupings whose special permission is required.

Such control as the electorate may exert will not exist insofar as there is any group or institution that can interfere with its electoral choices. If any such body or institution can 'remove, replace or replace' any choices, invigilating the range of choices open to the electorate, then such a body has the power of control. In Pettit's terminology, such a body or institution would be in a position of 'alien control' as regards the electorate. It will not however be in such a position if its interference is co-opted into the deliberative processes of the electorate, what Pettit describes as 'co-reasoning' (Pettit, 2008: pp. 114–116).

4 The nature of democracy

Introduction

We set out in the last chapter the theoretical toolkit offered by Philip Pettit to analyse whether relationships of domination exist, with an eye to establishing the conditions whereby the electorate may justly feel that they are able to exercise control over those who legislate and administer.

Philip Pettit's (2012: pp. 279, 302) theory of democracy, as abstracted from republican theory, is that there needs to be 'a properly individualized, unconditioned and efficacious system of popular influence', also described as 'suitably individualized'. It is individual participation by citizens that adds up to a majority, and no grouping or body has a right to place conditions on participation or what may be sought through participation. Electors choose, there is no censorship of what may be chosen and those choices (when taken) dominate.

But such participation must take place in a system. Such a system, to work, will recognise the practical limits and willingness of its citizens to actually participate. It will need to recognise that those who seek to build electoral support will not necessarily find in others the willingness to deliberate that is implicit in the hypothesis of 'If I can convince a majority of my fellow citizens that X is right, then we-over-time can do X'. The creation and maintenance of that system will be subject to constitutive decisions, which ought to be controlled by the people as the constituting power exercising control that is likewise 'properly individualized, unconditioned and efficacious', although the people may choose a system that limits those conditions in day-to-day legislative process. This, we shall see, is Pettit's 'dual-aspect' theory of democracy: that popular control must exist first at the level of the constituting people to set the rules of government, and then by the people as constituted within those rules.

We now turn to the question as to how such systems function (or not) to give public opinion a dominant power over legislation.

Public opinion and legislation – the mechanics

Thomas Paine (1791: pp. 2–3) said that: 'A Constitution is a *Thing* antecedent to Government, and a Government is only the Creature of a

Constitution. The Constitution of a Country is not the act of its Government, but of *the People* constituting a Government' [Emphasis in original].

Before someone can exercise administrative, executive or legislative power, the way of doing so must be established. A democratic constitution must be understood in terms of where the exercise of power stands in relation to the people, and not just in terms of inter-institutional relations. There is no democratic 'political constitution' without the people at its heart (Tierney, 2013: p. 2185).

Before we can apply the republican theory of government, we need to consider how democracies produce decisions. Frederick Schauer (1999: pp. 20–21) offered four 'decision procedures' by which power may be exercised in a state. Giving these in the order that we intend to use them, we find (1) 'public deliberation', decisions reached by a process or processes of deliberation that encompass the public as a whole; (2) 'a non-deliberative preference measurement, possibly by public opinion poll but more commonly by secret ballot' – the electors cast their votes (or not) for any reason (or none); (3) select-group deliberation, 'decisions might be made by deliberative processes within a select group, as with a representative legislature'; (4) 'expert (or elite) decision-making', which means that a particular issue is addressed by those with particular expertise.

Public deliberation

If the state belongs to the people, then our tour of the levels of decision-making should start with the people. There is 'public deliberation' to a greater or lesser extent as and when any issue arises. Anything can become a cause célèbre, and on anything the cry may come up that something must be done. Such public deliberation may involve a greater or lesser amount of the public deliberation. Few subjects elicit total indifference, and few will engage the entire population. Those who take an interest and reach a view may have closely engaged with the issues, they may have made themselves well-informed, or merely absorbed an opinion congenial to their preconceptions. Public ignorance may be remarkable to those who are engaged. Some may participate in public discussions by writing to the press, to their MPs, or in blogs; some may discuss the subject with friends and family, others may reach a decided view in the privacy of their own minds. It largely depends on how willing they are to pay the costs of becoming well-informed (Downs, 1957: pp. 141–142); for most people, it is an irrational investment of time and energy to involve themselves in the issues of the day (Dahl, 2000: p. 39). As such, 'public deliberation' does not just mean detailed discussions, for this would exclude the reality of how most of the electorate engage with politics prior to their voting decision (Mansbridge, 1999; Michelman 1988: p. 1531). Public deliberation encompasses what Jane Mansbridge (1999: p. 225) describes as 'everyday talk' in terms of being an unstructured marketplace of ideas where anyone can be heard to the extent that they make the effort to speak, and can find others willing to listen.

Members of the public have opinions, and they can share their opinions with the world, or such part of the world that they can reach. This is public opinion as public deliberation. They may share their opinions with the ballot box only: that is public opinion without involvement in public deliberation, except as a spectator. They may broadcast their opinions and influence others, yet not vote themselves: 'the man who talks loudest or most convincingly in the club or the pub may not vote at all' (Jennings, 1966: p. 197). They may keep their opinions wholly to themselves, in which case their opinions are kept from public opinion.

Public deliberation most obviously informs public voting, but it is also a necessary part of inhibitory control. If there is no public discourse, there is nothing (unless there are referenda) communicated to decision makers as to public opinion on particular issues, except that Party X is more popular than Party Y, but why this is so would be a mystery that confounds inhibitory control.

Public voting

Voting links public deliberation with the decision-making process of the legislators and government. We cannot in any realistic sense account for the importance of voting except as looking backwards to 'public deliberation', and forward to its effect on 'select-group deliberation'.

Public deliberation without voting will lead to a decision-making model like that described by the future Portuguese dictator, Antonio Salazar, when becoming finance minister (Gallagher, 1983: p. 48): '[L]et the country study, let it suggest, let it object and let it discuss, but when the time comes for me to give orders I shall expect it to obey'.

Studying, suggesting, objecting and discussing are all fine things, but unless such deliberation is brought to a decision there is no system which identifies public opinion and links it to legislative change. Without voting there is a closed oligarchy – the public's ability to 'throw the rascals out' is at the heart of the link between politicians and the electorate (Morton and Knopff, 2000: p. 51; King, 2007, p. 59). And in Pettit's terms, the electorate would have no form of collective counter-control over interference by political decision makers – there would be no virtual, inhibitory or interventional control by the electorate over the executive and legislators, at least none exercisable within the political system. It would be the public that stood, at best, in a position of co-reasoner should the political decision makers be inclined to listen. There can be no sense that citizens could think and think rightly that their views will carry the day ('over-time') if they can convince a majority of other citizens unless there is a formal and binding measurement of opinion. Applying Pettit's (2012: pp. 84–87; Maynor, 2003: pp. 45–46) notable 'eyeball test', there would be no sense in which the general populace can look their rulers in the eye as equals.

Select-group deliberation

Legislators may have expertise in particular subjects, but they are selected to represent, and representativeness is their closest thing to a core expertise (Laski, 1951: p. 37). Furthermore, the deliberation of legislators will be intertwined with the 'everyday talk' of public deliberation; the deliberation of judges will not. Politicians are meant to be approachable by their electors (Beetham, 1999: p. 165), judges must be independent. Voters may approach politicians in any number of ways in an attempt to influence them. They can write letters (and emails) to MPs or newspapers. They may visit their constituency MP. They may demonstrate. They may join a campaigning organisation. They may attend meetings. They may heckle. They may ask questions on television or radio current affairs programmes. Even the Prime Minister can be buttonholed by a mere voter, and should try to answer respectfully. Before a big measure reaches Parliament, it will have been subject to 'vigorous debate, public and private, up and down the country' (Laski, 1951: p. 31).

This contrasts with the position of judges – who Schauer (1999: p. 21) sees in terms of select-group deliberation, but are better seen as an example of 'expert deliberation', to which we shall turn next. Judges are chosen to be isolated from such popular pressures (Morton and Knopff, 2000: p. 51). They may be approached by fellow lawyers through the respectable medium of an academic article – which may serve as what Morton and Knopff (2000: pp. 137–147) call 'advocacy scholarship', a means of participation available only to specialists. The judiciary often view themselves as experts in the protection of liberty (*Belmarsh* [39], [178]; *RJR-MacDonald* [68]; Clayton, 2001: pp. 523–524; Clayton 2002: pp. 189–190), or as experts on criminal justice matters (*RJR-MacDonald* [68]), or otherwise as having a greater or lesser institutional competence to resolve issues.[1] Lawyers able to write learnedly in legal language will have an advantage in influencing the development of case law closed to ordinary citizens. The importance of judicial reasoning being conducted away from the passions of public opinion that may lead majorities to be tyrannical has been stressed (Kavanagh, 2009: pp. 351–352); and similarly, the American literature finds arguments that legal reasoning makes lawyers better at understanding how society works, and how it can safely regulated, than citizens who may feel strongly that something must be done (Friedman, 2009: pp. 1164–1166).

There is, however, a fundamental difference between a country constituting a system of government on the basis of identifying a group because it

1 For opposing views on these claims see Ewing and Tham, 2008: p. 690.

decides better in some way, and selecting a group to represent the citizens who make up the country. Arguments on institutional competence obscure the fundamental issue of the role of the electorate. In any case, if we remember that the relationship between a decision maker's deliberation and public deliberation is fundamental in a democracy, we see that deliberation by elected politicians cannot be equated with that between appellate judges.

Expert deliberation

Expert deliberation exists where types of decisions are confided in an authority with relevant skills. It might exist in areas where, for the time being, there is no meaningful public opinion, and where the reaction of legislators would be one of ignorance or indifference, with sporadic pockets of obsessively keen interest. It might exist to create authoritative advice for the legislature, as Pettit (2001–02; 2004: p. 55) argues should be the case where a difficult area of policy meets deeply entrenched instincts, such as criminal justice. This represents a division of labour, where a decision-making power (or recommendation-making role) is given to experts by reason that the select group cannot deal with the matter wholly itself, whether through want of expertise or time (or both).

Whereas select-group deliberation may be subsumed into the broader political process, where public deliberation and voting choices act upon legislators, expert deliberation ought to harness relevant skills and viewpoints in isolation from popular passions. Lay members may be part of expert panels, insofar as it is thought that a largely expert subject requires the input of those with a broader perspective, but such members are not appointed to represent the views of any constituency. Their representative role will be at the most that of providing virtual representation to a wider public that has largely never thought about the subject.

This is not to say that there is no equivalent of 'public deliberation', it is just that the public concerned will be appropriate to the expert group. For example, if a voter wishes to influence a judicial finding on a question of law, the only legitimate means of doing so is through arguments presented (typically by a lawyer) in a court. Lawyers have ways to influence jurisprudence through their 'learned capacity' (Beetham, 1999: p. 64): they can engage in the 'advocacy scholarship' mentioned earlier (Morton and Knopff, 2000: p. 53; see also Beatson, 2012: pp. 4, 8–9). They can devise litigation strategies to optimise the chances of case law developing in their favour, such as pro-abortion/choice campaigners in Poland (Bodnar, 2012: p. 158). Strategies may be fairly informal, such as Helena Wray's (2013: p. 859) suggestion that immigration lawyers, as well as representing their immediate clients, needed to think strategically about how running an argument might affect immigration jurisprudence.

'Expert deliberation' is a fact of life in the modern state. Schauer is correct when he points out that the wording on cigarette packets will largely derive from expert deliberation (Schauer, 1999: pp. 20–21). It is science that tells us the nature of health risk from smoking, not any deliberative process conducted by the public or politicians. Laski (1951: pp. 140–141) noted that decisions on allocation of funding to medical research lent themselves to decision by experts. However, this is not to say that the state should simply allow expert opinion to be determinative: the legislators (acting in response to their own and public deliberation) could take a minimalistic view of the role of the state in advising people not to harm their own health. Expert deliberation may have an almost exclusive role in setting out facts, probabilities, risks and costs. But experts cannot dictate responses. Amery (1964: p. 102) quotes Sir William Harcourt saying: 'the value of political heads of department is to tell officials what the public will not stand'. For example, how much people would pay to reduce a risk of cancer as opposed to that of heart attack is not reducible to expert analysis, such as a rationally standardised 'value of statistical life', but varies according to fears of different ways of dying (Sunstein, 2005: pp. 138–141).

The basics of democracy

Lord Sumption (2013: p. 11) recently argued that: 'Properly speaking, democracy is a constitutional mechanism for arriving at decisions for which there is a popular mandate'. At greater length, Dicey (2008: pp. 8–9) envisaged three ways in which public opinion may fail to direct legislation:

> [(1)] No 'opinion', in the proper sense of that word, with regard to the change of the law may exist; [(2)] the opinion which does direct the development of the law may not be 'public opinion'; and [(3)] lastly, there may be lacking any legislative organ adapted for carrying out the changes of the law demanded by public opinion.

The common theme is that of public opinion being connected to the end of products of government by some of sort of 'constitutional mechanism', per Sumption, or 'organ adapted' for the purpose of creating such a link, per Dicey.

David Beetham (1999: pp. 4–5, see also pp. 90–91) offered the following summary, which serves to unpack the ideas noted above as to the essential idea that there are 'decisions', a 'popular mandate', and a 'constitutional mechanism' in between:

> [A] system of collective decision-making can be said to be democratic to the extent that it is subject to control by all members of the relevant association, or all those under its authority, considered as equals. Popular control and political equality are the core principles of democracy …

Those principles of 'popular control' and 'political equality' have an obvious congruence with Philip Pettit's theory of democracy as abstracted from republican theory, that is, 'popular control exercised has to be suitably individualized, unconditioned and efficacious' (2012: p. 302, see also p. 279). Individualised because no family head or clan chieftain can exercise citizens' participatory rights for them; unconditioned in that no force can control which issues can be subject to deliberation and potential adoption; and efficacious in that popular control will direct the persons who directly hold political power. As seen in Chapter 3 ('Republican freedom vs republican participation'), the argument that citizens are not dominated by laws passed in a democracy is not that they can say the egotistical, 'I can get law X passed over time', but rather, 'If a majority of fellow citizens agree with me, then we-over-time can get law X passed'. There is no elite with an entitlement to thwart such an assumption, nor is there any group with special representation able to veto the majority.

This begs the question of whether a system is democratic when on many issues there is no public opinion to speak of and so no popular mandate except in the sense that the electorate's virtual control has given licence to the immediate decision makers. Similarly, it begs the question of whether it is realistic to talk of 'popular control' when decisions are in the immediate control of elites who may be unresponsive to public opinion on many issues. The idea that democracy should be seen as a process starting with the electorate and ending in legislation or policy is challenged by the realist (or elite) theory of democracy most associated with Joseph Schumpeter (Bacharach, 1971: pp. 9–10). Schumpeter (2011: pp. 269, 284–285) defined democracy thus:

> [T]hat institutional arrangement for arriving at political decisions in which individuals acquire the power to decide by means of a competitive struggle for the people's vote …
>
> Democracy means only that the people have the opportunity of accepting or refusing the men who are to rule them.

This approach narrows its focus to the act of voting and acts of electioneering. Instead of elections being the buckle that links public deliberation to select-group deliberation, elections merely choose the select group who will transact the affairs of state. In being required to submit itself to periodic popular election, the 'select group' of ministers and legislators will differ from a technical elite, but between elections such a select group should conduct itself as an elite independent of popular control.

We shall soon turn to Schumpeter's approach in detail, before applying the approaches of David Beetham's (1999: pp. 151–169) democratic audit and Robert Dahl's theory of polyarchy (Dahl, 1956: pp. 63–89; 1971a; 1971b; 1989: pp. 225–264; 2000) both (a) to reject Schumpeter's narrow view of democracy, and (b) to argue that the constituting power in a state is not only exercised by the legislature or the electorate when creating constitutional provisions or statutes, but is exercised continuously by the electorate's approach to its own opportunities for participation. In terms of formal constitutional rules, the electorate ought not to choose a system that limits the efficacy of popular control; but nor should it choose a system dependent on greater participation than it is willing to give. To a significant degree, the choices as to the degree of participation may be constitutive of a Schumpeterian constitution; but, equally, the ability to assert popular control through interventional control is an inherently legitimate choice in a democracy.

Dual-aspect nature of democracy

It is necessary to note the 'dual-aspect' nature of democracy which is set out by Philip Pettit (2012: pp. 252–279). The point is simple and targeted at the choice of constitution. In any democratic system there are the choices of the 'constituting people' who determine the form of government, and the choices of the 'constituted people', who will direct the government within that chosen form. Pettit recognises that the popular power in a democracy is often very much a reserve power in respect of its ability to direct government, but how distant such reserve power is from actual decision-making will be determined both by constitutional rules and participatory choices. A constitution may be structured in ways to facilitate or restrict the ability of public opinion impinging on legislative opinion (e.g. greater or shorter terms of office), and/or to affect individual citizens' cost/benefit analysis of participation (e.g. a system that offers representation for parties achieving 5 per cent of the vote nationally is more favourable to those wishing to participate for unrepresented ends than first-past-the-post, which requires candidates to achieve a plurality in a constituency). The constitutional rules are determined by the constituting power, which in a democracy will be the people themselves, at times through revolution, at other times through referenda, or constitutional conventions, or pressure on legislators.

It is important to note that republican theory does not view the people as being in anyway obliged to choose a republican form of government. They may experiment with direct democracy. If they value stability and leaders with independent judgment, they might introduce seven-year terms of office holders; or they might want their leaders never far from accountability, and go for three years. They might prefer a strong, appointed upper chamber for the legislature precisely to stand above democratic pressure. They may create a system of constitutional review or they might not. Then there is the constitutive effect of participatory choices. They might in their electoral preferences favour candidates who do what they think is right, over populists. Obviously, within any choice as regards the form of government and how to participate within that form, there are ways that are more or less republican in any tendency towards factional or oligarchic domination. But it is for citizens to decide which suits them best. It is thus not important that, ordinarily speaking for any democracy, Schumpeter (2011: pp. 284–285) will appear to be right that 'democracy does not mean and cannot mean that the people actually rule in any obvious sense of the terms "people" and "rule"'. The people will rule to the extent that they wish and should consent to a constitution that best suits their inclination to participate.

Hence, in respect of constitutional review, there are questions of whether Britain should move to a system where the courts can strike down statutes on human rights grounds or whether it should have constitutional review at all. Pettit's 'dual-aspect model of democracy' recognises that the republican requirements are not only, or even primarily, about whether the system of government increases or reduces the 'freedom as non-domination of the people'. The first question is whether citizens have a free and undominated choice to constitute and reconstitute their system of government. What Lord Bingham said in respect of a change to embracing strong-form constitutional reform is entirely in accord with Pettit's approach: '[i]t is one which should be made only if the British people, properly informed, choose to make it' (Bingham, 2010: p. 170; see also Hoffmann, 2002: [15]). Indeed, we may go further: republican theory demands that the people's role as the constituting power must be inalienable – to take terms from the debate around Parliamentary Sovereignty, the sovereignty of the people is 'ongoing', rather than 'self-embracing' (Young, 2009: pp. 66–68). A consequence of popular sovereignty is that questions of whether a legislature's sovereignty is self-embracing are not to be decided by constitutional theory, but will be open to determination by the choices of the popular sovereign – hence Jennings's derision at the idea of defining the powers of the Ceylonese post-independence Parliament according to constitutional theory as to the origin of its power instead of examining where power lay post-independence (Jennings, 1964). This is much as the German Constitutional Court has said when holding that 'eternity clauses' in Germany's written constitution could nevertheless be changed by 'the directly declared will of the German people' (*Lisbon Case*, BVerfG, 2 BvE 2/08 [228]).

This dual-aspect approach to democracy rejects Michelman's (1988: p. 1509) view of popular sovereignty as making a one-off appearance in a constitution's history to create a constitution 'entrenching substantive limits on the reach of their own sovereignty'. The popular sovereignty must endure – indeed, the same popular sovereignty did endure in the United States, and the reason why amendments are so few owes little to the will of the popular sovereign that enacted the original constitution, and everything to interplay between the conduct of subsequent generations and the formal difficulty of amendment. There result has been as a 'constitutional culture' against such amendments (Sinnott-Armstrong, 2003: p. 387). Michelman (1988: p. 1509) said that '[o]nce, however, is hardly enough' for 'the republican achievement of popular self-creation – of recollecting themselves as a people'; but the requirement of republicanism is more than this. The exercise of popular sovereignty at the level of the constituting power is something that the citizens must always have the legal and moral capacity to repeat.

The ultimate point is that the conditions of democracy ought to be satisfied and continue to be satisfied at both the level of the people as the constituting power, and the constituted people, that is, as the electorate in ordinary politics. However, there is no power to deny the people the right to choose a system that is less than democratic, and no power to deny the people the right to re-choose. As noted in Chapter 3 ('Republicanism and domination'), it may be rational to choose domination by the will of a third party if alternatives are likely to be more chaotic in practice, at least providing that choice can itself be retaken.

Schumpeter and classic realism

Democracy, for Schumpeter, does not start with the raw material of public opinion nor reach the end products of law and policies. There is nothing of what Waldron (2005: p. 445) describes as the 'complex and delicate interplay' between formation of public opinion, public voting and legislative debates and decisions. For Schumpeter democracy exists solely in the acts of seeking and receiving public votes, and is kept within the confines of those core activities. Schumpeter (2011: p. 145) argues that public opinion does not direct political action:

> [T]he mass of people never develops definite options on its own initiative. Still less is it able to articulate them and to turn them into consistent attitudes and actions. All it can do is to follow or refuse to follow such group leadership as may offer itself.

It is not denied that the electorate has opinions, however, '[e]ven if strong and definite they remain latent, often for decades, until they are called to life by some political leader who turns them into political factors' (Schumpeter, 2011: p. 270). Potential leaders bid for power and '[v]oters confine themselves to accepting this bid in preference to others by refusing to accept it' (p. 282), and 'once they have elected an individual, political action is his business and not theirs' (p. 295). Indeed, the principle that electors do not seek to influence those that they elect is presented by Schumpeter not just as part of a realistic view as to how democracy normally works, but as an aspect of 'Democratic Self-Control' which he argues is a precondition for successful democracy (pp. 294–295). The electorate should have no inhibitory control over government and legislation, as elected politicians should have a free hand before submitting themselves to 'interventional' control represented by elections. The electorate have none of what Pettit (2012: pp. 230, 268–269) described as a 'reserve' power over issues, because electors should avoid inhibiting their leaders' judgements, and should not think of participating to procure particular outcomes. Schumpeter envisages the electorate to be passive and awaiting leadership. The effectiveness of the 'interventional' control depends wholly on the choices granted by the elites.

Schumpeter was right to see democracy as centred on the competition for votes – he was wrong to isolate voting from the deliberation (public, select group and elite) that surrounds it. A democracy exclusively centred on competition for votes can, like any market, be undone by anti-competitive practices. In such conditions, it is entirely possible for normally competing elites to decide between themselves that leadership should not be granted in a particular direction forming an oligopolistic market controlled as a cartel. This will happen 'if political supply does not adjust competitively to changes in demand and voters perceive that their demands are not satisfied' (Pelizzo, 2003: p. 173). Such political cartels may exist by way of grand coalitions either excluding minority opinion groups from the bargaining process such that they need not be taken into account, as happened with the exclusion of Social Democrats in 1930s Switzerland (Dejung, 2010: pp. 104–105). Alternatively, 'effective political competition' may be undermined by bringing all parties within a 'Grand Coalition', a dynamic that was feared in late-1960s West Germany (Kalterfleiter, 1970: pp. 596–597), although not realised in practice because normal competition resumed at subsequent elections. As well as formal coalitions of parties, there may be issue-specific agreements between those competing to hold power. Before the 1992 British General Election, the major parties agreed not to outflank each other in respect of immigration control, an agreement which some have praised (Hodges, 2014), but was essentially a cartel agreement. The decision of a party elite to take a stance that is potentially unpopular with its supporters is part of the vicissitudes of representative democracy – the party 'takes its chance of the nation following or not following' (Bagehot, 2007: p. 131). If *all* parties agree to take the same stance (or to take stances within an agreed range of choices), then there is a deliberate removal or reduction of effective choice. Instead of representing the public, legislators would be exerting alien control over the electorate. Cartels, of course, are liable to break down – but, as long as they hold good, the only systematic way of breaking a political cartel is the entry of a new product (i.e. a new party) into the electoral market. This is a particularly difficult step to take, particularly in a first-past-the-post electoral system such as that used to elect the Westminster Parliament.

Schumpeter also argued that, as a precondition for successful democracy, the involvement of politicians themselves should not reach wholly to the end of the creation of legislation and policy. He argued that politicians must restrain themselves from interfering with matters of complexity which are very much in the realm of experts. In contrast to Philip Pettit's (2002) view that criminal law would benefit from authoritative *but non-binding* advice from experts to legislators, Schumpeter (2011: p. 292) argued that in determining the detail of a criminal code 'parliament will have to accept the specialist's advice whatever they may think themselves'. This argument contrasts starkly with Walter Bagehot's (2007: p. 181), who saw 'no limit to the curiosity of Parliament', and that 'all branches of administration' must give an account to Parliament 'to say why they act when they do, and they do not when they don't'. In contrast to Schumpeter, Bagehot (2007: pp. 171–172) argues that there is no class of experts or intellectuals who could claim a special power in determining the laws of the country.

Schumpeterian democracy critiqued

Peter Bacharach (1971: p. 9) argued that the Schumpeterian view would mean that 'democracy should not be conceived as a political theory that encompassed both ends and means'. The result is a disconnection between the Schumpeterian approach and any popular desire to demand legislative change. Bacharach explains the tension that many see between the classic understanding of democracy as rule by the people, and an apparent reality that democracy extends only to electors choosing between which elite individuals will dominate them (1971: pp. 9–10):

> The difficulty with the classical theory [of democracy], as understood by the realists, was that it had little relationship to the real world. The evidence compiled by various studies consistently showed that the majority of people are politically apathetic and ignorant and that they simply do not choose to participate actively in political life. Confronted by this evidence, the contemporary democratic theorist had the option of embracing a normative theory of democracy which has little resemblance to the real world or of revising the theory to accord with the prevailing facts.

If accepted, this is a potent argument undermining the basic premise of seeking a balance between the protection of human rights and democracy, and would thus question the utility of enquiring into that balance. It goes beyond familiar pessimistic assertions as to the reality of British democracy being that decisions are often taken with minimal democratic credentials (Steyn, 2005a: pp. 346–347; Clayton, 2004: p. 40; Kavanagh, 2009: p. 376). Such arguments tend to invite John Hart Ely's (1980: p. 67) rebuke: 'Sophisticated commentary never tires of reminding us that legislatures are only imperfectly democratic … the appropriate answer is to make them more democratic'. The realist approach to democracy denies that 'more democratic' is an option – Schumpeter might overstate the position by suggesting that the public are only engaged to the extent required to cast a vote, but popular interest in democratic decision-making is inevitably weak in respect of many important decisions and non-existent in respect of most of the remainder. Criticisms of the democratic (or, indeed, undemocratic) nature of the British Constitution in the here-and-now would cease to be just a critique of contemporary, local and (therefore) remediable phenomena, but would instead reflect contemporary and local occurrences of the inevitable failure of the democratic political method to result in popular rule. On this view, it would not be a choice between judicial power (under constitutional review) as against popular power (by way of democracy): the constitutional choice would be as to what decision-making roles should be possessed by which elite (i.e. the politicians and the judges).

When academics discuss what approach elite judges should adopt when determining the scope and application of the Human Rights Act, factors which have loomed large include those of relative institutional competence (Steyn, 2005a: pp. 360–361; 2005a, p. 352; Jowell, 2003: pp. 598–601; Lester and Pannick, 2004: [3.19]) and the limitations of adjudicative decision-making (Edwards, 2002: p. 859; Fuller, 1978: pp. 394–395). A society that accepts the realist critique of democracy will believe that, however it might design its constitution, it will not create popular rule, and so we should not have democratic scruples about replacing an elected elite of politicians with an appointed judicial elite of lawyers, if the latter is more reliable. There is a decision to be made where expertise lies – so the competence issues addressed in the 'judicial deference' debate are the correct issues, even if the judges are not the rightful constitutive power to determine where the line for judicial competence or the proper limits of adjudication should be drawn in any particular society. The role of elections shrink to one of governance: in the 'economics of civic virtue', the electorate may lack sufficient virtue to be truly self-governing, but may nevertheless be able monitor a high-profile elite of elected legislators for such a quality (Michelman and Sullivan, 1986: pp. 58–60; see also Sunstein, 1988: p. 1556).

The extremity of the disconnect anticipated by Schumpeter between legislative/executive action and public opinion can be illustrated by noting the contrasting views of Edmund Burke, normally cited for his rejection of the role of MPs as carrying out mandates from their electors (e.g. Hailsham, 1978: p. 99; Cowley, 1996: p. 218; Colon-Rios, 2014: p. 307). Yet Burke also argued that it would be wholly wrong if an elected legislature saw its task as being purely objective, unfettered by public opinion (Burke, 1808: pp. 287–288; cited Dicey, 1982: p. 35):

> It would (among public misfortunes) be an evil more natural and tolerable, that the House of Commons should be infected, with every epidemical phrensy of the people, as this would indicate some consanguinity, some sympathy of nature with their constituents, than that they should in all cases be wholly untouched by the opinions and feeling of the people out of doors. By this want of sympathy they would cease to be a House of Commons.

A democracy that *perfectly* tracked public opinion through every peak and trough might well be a form of democracy that the people would not wish on themselves; but a form of government where legislators were wholly objective would not be much of a democracy.

The problem with the realist approach to democracy, or at least the Schumpeterian version, is that it does not itself represent reality. If classic democratic theory idealised popular participation and the responsiveness of politicians to elections, the Schumpeterian view relies on the restraint of electors not to seek to influence politicians, and idealises politicians in not being guided by public opinion despite competing for votes. As Beetham (1999: p. 42) said, 'elections exert an effect well beyond the time when the actually take place ... [t]he fact of the vote casts a long shadow in front of it'. Therefore, Schumpeter's approach, 'far from being realistic as is claimed, is simply inaccurate'. Inhibitory control of politicians by the electorate is inevitably a real factor, and made inevitable by the interventional control that electorates inevitably have by the choice of who governs.

It should also be noted that the Schumpeterian view of democracy sits poorly when the competing political parties are seen as mass political movements. To view democracy purely as competition for votes, taken to its logical conclusion, views political parties as companies competing for market share (Parris, 2015). Companies are not necessarily interested in the quality of their product, but in volume and margin. Insofar as political parties are still to some extent mass political movements, the flexibility of politicians to branch out into new products is restrained by a membership that is interested in winning for a purpose. If accountability is only in a choice between elites, then elites can divide up the spoils. This is an aspect of the cartel party hypothesis (Katz and Mair, 1995) that Peter Mair (2013) developed shortly before his death. Where party elites are 'either governing or waiting to govern' then we are left with Schumpetarian 'competing teams of leaders'. Mair (2013: pp. 88–89) concludes that: 'What remains is a governing class', and (p. 98): 'The result is the beginning of a new form of democracy, one in which citizens stay at home while parties get on with governing'. If party elites are accountable also to mass movements, where the only spoils enjoyed by party members is in their favoured policies triumphing, then competition is real. Any viewpoint capable of gaining a mass movement enters the contest whether it be red, blue, yellow, gold, green or purple. Of course, if the public cease to want to participate, then they create the conditions for cartelisation.

Polyarchy

An approach which neither idealises democracy so as to ignore the indifference of most electors to most issues, nor turns realism into cynicism by treating such indifference as a universal characteristic of any putatively democratic system, is Robert Dahl's theory of polyarchy. There are seven conditions for polyarchy (Dahl, 1989: p. 221):

1. *Elected officials.* Control over government decisions about policy is constitutionally vested in elected officials.
2. *Free and fair elections.* Elected officials are chosen in frequent and fairly conducted elections in which coercion is comparatively uncommon.

3. *Inclusive suffrage.* Practically all adults have the right to vote in the election of officials.
4. *Right to run for office.* Practically all adults have the right to run for elective offices in the government, though age limits may be higher for holding office than for suffrage.
5. *Freedom of expression.* Citizens have a right to express themselves without the danger of severe punishment on political matters broadly defined, including criticism of officials, the government, the regime, the socioeconomic order, and the prevailing ideology.
6. *Alternative information.* Citizens have a right to seek out alternative sources of information. Moreover, alternative sources of information exist and are protected by laws.
7. *Associational autonomy.* To achieve their various rights, including those listed above, citizens also have a right to form relatively independent associations or organizations, including independent political parties and interest groups.

Viewed from the perspective of the citizen, Dahl (1971a: p. 2) describes the following:

> [A]ll full citizens must have unimpaired opportunities:
>
> 1. To formulate their preferences
> 2. To signify their preferences to their fellow citizens and the government by individual and collective action
> 3. To have their preferences weighed equally in the conduct of the government, that is, weighted with no discrimination because of the content or source of the preference.

Polyarchy thus describes what we would recognise as a functioning representative democracy, whilst qualifying the concept of popular power intrinsic to the word 'democracy'. Under the theory of polyarchy, '[d]emocracy is a goal, not an achievement' (Dahl and Lindblom, 1953: p. 41): even in a system that seeks to be democratic, *direct* power is held by different groups, individuals, organisations and institutions. The 'unimpaired opportunities' to participate described above by Dahl may go unused, as is increasingly the case in the established democracies (Dahl, 2000: p. 39). For a system to be a 'polyarchy' there are no limitations on who may come to hold to power nor indeed on who might cease to hold it. If the electorate as a whole choose to participate within the system, there would be no holder of power who could resist the will of the majority. Lindblom (1977: p. 138) presented a ladder of power holders in a political system, which, translated into British politics, would be as follows:

- The Prime Minister

- Cabinet Ministers
- MPs
- Party officials
- Politically active citizens
- Voters
- Non-voters

The democratic moments are when the ladder is collapsed and all stand in a position of equality, as at a general election or referendum, where each citizen has one equal vote. A system may be constituted to increase or reduce the number of such events, for those equal moments to directly address specific issues through referenda, or act on issues less directly, i.e. through interventional or invigilatory control exerted by voting choices at elections.

The antithesis of a system of 'polyarchy' is that of 'closed hegemony', where the particular holders of power would be able to resist the participation of the electorate in general – creating a scenario where either the electorate must submit to or reject the system (Mair, 2013: p. 138).

A polyarchy may operate outwardly on an elitist model where there is a lack of actual participation: a lack of general public participation leaves the populations in Western democracy open to elite domination (Mair, 2013: pp. 75–98). However, Dahl emphatically rejected the suggestion that he sought to promote popular passivity, although such accusations have persisted (Robinson, 1996: pp. 20–21). Dahl (1971a, p. 112 fn. 13; Dahl and Lindblom, 1953: p. 314) picked out this quote to affirm that an elite holding legislative and executive power could not resist a majority of the populace that wishes to exert itself:

> [M]any policy decisions cannot actually reflect any specific preferences of the greater number. About the most that can be said for polyarchy is that, if the opportunities for political action are kept open to a representative section of the adult population, specific policies will rarely violate *highly ranked, intense, stable, and relatively broad preferences* of the greater number for a longer period than about the interval between elections.
>
> [Emphasis added]

Lindblom (1977: p. 143), Dahl's original collaborator, would restate the point:

> The outcome for majority rule is that the majority volition normally prevails only on issues on which there is an unmistakable massive long-standing majority opinion – a grand majority – to which both parties commit themselves. Secondary majorities – that is to say, majorities favoring a position on a secondary volition that is at issue do not necessarily prevail.

One may doubt some of this. A clear majority may be established even if one or more major parties continues to oppose. However, the basic sentiment is the same: representative democracy is designed so that the majority public view is acted upon when strong, stable and unmistakable; it is not designed (i.e. constituted) to be responsive to every peak and trough of public opinion.

Dahl is not arguing that the power of elites should be insulated from the electorate, but rather that an effective opportunity for political action is open to the majority of the electorate on any issue where the majority of the electorate is motivated to participate. In the absence of such participation, power holders get on with the business of wielding power. However, as Ivor Jennings (1966: pp. 209–211) argued in respect of the lack of revolutionary change in recent British constitutional history: a lack of popular involvement achieving major changes is not conclusive evidence of elite domination over the populace; it would be equally consistent with popular contentment. The popular power will often operate as what Pettit (2012: pp. 230, 268–269) described as 'a reserve power'. Public opinion is not the fountain of all law and policy, and thus many a system may operate outwardly as if it were a hegemony when in fact operating within boundaries referable to virtual and inhibitory popular control, as was explained in Chapter 3 ('The framework approach').

Democracy is never fully achieved in creating a political system, partly because of the impossibility of the electorate's opinions guiding all law and policy making. The extent to which the goal might be thought to be achieved is at all times contingent on the behaviour of the actors within the system. It is rather that a system that allows for polyarchy will promote an approximation to democracy (Dahl and Lindblom, 1953: p. 41). Creating a system that allows for a close approximation permits a society to operate its constitution in a democratic way. Crucially, in terms of the creation of a democracy, it is never simply a matter of (a) the constitutive power creating institutions adapted to translate public opinion into legislative action, and (b) there being public opinion. If the electorate does not participate sufficiently to control the selected group of legislators and governors, then Dicey's (2008: pp. 8–9) second condition for the failure of representative government must apply: the select group is free to act as a hegemonic elite, guided its members' own opinions rather than public opinion. This is essentially the dynamic that the late Peter Mair (2013) lamented in his final work developing the 'cartel party' hypothesis (Katz and Mair, 1995) on how electorates were abandoning politics to elite.

Writing over forty years after first expounding the concept of 'polyarchy', Dahl raised a paradox in democracy which sheds light on key issue of how far the existence of democracy depends on active participation. The paradox Dahl (2000; p. 35) highlighted was that '[i]n many of the oldest and most stable democratic countries, citizens possess little confidence in some key democratic institutions. Yet most citizens continue to believe in the desirability of democracy'.

The belief that the democratic institutions ought to be the route by which they are heard also remains. The crucial point that Dahl makes is that (a) there is what he calls the 'first dimension' of democracy which is the existence of the 'rights and opportunities' to participate, and (b) there is the 'second dimension' of using those rights and participating in those opportunities (pp. 38–39).

Dahl's conclusion, albeit expressly noting the limited empirical evidence on the subject, is that the public are more likely to value the existence of the opportunities to participate than to use those opportunities (p. 39):

> Although a majority of citizens in most democratic countries may view participating in political life as *neither very urgent nor particularly rewarding, and though many may be dissatisfied with the way their government works, overwhelming majorities of citizens do value the rights and opportunities their democratic system of government provides to them.* To be sure, they may choose not to exercise their rights and seize their opportunities very often. Yet their views are definitely not internally inconsistent.
>
> [Emphasis added]

Sir David Edward (2008: p. xxi) argues (emphasis added) that 'Democracy is something more than permitting us to choose, every few years, between candidates selected by self-selecting party machines. '*We wish to be heard*'. Dahl's refinement to this is that this 'wish to be heard' is no less strong simply because electors are silent most of time: they wish to be heard when something is important enough to them to speak. And as Bagehot (2007: p. 135) argues: '[T]he most dull government is a free government on matters its ruling classes will not hear'.

Dahl (2000: pp. 39–40) notes that the rational responses to a problem of not being heard will be either to reduce support for democracy or to increase participation:

> Dissatisfaction with the way their government works might in the long run weaken the confidence of some citizens in the value of the first dimension of democracy and thus weaken their support for democracy. Other citizens may conclude that they will simply have to participate more actively in political life in order to mend the defects they see in the operation of their democratic government. They are less likely to do so, however, unless they possess some idea of plausible remedies and solutions.

If an individual has no prospect of advancing their beliefs through the democratic process have the options of (1) submit, and (2) rebel (Mair, 2013: p. 138, citing Dahl, 1965).

The democratic audit

In terms of systematising the requirements for democracy, the leading British theorist is David Beetham, who gives 'popular control and political equality' as being the central principles of democracy (Beetham, 1999: pp. 5, 90–91).

Beetham's (1999: pp. 162–167) democratic audit sets out thirty indices of democracy which are divided into four areas:[2]

i. Free and fair elections – criteria 1–6;
ii. Open accountable and responsive government – criteria 7–18;
iii. Civil and political rights – criteria 19–23;
iv. Democratic society – criteria 24–30.

In Beetham's analysis there are four dimensions to a democracy: (1) popular election, (2) open and accountable government, without which it would be impossible to know what those who are elected have done, (3) civil and political rights, without which debate of political issues could not be conducted independently of the state, and (4) civil society through which the people participate whether it be by joining political parties or single-interest campaign groups, or by discussing politics with a neighbour before deciding how to vote (Beetham, 1999: pp. 154–156). Dimensions (1)–(3) set out the legal and political structures that create a connection between government and the people at large; and dimension (4) deals with the people actually involving themselves. Without (4), the legal and political structures in (1)–(3) will operate without the people, and thus fail to be democratic regardless of their outward form. Dicey argued that the public cannot control legislative change if there is no public opinion; Beetham provides the refinement that there is no public opinion until private opinions are made public. Beetham's (1999: pp. 166–167) final category concentrates on social matters in that 'the quality and vitality of a country's democracy will be revealed in the character of its civil society as well as its political institutions'. We find *ability* as well as *opportunity* to participate in political life stressed. Electors must belong to the same society as opposed to discrete factions, and must believe in their own ability to influence the political system – which in a democracy includes an ability to influence fellow citizens, which is difficult if discreet groups regard each other with hostility or indifference. This is essentially the same idea as Dahl's (2000: pp. 39–40) argument that citizens require 'some idea of plausible remedies and solutions' if they are to participate. Dicey (2008: pp. 37–39) had noted that democracy is used in two senses: political and social. We see from Beetham's analysis that the two are intertwined.

2 An earlier version of the "democratic audit" is set out in Beetham (1994: pp. 36–41).

In any representative democracy there is a division of labour. Elected legislators and ministers spend considerably more time on political matters than those who elect them (and, it must be added, the total time that legislators and ministers spend on any issue is dwarfed by the hours that unelected officials devote to formulation and implementation of policy.) But how much is this a matter of 'time' restraining the public from becoming involved, and how much is it a matter of 'capacity', i.e. lack of capability means that the public ought not to become involved even if they had time and motivation. Beetham (1999: p. 9) argues:

> The distinction between the argument about time and the argument about capacity ... is much more blurred in the practice of election to public office, with the possibility of unlimited re-election, where political decision-making becomes in effect a profession. Like all forms of the division of labour, the monopolization of a given practice by a special group conveys the illusion that they are uniquely fitted to engage in it, and everyone else is unfitted. This illusion even confuses many democrats, who believe that political representatives possess some special competence or capacity which they do not.

This warning accords with Laski's (1951: p. 37) argument that the true competence of elected representatives is their representativeness itself. Beetham (1999: p. 81) reiterates the point in a manner more obviously applicable to human rights adjudication:

> [A]ny form of belief, whether sacred or secular, is incompatible with democracy if it claims that the final truth for society lies in some superior and esoteric knowledge that is beyond question by the uninitiated, and to which political authority must be subject.

Democracy starts with the belief that the people are capable of governing themselves, not with the question of which body of people has technical or moral superiority (Beetham, 1999: pp. 90–91): 'The core idea of democracy is that of popular rule or popular control over collective decision-making. Its starting point is with the citizen rather than with the institutions of government'.

This principle is entirely in keeping with Pettit's (2012: p. 302) view that 'popular control' should be 'individualized, unconditioned and efficacious' and with Dahl's (1971a: p. 2) approach that democracy will exist when the populace use 'unimpaired opportunities' to participate equally; it is not simply a matter of institutional design. Even though, as Michelman (1988: p. 1499) said, democracy will give authority to decisions, democracy does not exist for the purpose of giving authority to decisions taken by the state. Democracy arises from the authority of the citizen. The democratic audit is about the ability of the public to exercise that popular control.

The audit starts and ends as follows (Beetham, 1999: pp. 162, 167):

> 1. How far is appointment to legislative and government office determined by popular election, on the basis of open competition, universal suffrage and secret ballot, and how far is there equal and effective opportunity to stand for public office, regardless of which social group a person belongs to? …
>
> 30. To what extent do people have confidence in the ability of the political system to solve the main problems confronting society and in their own ability to influence it?

The audit starts with a factor without which there is no democracy, and which taken in isolation would amount to the Schumpeterian view of democracy as competition for votes alone. The audit ends with a factor whose absence would be a significant, long-term weakness in democracy. As the audit moves from criterion 1 to criterion 30, it moves from factors that might cause a democracy to be utterly debased through to various factors which would represent genuine weaknesses, albeit of a generally diminishing immediacy. However, it is not that social factors are of minor importance compared to political structures in his approach to democracy. Beetham (1999: p. 5) argues that a democratic society's 'associational life should be internally democratic, and that it should provide the socioeconomic conditions for political equality to be realised in practice'. As Bagehot (2007: p. 147) pointed out, labourers living under a squirearchy were not free when exercising any participatory rights, as their votes are liable to be controlled by local elites. And, as Dahl (1989: p. 221) argued, 'associational autonomy' is necessary to polyarchy.

Hence, the thirtieth and final criterion for the democratic audit is necessary for the opinions of the populace to exercise the role implicit in the first criterion: open competition for votes requires electoral engagement, not hopeless disillusionment. It is necessary that the public have confidence in themselves and in the system in order for the first part of the fifth criterion, 'what proportion of the electorate votes', to be answered positively. But talk of public confidence is less easy to audit, which is likewise true of the sixteenth criterion (Beetham, 1999: p. 165), the accessibility of elected politicians and their effectiveness in representing the interests of voters.

Many criteria from Beetham's democratic audit touch closely on the social rather than the institutional side of democracy (Beetham, 1999: pp. 166–167). We find factors such as:

- the extent to which issues of social and economic status allow for equality in the practical exercise of 'civil and political rights' (20th criterion);
- effectiveness of information and education relevant to the exercise of those rights 22nd criterion);

- whether associations of citizens are controlled by their own members or dependent on government (26th criterion).

With the 26th criterion, we should note the link with Katz and Mair's cartel party thesis: mass participation movements should be the means by which politically concerned citizens organise and press their concerns on those closer to the reins of actual executive and legislative power (Mair, 2013: pp. 75–98). Party leaderships should not achieve independence from the memberships, nor gain dependence on the state.

To revert to Robert Dahl's idea of 'polyarchy', a constitutional system outwardly structured to allow electors to take an equal share of the power would fall well-short of the democratic ideal if a failure in the social factors of Beetham's democratic audit meant that direct power holders would be left in peace. This is unsurprising, as Beetham is covering in detail ground outlined in Dahl's 5th–7th criteria for polyarchy. If we consider Beetham's 28th and 29th criteria – plurality in the media, and citizens being equally equipped 'to participate in economic, social, cultural, as well as political life' – these factors do not relate to the form of the democratic system (Beetham, 1999: p. 167). However, no form of democratic system would long survive a total failure to achieve these criteria. It is not about a 'morally overlain' or 'fat' view of democracy incorporating broad, substantive freedoms (Allan, 2006: pp. 535–536), it is rather that popular rule will not operate within the system absent the social factors that Beetham identifies.

A point that flows from this is that the same measure (such as the Human Rights Act) may act to reduce the democratic credentials as measured in respect of one audit factor, whilst increasing the presence of another factor. Hence, the impact of constitutional review on democracy is not simply measured by the immediate counter-majoritarian effect on restraining the majority view of legislators. It is necessary to consider the entirety of the picture and to look from the citizen's perspective. Ultimately, the question is about the effectiveness of participation as a *citizen* in the political process, not the effectiveness of judicial process to an individual *subject* who wishes to be relieved of a particular burden. Democracy is certainly not about the utility of judicial process for providing *citizens* with outcomes that the political process has not provided.

Willingness to participate and Downs's hypothesis

Given the importance of popular participation, the willingness to participate is something of a spectre at the feast of democracy. A constitution can only provide the means for participation, it cannot force participation. It cannot be predicated on participation which is unlikely to be forthcoming.

The economic theory of democracy put forward by Anthony Downs (1957) provides a useful critique to what may be expected in terms of participation – and thus what may be achieved in terms of democracy. The 'cost of voting is very low', but the cost of informing oneself so as to make the right choice is far in excess of any expected gain (Downs, 1957: pp. 146–147). The same applies as regards the cost–benefit analysis of citizens, having already spent the time costs of informing themselves, then lobbying government for specific changes (pp. 148–149). Ideologies provide a shortcut so that citizens (and, indeed, decision makers) need not expend the costs of fully informing themselves on everything (pp. 141–142). An obvious inference from this is that anything that raises the cost of citizens informing themselves (e.g. as to the appropriateness of their usual ideological shortcut in particular circumstances) acts as a hindrance to participation. Citizens need to 'possess some idea of plausible remedies and solutions' (Dahl, 2000: pp. 39–40). The greater the information costs, the more remote the prospect of remedies and solutions and the harder it is to see participation as a rational investment of time and energy. Should a political issue require specialist knowledge (or be presented as such), citizens become poorly equipped to participate with confidence: the 29th criterion of the democratic audit (Beetham, 1999: p. 167). The difficulties created by political issues being translated into the form of human rights law creates obvious issues for popular participation, which we shall consider later.

Nevertheless, given the practical disinclination of the public to use the rights and opportunities to participate (Dahl, 2000: p. 39), there is nothing unusual in creating a system with a division of labour to keep the day-to-day practice of power in check (Kyritsis, 2012: p. 323), whilst trying to avoid blocking popular participation when it occurs. We see a clear parallel with the 'dual-aspect' approach to democracy of Pettit (2012: pp. 252–279). Pettit's approach separates out 'the constituting people' and 'the constituted people'. They are the same people, but the latter operates on a day-to-day basis under the constraints that they have chosen, and may amend. The people as 'the constituting people' have all the power that they could ever want; but they seldom act in such a capacity, and when they do so, they may well choose a system of government where that power will be largely mediated through representatives. What Robert Dahl's approach brings to the fore, and is implicit in Pettit's recognition of popular power as a reserve power, is that the nature of the constitution will be largely constituted out of the behaviour of the people towards elites, and the elites' tendency to adopt an oligarchical role within the constitutional structure. The electorate will constantly act as a constituting power in the ebb and flow of its willingness to participate, for that will determine the democratic nature of the constitution as much as any formal constitutional provision. In so far as citizens are active, they exercise inhibitory or interventional control. If citizens are inactive, the only sense of control is 'virtual control' as the absence of a popular reaction will demonstrate that the elite is still acting with the yet-unknown limits of popular acceptability.

Conclusion

Philip Pettit (2012: p. 302) argues that democracy requires 'popular control' that is 'individualized, unconditioned and efficacious'. David Beetham (2003: pp. 4–5, 90–91) similarly sees democracy in terms of 'popular control' and 'political equality'. In a purely representative democracy, popular control will amount to nothing higher than what Dahl and Lindblom (1953: p. 314) describes: the 'highly ranked, intense, stable, and relatively broad preferences of the greater number' of the electorate that will prevail over time (meaning 'a longer period than … the interval between elections') as against the preferences of elite and select groups.

The exercise of that control through the act of public voting is the forum where all citizens can be brought to a position of equality (and with public deliberation creating the shadow of future public votes). The essence of democracy is that there is a process where all may participate on equal terms, and this process has the power to dominate the legislative decisions of the state. How far in practice the domination exerted by the process extends into the range of legislative decisions may be greater or lesser. Direct democracy may give legislative power to referenda where all voters are equal. Due to the imprecision of electing a government on a broad manifesto, representative democracy relies significantly on inhibitive and virtual control in respect of linking public opinion to individual legislative and policy aims, and these forms of control will wither for lack of mass participation outside of the act of voting (Mair, 2013: pp. 75–98).

But constitutional design is only the start of the picture. John Stuart Mill (quoted by Jennings, 1938: p. 79) said: 'Political institutions are the work of men; owe their origin and their whole existence to human will … In every stage of their existence they are made what they are by voluntary human agency'.

The point is that the formal rules of governance are operated by human actors. A constitution may permit or prevent democracy, but of itself it can only promote 'polyarchy' by allowing for equal participation at a fundamental level of decision-making. As Tushnet (2003a: pp. 2786–2788) explains, 'institutional choice' does not end with institutional design, it continues with the activities of the participants.

It is thus contradictory for the electorate to use its constituting power to choose or maintain a system of government that requires a higher degree of their participation than the electorate is willing to give. It follows that it is by no means undemocratic for the constituting power to adopt a system of constitutional review that recognises that such review will often interfere with the choices of politicians and not, in any meaningful sense, the choices favoured by the electorate (Honohan, 2009: pp. 100–101).

It follows that the analysis of the impact of constitutional review, and how far it interferes with the electorate's favoured choices, only *starts* with institutional design, such as the judicial power falling short of striking down primary legislation. It is also necessary to consider how the system will impact on electors' evaluation of the availability of effective participation, and on whether the existence of constitutional review will interfere with the relationship between electors and the electorate. Constitutional review creates a counter-majoritarian force on legislation. How far that force is stronger than the force that electorates may realistically bring to bear on legislators is crucial to whether electorates can choose to control legislators, or whether legislative choices are invigilated by the judiciary. To use the phrase common to the literature, 'political cost', does constitutional review create a political cost deriving from, or external to, the electorate; and, if external, does that cost exert alien control over the ability of public opinion to control legislation?

Importantly, from a republican perspective, political elites are not free from domination by the electorate simply because the electorate seldom participates so as to enforce the will of the majority of citizens against the inclinations of the elite. As we saw when considering the extreme example of slavery in Chapter 2 ('Counter-majoritarian effect'), domination derives from the nature of the power relationship, not the exercise of the power per se (Skinner, 2008: pp. 92, 96–97). However, if the acceptance of the Human Rights Act inherently entails an acceptance of a hindrance to the electorate's exercise of that power, such that the hindrance can only be removed by the removal of the Act, then the reconciliation between rights protection and democracy offered by the 'elegant balance' thesis cannot stand. The 'elegant balance' requires the Human Rights Act to coexist with the electorate having a meaningful invigilatory power over the results of constitutional review so as to exercise counter-control when it chooses.

5 Constitutional review – a rights-protection pact

Introduction

This chapter outlines the component parts of a system of constitutional review and how they create a counter-majoritarian effect.

By a counter-majoritarian effect we mean that constitutional review interferes with what would otherwise be the political process, whether that process is confined to the political institutions or involves an interaction between those institutions and the electorate. Interference may create a hindrance to a greater or lesser degree. Broadly speaking, constitutional review may interfere by restricting choice, or it may interfere in the evaluation of choices. A key phrase from Pettit's analysis is that of 'alien control'. Judicial opinion is 'alien' in relation to public opinion being external to it, but does it 'control'? If it does control, how far does that control spread?

The aim of this chapter is not to set out the detail of the different forms of constitutional review found in various common-law jurisdictions and their particular impact on the interpretation of those territories' respective bills of rights. That is a subject covered with formidable detail recently by Kris Gledhill (2015). The purpose of this chapter is rather to set out the basic constitutive choices that are to be made that either determine directly the extent of the counter-majoritarian effect of a bill of rights, or place that effect in the hands of a force external to the electorate, such as the judiciary (domestic or international).

The most fundamental choice in terms of the nature of a system of constitutional review is illustrated by Mark Tushnet's useful division of systems of constitutional review into two categories: 'strong' and 'weak'. In a 'strong' form of constitutional review, an adverse decision by the courts cannot be ignored by the legislature, nor can it by overturned by using ordinary legislation to either amend the bill of rights or to create a particular an exemption for the legislation concerned. In 'weak' constitutional review, the legislature may set aside any judicial defeats using its ordinary legislative process (Tushnet, 2003a: p. 2786; 2003a: pp. 356–357). It engages both the entrenchment and the enforcement of bills of rights, but it does not tell the full story of the importance of constitutional review in a particular country.

As Tushnet (2003a: p. 2786) himself stresses, the question of whether a constitution follows weak-form or strong-form review is independent of the 'scope' of the subject matter which may be subject to review in the courts. So, whilst the 'weak-form'/'strong-form' dichotomy is important, we need to outline the issues that will determine the nature of the protection of rights, and the impact on majoritarian decision making.

The extent of the hindrance is only in-part legal. Except insofar as the constitutional review system may entrench a bill of rights, nothing in analysing the constitutional law per se will of itself explain any 'political costs' or other forces persuading legislators not to counter-control constitutional review decisions. No constitutional provision is immune to amendment if the electorate are sufficiently resolved to make a change, even those formally expressed to be beyond constitutional amendment such as Article 20 of the German Constitution, the 'state sovereignty' provision (*Lisbon Case* [228]). Therefore consideration of the counter-majoritarian tendency of a system of constitutional review requires consideration of the relationship between a country's electorate and its constitution. Judicial decisions cannot be said to exercise 'alien control' over legislative change if such decisions are invigilated and subject to counter-control by the electorate.

Extent of counter-majoritarian impact

As we saw in Chapter 2 ('Counter-majoritarian effect'), the choice to create a system of constitutional review within a democracy is a choice to create a counter-majoritarian system precisely because of perceived difficulties with majoritarianism, particularly fears of majority tyranny (Ely, 1980: pp. 7–8). As such, the legal rules and interpretation of such a system represent a balance between the concerns of rights-protection and democracy (Hale, 2011: p. 21; Fredman, 2013: p. 292). It represents the conscious choice of the constituting power.

For the moment, we therefore limit ourselves to the constitutional form (national and international) given to the system of constitutional review as interpreted by the judiciary in terms of:

(i) Entrenchment
(ii) Enforcement
(iii) Scope
(iv) Rules for interpretation
(v) Judicial approach to interpretation
(vi) Rules for justification
(vii) Judicial approach to justification
(viii) Internationalisation.

We consider these factors now in turn.

Entrenchment

A system of constitutional review is 'entrenched' when the bill of rights itself cannot be amended without a special constitutional process. Entrenchment is common, but not essential: the Human Rights Act 1998 and the Bill of Rights (New Zealand) Act 1990 are both ordinary statutes, as was the Canadian Bill of Rights 1960. Article 28 of the French Declaration of the Rights of Man and Citizen (1793) specifically denounced the concept of entrenchment: 'A people has always the right to review, to reform, and to alter its constitution. One generation cannot subject to its law the future generations'.

With entrenchment, ordinary democratic process is hindered by a system of constitutional review to the degree that 'supermajority' requirements are imposed. Such requirements may make it appear that the hindrance is insuperable, as Dworkin (1998: p. 140 fn. 7) argues is the case with the US Constitution. Allied to strong-form enforcement against primary legislation, entrenchment means that judicial opinion expressed through constitutional review cannot itself be counter-controlled through the ordinary political process, but only by formal constitutional change. In contrast, constitutional review in both New Zealand and the United Kingdom rest on statutes which can be amended or repealed by ordinary legislative process.

Enforcement

Enforcement provisions determine what happens after a judicial finding that a particular executive or legislative action is contrary to the bill of rights. There are three obvious forms of enforcement that the bill of rights may provide for in respect of primary legislation: a) setting aside, b) declarations of incompatibility, and, c) interpreting the legislation against its natural meaning so as to achieve compatibility.

The strongest form of enforcement is that anything held to be contrary to the bill of rights will be illegal. Executive action will be quashed, primary and secondary legislation will be set aside. Normally this will amount to a strong-form of constitutional reform, but where there is a procedure for a statutory override (as in Canada) it can still be seen as weak-form review. Particular courses of action may be ordered (*Swann v Charlotte-Meklenburg* (1970) 402 US 1). Damages may have to be paid to those affected. It may be that compliance with the bill of rights need not be instantaneous, most famously this was the case with desegregation rulings by the US Supreme Court (*Brown v Board of Education of Topeka (No. 2)* (1955) 394 US 294, see also a Canadian example in *M v H* [1999] 2 SCR 3 [145]–[147]). But in such a strong-form of enforcement, the offending act or law must sooner or later be repealed or appropriately amended, as it will be set aside by the courts.

It is important to stress that the possibility of striking down legislation is only one form of enforcement. Where statutes cannot be struck down – as is the case under the Human Rights Act and the Bill of Rights (New Zealand) Act 1990 – the 'bill of rights' may be enforced to a significant extent by way of purposively interpreting primary legislation. This means that a statute is given a meaning that it normally would not bear to make it rights-compatible. Creating such an interpretative duty provides a bill of rights with immediate effect (or at least potentially so) in the absence of a power to set aside legislation (Gardbaum, 2001: p. 728).

However, it must be stressed that where a bill of rights does not permit the setting aside of primary legislation, it may nevertheless be that 'more difficult and testing tracks' (Pettit, 1997; p. 232) have been created for legislating contrary to fundamental rights. Primary legislation is far from being the be-all and end-all of state activity, so it is possible to overestimate the significance of how a bill of rights interacts with such legislation. Given the size of the modern state, much that affects rights is carried out under administrative discretion or by secondary legislation passed using fairly broad statutory powers. If the bill of rights closes off these approaches for achieving incompatible legislation, then the easiest tracks for infringing rights are prevented. The natural meaning of legislation is struck down, allowing the court to go directly to a rights-friendly outcome, with the legislature needing to positively enact legislation and paying the political costs for doing so (Gardbaum, 2001: p. 729).

Scope

Bills of rights may be wide or narrow depending on their history and context, e.g. (1) The Bill of Rights which arose out of the Glorious Revolution of 1688 would not by modern standards represent constitutional review – it was an ordinary statute dealing with the immediate issues arising out of abuses by Charles II and James II. Similarly, as Lord Sumption (2015: pp. 3–4) explained, the Magna Carta dealt with specific concerns of the day, not general principles. (2) A deliberately general approach, and more recognisably modern, is found in France's *Declaration of the Rights of Man and of the Citizen (1789)*, which sought to be exhaustive and which dealt with the question of the justification of the infringement of the enumerated rights (Sumption, 2015: pp. 4–5). (3) The 'small bill of rights' in the British North American Act 1867, the original Canadian Constitution, where security of judicial tenure and certain issues around protecting denominational schools represented problems whose resolution was of foundational importance to the coming together of the Canadian provinces (Greene, 1989: p. 15). This demonstrates that any issue may be made subject to constitutional review if it is important enough to the people who are to live under the constitution.

It is thus possible to prescribe a very narrow set of rights as requiring special constitutional protection; and it is possible to have a bill of rights covering all freedoms that a society believes to be important. In-between, it may be that a bill of rights covers those important rights that are seen as threatened at a particular time. The scope of what is protected under a system of constitutional review is, to state the obvious, found in the first instance in the text of the bill of rights as approved by the constituting power.

Rules for interpreting

When setting the scope of a bill of rights, the constituting power will not just prescribe what falls within the protection (conditional or unconditional) of the document, it will in its choice of drafting create a greater or lesser potential for further subject matter to be included by way of interpretation. The subject of interpretation starts with the choice of how to define the scope of the substantive rights that the constituting power has chosen to protect. Those behind a bill of rights might seek to define the rights with such precision as to limit the scope for interpretation. During the negotiations for the ECHR the British Government introduced greater detail into the clauses precisely so as to restrain the potential for unexpected interpretations, although '[a]rguably the detailed substantive text reinforced the idea that the Convention was not merely a safeguard against outrageous violations' (Bates, 2012: p. 388, fn. 39). This underlines the difficulty in regulating judicial interpretation prospectively. Also, if the aim of the project is to state important principles regarding human rights, then adding sufficient prescriptive detail to close off potential judicial activism might have meant abandoning that goal in favour of one that used particular provisions to condemn particular vices.

It is possible to create general provisions to limit the scope of a bill of rights. Article 14 of Chapter 21 of the Swedish Constitution 1982 required the court to set aside legislation 'only if the fault was manifest' (Tushnet, 2003a: p. 2786, fn. 25), effectively enacting a system of what in US jurisprudence is known as 'Thayerian-review' (Thayer, 1893: p. 144). Essentially, whatever the court might think is the *natural* interpretation of a bill of rights or constitution, the court's second and real interpretative task is in identifying what the constitution *necessarily* requires.

Judicial approach to interpretation

Of crucial importance to the practical scope of a bill of rights, and thus its importance in the constitution of the state concerned, is the judicial approach to interpretation.

In 1975, Andrew Ashworth (1975) wrote an article on the possible effect of the European Convention on the English self-defence; Steve Foster and Gavin Leigh (2016) returned to the subject forty years later. Whereas Ashworth could only work from the text of Article 2 of the Convention ('right to life') to suggest how the issues of self-defence might be framed in human rights terms, by 2016 Foster and Leigh could draw on jurisprudence.

Interpretative choices had been made by judges, and from the vague possibilities of the text identified by Ashworth, the Convention's meaning had taken greater shape in this area.

A bill of rights will normally be generally worded, briefly setting out principles, which will be interpreted in a more expansive way than a normal statute. The US Constitution provides examples of the impact of interpretative choices: a provision can be interpreted as having no legal effect (e.g. Article 4, the guarantee of republican government (*Luther v Borden* (1849) 48 US 1)); the scope of a provision may expand by analogy with the concept originally described, as with the Fourth Amendment's reference to protecting 'papers ... against unreasonable searches and seizures' being interpreted to cover electronic interceptions that did not exist when the provision was drafted (*Katz v United States* (1967) 389 US 347); and the interpretation of 'due process' to encompass something called 'substantive due process', which on its face is a contradiction in terms (Ely, 1980: pp. 15–16). The 'living tree' analogy of Lord Sankey in *Edwards v Attorney General for Canada* [1930] AC 126, 136 can be applied according to the judicial will to interpret provisions restricting government and legislative power.

Judicial interpretation may at times be precisely opposite in different countries – as for example the American and German courts' approaches to abortion and foetal personhood (*Roe v Wade* (1973) 410 U.S. 113; *BVerfGE 39*, 1).

Which is all to say that the scope of a bill of rights may in the first instance be set by the constituting power, but afterwards the scope can expand or contact depending on the judicial approach to interpretation in respect of particular clauses and concepts.

Rules for justification

The real heart and soul of a 'bill of rights' often pertains to whether the particular legislative or executive action will be held to be justified. As with scope, the first place to consider for the approach to justification is in the document itself. The ECHR adopts many forms of wording as to the level of necessity and the factors that may be used as justifications such as 'necessary in a democratic society' (Articles 8 and 10), 'to the extent strictly required' (Article 15) and 'as it deems necessary' (Article 1 of Protocol 1), with each provision itself differing on the breadth of factors that may relevant to public necessity.

We thus see great differences within the ECHR in terms of the justificatory hurdle and in the situations that may legitimately give rise to a rights-limiting measure.

By contrast, in the US Bill of Rights, the First Amendment provides that 'Congress shall make no law ... abridging freedom of speech, or of the press', which on its face provides for no restrictions, not even for libel, risks to national security, or incitement to commit a crime. Nevertheless, the US

Supreme Court has adopted a 'clear and present danger' test for identifying exceptions to free speech (*Schenck v United States* (1919) 249 US 47, 48).

It would be perfectly open to create rules to tell the courts how to construe general principles. For example, Human Rights Act sections 12 ('particular regard to ... freedom of expression') and 13 ('particular regard to ... of freedom of expression, and freedom of thought, conscience and religion') contain instructions to the court as to how to approach certain issues. In reality, these provisions have had no real impact on the application of the Act, beyond the approach to interim relief (Tomlinson, 2003; *Cream Holdings Ltd v Banerjee* [2003] EWCA Civ 103; [2003] Ch 650 [51]). The difficulty with the provisions, and the reason for their limited success, is that it is difficult to differentiate 'particular regard' for a right with the actual requirements of proportionality when it is the only right in issue. This highlights the difficulty in elaborating what is meant by 'justification' unless it is to adopt a Thayerian approach to constitutional review, such as the old Swedish standard of whether 'the fault was manifest' (Tushnet, 2003a: p. 2786 fn. 25). Even then, it may take more to stifle judicial ingenuity in putting the merits of a measure into more direct consideration. It is worth noting that a similarly Thayerian (albeit judicially created) formulation of 'manifestly without reasonable foundation' is used in ECHR disputes relating to social security. This formulation has proved far from an insuperable hurdle to close judicial scrutiny, *Mathieson v Secretary of State for Work and Pensions* [2015] UKSC 47; 2015 1 WLR 3250. Indeed, even on a politically contentious issue such as the strictness of the benefit cap, two of the Supreme Court judges believed applying the cap to child benefit to be 'manifestly without reasonable foundation', and reached that conclusion by holding certain interests (in that case children's) to be of particular importance, see *SG v Secretary of State for Work and Pensions* [2015] UKSC 16; [2015] 1 WLR 1449 [210]–[229], [268].

Judicial approach to justification

Of key importance in human rights instruments, is the approach to justification in the case-law. Just as with our discussion of the formal scope of the protected right and the judicial interpretation of the right, whilst any human rights instrument may or may not set down rules to approach justification, judicial practice will be all-important.

In respect of abridging property rights (Article 1 of Protocol 1), the ECtHR has effectively replaced this ostensibly permissive approach of 'as it deems necessary' found in the Convention's wording with a 'fair balance' test (*Sporrong and Lonnroth v Sweden* (1983) 5 EHRR 35 [69]), which can justify the court taking a more restrictive view of what can be allowed (Nicol, 2010: pp. 138–140). Likewise, the jurisprudence of the ECtHR shows that immense differences in outcome may result from the judges giving ostensibly the same 'margin of appreciation' as to whether a measure is justified

(*Hirst*, Dissent Wildhaber et al. [5]). At national level, the equivalent issue of how far judges should defer to the local legislature on questions of necessity is an important and vexed issue, according to Jowell (2003: p. 592) 'the most difficult question for the courts in the interpretation of the Human Rights Act'. To give examples from the USA, there is a world of difference between the 'strict scrutiny' standard of review of justifications in 'suspect category' discrimination cases, and Wendall Holmes's 'does it make me puke' approach (Wiecek, 2002). Often, it is as Dworkin (1998: p. 357) said of modern US Constitutional debate: '[t]he capital question … is not what power the Court has but how its vast power should be used'.

However, as seen in Chapter 3, any apparent reduction in judicial interference should not be seen as a removal of domination. If the judges have a power of invigilation that amounts to alien control, then they are no less dominant because there exists a possibility of the judges being persuaded as to justification in the future. The invigilated party (the legislature and, possibly, the electorate itself) will still exercise its choices in a position where the invigilator has a power to exercise control. Absent of effective counter-control, the initiative remains with the courts.

Internationalisation

The final factor to be considered is internationalisation. Bills of rights may be embedded into international law and politics, and thus to some extent underpinned and influenced by external power. Such links can be part of the original constitutive choice, as for example the express mention of particular international conventions, as is the case with Human Rights Acts of the United Kingdom, or by a general reference to international human rights obligations in the case of Australian Capital Territory and Victoria (Gledhill, 2015, pp. 152–158). Even where there is no constitutional reference to international norms, the fact of a state being a party to international human rights conventions may nevertheless form an important part of the context of internal human rights dynamics, as is most obviously the case with the relationship between many Caribbean states and the Inter-American Commission on Human Rights (Carter and O'Brien, 2000).

We have so far sought to divide up the various ways in which constitutional review may be created *within* a constitution, and the factors that determine its importance. It has been argued that national constitutional forms may be rendered academic in the face of external legal and commercial obligations. This is essentially Danny Nicol's (2010) critique of how subscribing to international governance may create a high level of constitutional entrenchment, either rendering the power of national legislatures and electorates empty, or at least materially weakening it. We cannot, therefore, simply look to national constitutional forms to establish practical constitutional significance; indeed, national constitutional theory may be misleading as to the effect on domestic law of internationalising measures (Sand, 2007: p. 288).

It is worth noting that internationalisation may expand beyond the bill of rights directly in issue. Other rights treaties (e.g. the UN Convention on the Rights of Children) may be used as a means for interpreting human rights conventions and bills of rights. The court may seek to achieve 'harmony' of approach between general human rights principles in a bill of rights and other international conventions, *Mathieson* [42]–[44].

The linking of issues – constitutional review as a rights-protection pact

At the heart of the power of constitutional review is that the linking of issues can entrench individual policies beyond their individual importance. We see this in Danny Nicol's (2010: p. 21) argument that international free-trade agreements will mean that adherence to each particular provision becomes necessary to ensure access to world trade. A state cannot be partly loyal to free-trade principles without it appearing to be in principle unfaithful to free trade. The very fact of disparate issues having been linked means they are seen as an indissoluble package (Nicol, 2010: p. 8). Similarly, can a polity be 'partly' loyal to a bill of rights? The UN High Commissioner for Human Rights (UNHCR, 2015) may argue that human rights are 'all interrelated, interdependent, and indivisible', but it is the practicality of rights having been brought together within the same system of constitutional review that creates the real indivisibility.

What we wish to note here is a structural dynamic potentially created by any broad ranging rights instrument: the concept that the integrity of the entire instrument must be upheld, or every part is weakened. This can represent a challenge to the Human Rights Act's putative 'elegant balance'. The Act ostensibly and deliberately internalises the possibility of it being overridden, its provisions contemplate such steps being taken. But is such an override power an inherent contradiction for a bill of rights, such as can only be resolved by either disavowing (or removing) the flexibility, or by discarding the Act?

The importance of linking rights issues may be illustrated if we go back eight-hundred years, and consider the Magna Carta. There were clauses on such disparate issues as protecting widows from forced remarriage (clause 8), removing fish weirs from certain rivers (clause 33), as well as more celebrated clauses against such as '[t]o no one will we sell, to no one deny or delay right or justice' (clause 40). Although the enforcement mechanism of a council of barons (clause 61) was never brought into effect, the Magna Carta could nevertheless galvanise broader political opinion through the centuries, joining disparate issues of freedom together under one rhetorically powerful banner (Sumption, 2015: pp. 3–4). Rights were linked in the Magna Carta not because they were 'interrelated, interdependent and indivisible' at an abstract level, but because creating an interrelationship through the Magna Carta, treating them as indivisible, was mutually beneficial. The only real relationship was that each proposition was threatened by an over-mighty King, and so a united front was the best defence.

Manfredi (2001: pp. 186–188), a critic of judicial power, attributes an equivalent dynamic to why Canadian legislatures are averse to overturning decisions under the Charter by way of attaching a notwithstanding clause. Manfredi argues that use of the clause was discredited of its 'misuse' by the Quebec legislature, in particular Bill 178 which prohibited businesses from displaying external commercial signs in English. As a result, as regards using notwithstanding clauses to restrict the Charter's application, 'constitutional convention virtually prohibits its use'. The Premier of Alberta explained when withdrawing a notwithstanding clause aimed at protecting entirely reasonable compensation legislation for victims of historic eugenic practices from Charter challenges (Manfredi, 2001: pp. 187–188):[1] 'It became abundantly clear that to individuals in this country the Charter of Rights and Freedoms is paramount and the use of any tool ... to undermine [it] is something that should be used only in very, very rare circumstances'.

Hence, the same Alberta government 'summarily dismissed the idea of invoking the notwithstanding clause after the Supreme Court's *Vriend* decision' (Manfredi, 2001: p. 188). The point that Manfredi makes is very much in line with what we shall call our 'rights-protection pact' hypothesis. In Canada, legislatures have declined to override the Charter precisely because to do so would undermine the Charter generally. Hence, following the decision in *M v H* that 'same-sex partners are entitled to the same rights and responsibilities as common-law couples', the Ontario legislature's response was entitled 'Amendments Because of the Supreme Court of Canada Decision in *M. v. H. Act*'. The Ontario government further disassociated itself from its own legislation: government MPs did not attend the debate; even the Attorney General vacated the chamber after presenting the legislation (Ontario Deb, 1999). There is no clearer example that the principal of Charter sanctity dwarfed objections on individual issues, however strongly held those objections were. The perceived duty of Charter compliance also allowed the government to present itself as not responsible (and so not accountable) for legislation. Logically, if interference comes by way of co-reasoning, then the ultimate decision maker cannot disavow responsibility. Only by presenting (rightly or not) oneself as being in a position of lacking the reality of choice is it possible to avoid accountability.

Bills of rights can thus be seen as 'rights-protection pacts' for different issues of liberty and civil rights. In terms of the republican analysis, by creating a link between issues and risks, a bill of rights alters the nature of the decision that the legislature must take, and thus the electorate may respond

1 The legislation provided a clear and certain path to compensation. The concern was that the legislation violated the Convention by barring access to the courts, albeit that the success of claims and quantum was unclear.

to. A determination that a policy is contrary to a bill of rights – a decision possibly taken by the constituting power in promulgating the bill of rights, but often by the judiciary in its interpretative decisions – reduces the probability of that decision being taken. To that extent, there is prima facie alien control over the democratic process; subject to the possibility of a free choice of counter-control.[2]

Conclusion

What we have examined here are the legal factors that affect how a system of constitutional review will operate to restrict the choices in the ordinary legislative process and thus create (for better or worse) a counter-majoritarian effect. Essentially these factors are: (1) Entrenchment, (2) Enforcement, (3) Scope, (4) Rules for interpretation, (5) Judicial approach to interpretation, (6) Justification, (7) Judicial approach to justification, and (8) Internationalisation.

The basic theme is that the counter-majoritarian consequences of constitutional review will often be largely independent of the original choices of the constituting power. Issues of scope and justification will be more responsive to judicial interpretation than constitutive attempts at fine-tuning the bill of rights.

Constitutional review may operate as a system which puts rights infringements to more testing tracks than would normally be the case. A system of constitutional review may be structured to promote deliberation, particularly in shedding light on administrative and executive action by requiring primary legislation to ratify rights infringements. Similarly, this may be the case where constitutional review scrutinises the justifications given whilst avoiding making a specific ruling on the merits of the issues. However, whether this works as a system of co-reasoning depends on the reality of choice as to legislative counter-control – not whether the judges can put off confronting the electorate with a reality that no reasons for a given choice will satisfy the judiciary. Ultimately, in any bill of rights, there is an inherent possibility of an impasse between reasons that the judiciary will accept and those of public opinion, with neither side being unreasonable. In respect of weak-form systems of constitutional review such as the Human Rights Act, the existence of a position of judicial domination is determined not by considering inter-institutional dialogue as long as it lasts, but by, a) whether the courts must cease to interfere before the co-reasoning of dialogue hardens to alien control by the judges, and b) the approach of the legislature and the electorate towards exercising counter-control in those circumstances.

As discussed in Chapter 2 ('Political costs'), it is often said that the 'political costs' explain the reluctance of legislatures to overturn or ignore the

2 Chapter 3 (third axiom), and (fourth theorem), above.

results of constitutional review. This begs the questions: what are these political costs, who exacts them, and how does this interrelate with the legal aspects of the constitutional review system? Nothing in a country's formal system of constitutional review, whether in the choices of the constitutive power that passed the bill of rights or in the subsequent interpretative choices, will provide the explanation of these questions of political behaviour and popular participation. It may, however, be that bills of rights, by grouping together rights, confer increased importance on all affected rights. This 'rights-protection pact' argument would lead to compliance being a structural necessity for an effective bill of rights even if its legal form permitted flexibility.

6 The classic constitution

Introduction

When considering the effect of the Human Rights Act on democracy, the question is whether the Act tends to clear channels for participation such that the constitution operates more as a 'polyarchy', to use Robert Dahl's terminology; or, alternatively, does the Act tend to frustrate the electorate asserting itself against those that hold immediate power? Has it given the judiciary an oligarchical position where their decisions are enforced and entrenched independently of public opinion, or is judicial opinion simply a source of influence which may be set to one side when the public exercise their participatory rights in earnest? If, as Laski (1921: p. 23) said, sovereignty tends to flow to the administrative centre, how does the Human Rights Act affect this flow? Lord Kerr argued that, in respect of primary legislation, the Act directs attention to Parliament, the source of the incompatibility and the only cure (*Nicklinson* [365]). But Parliamentarians have at times redirected the attention back to the courts by presenting themselves as having no choice but to comply, for example, in the legislative response to *F and Thompson* (HL Debate, 2012: col. 886). To answer these questions we must understand the constitutional system in which the Human Rights Act operates, for it is within this system that the Act will restrict or promote, create or destroy avenues for 'popular control', which is 'suitably individualized, unconditioned and efficacious' (Pettit, 2012: p. 302, see also p. 279). Therefore, we shall consider the operation of the classic British Constitution.

The classic constitution

Anthony King (2007: pp. 15–38) argued that there was a canonical sextet of theorists of the classic constitution: A.V. Dicey, Ivor Jennings, Walter Bagehot, L.S. Amery, Harold Laski and Sidney Low. Those writers covered almost exactly one hundred years from the publication of Bagehot's *The English Constitution* in 1867 to the death of Ivor Jennings in 1965. Of the canonical sextet, two were legal academics (Dicey and Jennings), two were journalists (Bagehot and Low), one was a Conservative politician of cabinet rank (Amery), and one was a Labour activist and academic (Laski). Their opinions greatly differ: Jennings criticised Dicey's views on the nature of the rule of law and the importance (but not existence) of Parliamentary Sovereignty; and Amery and Laski differed greatly as to the health of parliamentary democracy in an age of strong party discipline. Their writings span a period when the franchise expanded greatly. Yet Anthony King was able to use Bagehot, Laski, Amery, Low, Jennings, and Dicey as all essentially providing perspectives on the same thing: the classic constitution.

The difficulty in describing the 'classic constitution' is not in describing the 'structural elements', which as Sidney Low (1920: p. 5) states, 'exhibit a wonderful superficial permanence'. As Jennings (1938: p. 67) puts it: 'the legal basis of the constitution was settled by the Revolution of 1688'. It is rather that what Bagehot (2007: p. 97) describes as the 'literary theory' of the constitution often does not represent reality. Bagehot (2007: pp. 240, 284–285) noted as early as the 1860s that the House of Lords power of veto over legislation was theoretical, and the monarch's power to freely appoint her own ministers was so theoretical that its use would be as startling as a 'volcanic eruption in Primrose Hill'. Dicey (1982: p. xlii) saw the importance of the Lords' veto as allowing it to insist on involving the people in decisions of constitutional importance, but not to thwart the House of Commons or public opinion. Low (1920: p. x) himself argued in the first edition of *The Governance of England* that the Lords' legislative veto was illusory, as it would be removed in the conflict resulting from its actual use; and reported that precisely this had come to pass when he wrote the second edition. Dicey (1982: pp. cxxx–cxxxi) at length berated Blackstone for describing the royal prerogative as if it were still exercised by the monarch, as even by the mid-eighteenth century this was 'the direct opposite to the truth'. Amery (1964: pp. 6–7; 1952: p. 59) argued that whether the monarch's personal powers could be used constitutionally or not would depend on the outcome of the resultant political controversy: 'the verdict of the nation alone will settle whether such an assertion of the royal authority will have been constitutional or not'. As we noted in Chapter 4, whether viewed in terms of Dahl's polyarchy or Beetham's democratic audit, whatever the legal constitution, the behaviour of political actors from the elector to the minister will be constitutive of the nature of the constitution.

The division between legal powers and the reality of power has been variously described. Anthony King (2007: pp. 5–9) talked in terms of a 'Capital-C' and a 'small-c' constitution. The Capital-C constitution is the codified constitution, and a small-c constitution is everything else – but even where a constitution is codified, not everything that is important is codified or even written down. Dicey (1982: pp. 277–291) discussed a similar distinction between legal and non-legal rules when describing the importance of conventions which of themselves lack force of law, although he demonstrated that the division is blurred in that conventions will be strong if they cannot be flouted without eventual illegality (Dicey, 1982: pp. 296–300). Sidney Low (1920: pp. 8 and 14) argued that 'our formal constitution is strictly a legal one', but that this picture was incomplete. He divided the constitution into 'formal, conventional and actual' parts, i.e. legal rules, non-legal rules, and actual behaviour for which no rules are prescribed but clear patterns of behaviour are observable. But whether we draw a divide between Capital-C and small-c constitutions, or between formal, conventional and actual parts, or between juridical and behavioural methods, they are describing much the same point.

The starting point for considering the 'classic constitution' is to be found in what Sir John Laws (2012: p. 576) referred to as 'A.V. Dicey's twin peaks, parliamentary sovereignty and the rule of law'.

The classic (formal) constitution

What we shall see is this: Parliamentary Sovereignty tells the courts of their relationship to Acts of Parliament; and the rule of law tells officials of their relationship to the courts, and upholds their relationship to Acts of Parliament. The rule of law does not restrain Parliament, but is a necessary part of Parliament's commands requiring or forbidding particular conduct.

Parliamentary Sovereignty

Dicey (1982: p. xxxvi, see also pp. 3–4) set out the classic definition of Parliamentary Sovereignty:

> The sovereignty of Parliament is, from a legal point of view, the dominant characteristic of our institutions. ... The principle of parliamentary sovereignty means neither more nor less than this, namely that 'Parliament' has 'the right to make or unmake any law whatever; and, further, that no person or body is recognised by the law of England as having a right to override or set aside the legislation of Parliament'.

It is true that recently writers have argued against the existence of Parliamentary Sovereignty. It might be that the principle is said to be one of common law, and thus inherently subject to judicial development (*Jackson* [102]; Hope, 2011: pp. 11–12). Tapping a thin line of precedent dying out in 1701 (*Day v. Savadge* (1614) Hobart 85, 87; *Dr Bonham's Case* (1608) 8 Co. Rep. 107a, 118a; *City of London v. Wood* (1701) 12 Mod. 669, 687–688), there are arguments from history that the courts once asserted a power to set aside statutes (Allison, 2007: pp. 131–140; Joseph, 2001: p. 365; Knight, 2009: pp. 375–377) – although the better view is that such arguments are wrong as a matter of legal history (Williams, 2006; Goldsworthy; 1999: pp. 109–124, 197–204) and anachronistic as a matter of the history of political thought (Skinner, 1969: pp. 7–8). It may be suggested that the rule of law must take precedence over Parliamentary Sovereignty, and so statutes that violate the rule of law may be set aside – Sir Stephen Sedley's 'bi-polar sovereignty' thesis (Sedley, 1995: p. 389; Knight, 2009; pp. 365–367). Such arguments are controversial enough today when Parliamentary Sovereignty may be under pressure (Elliott, 2004: p. 554) and no judicial power to set aside statutes has ever been employed, other than one granted by Parliament under the European Communities Act (*R v Secretary of State for Transport, ex parte Factortame Ltd (No. 2)* [1991] 1 AC 603, 658–659, *Thoburn*). The orthodoxy is that Parliamentary Sovereignty remains the 'bedrock' of the British Constitution (*Jackson* [9], per Lord Bingham) – and there was no doubt as to this principle as being part of the 'classic constitution'. The principle can be glimpsed in Bagehot's (2007: p. 181) description of Parliament as a 'despot'. It was expressly stated in the Privy Council's advice in *Logan v Burslem* (1842) 4 Moo. P.C. 284, 294–295. Ivor Jennings doubted Dicey's view that Parliament could not bind itself, but had no doubt that Parliament could bind the courts (Jennings, 1938: p. 135). The White Paper (1997: [2.13]) that led to the Human Rights Act did not doubt the existence and utility of Parliamentary Sovereignty, even whilst seeking to address its risks. Lord Hope (2011: p. 9), whilst proposing limits on Parliamentary Sovereignty, expressly admitted that 'the traditional answer, of course, is that no judicial review of legislation enacted by parliament is possible'. That Parliamentary Sovereignty is a starting point of the 'classic constitution' cannot be seriously doubted.

This conclusion is unchanged by the recent 'constitutional statute' approach. In the case of *Thoburn* ([60]–[67]), Lord Justice Laws expounded a refinement to the theory of Parliamentary Sovereignty. He held that the common law recognised a class of constitutional statutes which were immune from the normal principle of implied repeal, challenging the Diceyan orthodoxy (Dicey, 1982: p. 78). However, it must be questioned whether *Thoburn* went to the basic definition of Parliamentary Sovereignty, i.e. that Parliament can make and unmake any law whatsoever (Dicey, 1982: pp. 3–4; Jennings, 1938: pp. 148–149). What needs to be appreciated is the marginality of the doctrine of implied repeal in terms of ordinary lawmaking. Rebecca Prebble (2005: pp. 299–300), having recounted the view that the decision in *Thoburn* 'seems only a few degrees removed from actually declining to apply particular statutes', then noted that implied repeal has long been a doctrine of 'last resort'. Put simply, it is a defect in drafting not to expressly repeal or amend contradictory pre-existing statutes. Were it not for Dicey's emphasis on implied repeal, it could hardly be thought to be a defect in Parliament's sovereignty to protect Parliament from accidentally repealing Acts such as the Magna Carta, the Bill of Rights 1689, the Act of Union, the Reform Acts, the Human Rights Act, the Scotland Act 1998 and the Government of Wales Act 1998, and the European Communities Act (*Thoburn* [62]; *R (HS2 Action Alliance Ltd) v Secretary of State for Transport* [2014] UKSC 3; [2014] 1 WLR 324 [208]). Alison Young

(2009: pp. 40–45), in a lengthy treatment of *Thoburn*, thought the concept of constitutional statutes was about 'principles of interpretation' rather than implied repeal itself, a presumption that certain things are too important to risk happening by oversight. Despite the immense significance attached to *Thoburn* and 'constitutional statutes' by some eminent writers (e.g. Bogdanor, 2009: p. 278), the decision, as Farrah Ahmed and Adam Perry (2014: pp. 534–535) conclude, does not change anything fundamental in the constitution such as the principle that statutes are the highest form of law.

In respect of the limits on parliamentary power, Jennings (1938: pp. 148–160) talks of (1) 'legislation changing foreign law', 'conventional limitations in regard to the dominions', 'other responsible legislatures'; (2) 'international law' in that a *domestic* sovereignty does not alter the reality that Parliament will as a matter of *international* legal obligation seek to avoid passing legislation contrary to international law; and (3) 'the mandate theory' that 'fundamental changes of policy must not be effected unless they have been in issue at a general election'. It is notable that when Jennings sets out these 'limitations upon Parliamentary authority', they divide between scenarios where (i) Parliament would itself be seeking to assert alien control on those outside its jurisdiction, (ii) the alien control that Parliament may be subject to by way of outside interference, in this case international law, and (iii) the non-alien control that an electorate has in respect of its representatives. The difficult relationship between international affairs and popular control of government will be considered later in Chapter 8 ('Internationalisation, statecraft and accountability').

Rule of law

The 'rule of law' is the second of the two key principles of the British Constitution, viewed juridically. Dicey (1982: pp. 110–115) argued that the rule of law as existing in Britain guaranteed personal safety and security of possessions as against the state by means of ascertainable legal rights (not overarching general principles), which were enforceable against the officials concerned:

> [1] … no man is punishable or can be lawfully made to suffer in body or goods except for a distinct breach of law established in the ordinary legal manner before the ordinary courts of the land. In this sense the rule of law is contrasted with every system of government based on the exercise by persons in authority of wide, arbitrary, or discretionary powers of constraint … [2] We mean … when we speak of the 'rule of law' as a characteristic of our country, not only that with us no man is above the law, but (what is a different thing) that here every man, whatever be his rank or condition, is subject to the ordinary law of the realm and amenable to the jurisdiction of the ordinary tribunals … [3] We may say

> that the constitution is pervaded by the rule of law on the ground that the general principles of the constitution (as for example the right to personal liberty, or the right of public meeting) are with us the result of judicial decisions determining the rights of private persons in particular cases brought before the courts; whereas under many foreign constitutions the security (such as it is) given to the rights of individuals appears to result from the general principles of the constitution.

It is necessary to consider what Dicey was describing in its own context (Craig, 1997: pp. 470–474), and not to mix it with anachronisms such as equating Dicey's theory with modern day dialogic theory (Hickman, 2005: p. 325 fn. 86), or arguing that Dicey 'associated the Rule of Law with rights-based liberalism and judicial review of governmental action' (Fallon, 1997: p. 1). It is true that a legislature would keep best within Dicey's concept of the rule of law if it practised laissez-faire liberalism and did not confer the sort of discretions necessary in a modern regulatory state. But the principles of the rule of law that Dicey observed from British constitutional practice belonged to, as Laski (1919: p. 451) wrote, 'the days when the functions of government were negative rather than positive in character'. It is, after all, one thing to make an official liable for breaking a clear law as regards entering a property without a warrant; another thing to impose liability on the same official when exercising a discretionary power that exists to promote public health or welfare.

Jennings (1941: pp. 369–370 fn. 20) pointed out a remarkable thing in respect of Dicey's exposition of the rule of law: it entirely omits the 'separation of powers'. Dicey's rule of law arguments were focused on the use of executive discretion, which overlaps but is crucially different. The rule of law, in Dicey's view, is violated by acts of executive discretion. However, it is not obvious why the principles of legality were interested in whether a particular general law owes its creation to Parliament or to delegated legislative powers.

The focus of this approach to the rule of law is on the relationship between the citizen (as a subject of governmental power) and the executive as controlled by the courts. The courts did not exercise control (alien or otherwise) over Parliament, let alone over citizens in their legislature-making and legislature-controlling abilities. Dicey's rule of law is not focused on the role of Parliament nor interested in arguments based on how the executive may control Parliament through party discipline (e.g. Neuberger, 2015a: [48]). Modern theories around constitutional review have focused on the relationship between the legislature and the courts. That Dicey's theory of the rule of law in the British Constitution did not presuppose any law for Parliament is made emphatically (Dicey, 1982: pp. 314–315):

> This rule of law, which means at bottom the right of the Courts to punish any illegal act by whomsoever committed, is of the very essence of English institutions. If the sovereignty of Parliament gives the form,

> the supremacy of the law of the land determines the substance of our constitution ... The supremacy of the law of the land means in the last resort the right of the judges to control the *executive* government ...
> [Emphasis added]

The ordinary law of the land includes statutes, and the ordinary law can only be dispensed with by the authority of Parliament – Dicey is clear that there is nothing unconstitutional even with an Act of Indemnity which forgives illegality by officials. That a formal law is required to suspend the application of an ordinary law maintains, argued Dicey (1982: pp. 142–145), the supremacy of law.

It is nevertheless argued by Tom Hickman (2005: p. 324) that Dicey succeeded in 'bringing common law reason to bear on legislative projects', and thus that 'Parliament is thereby required, as a general matter, to face squarely the prospect of infringing rights'. However, this dialogic dynamic was not how Dicey described the interaction between public, legislative and judicial opinion. Dicey (2008: p. 263) described judicial opinion as a cross-current which may tell on public and legislative opinion. The quality or otherwise of judicial legislation was not the point, it was 'the fact that judicial legislation may be the result of considerations different from the ideas which influence Parliament'. Judicial opinion was apt to generate different ideas to public opinion, which might affect public opinion. At no point are the judges promoted as a check on the link between public opinion and legislation, nor is it suggested that legislative opinion should be settled by way of a private conversation between the political and judicial branches of the state. Even were Hickman's view of legislation as a joint project between judges and Parliament true as regards Dicey, such a common-law dialogue approach is not found in the other writers amongst the 'canonical sextet'. Harold Laski (1951: pp. 44–45) was particularly scathing of judicial influence in the legislative process:

> [S]ince the famous *Arlidge* case, the judges seem to me to have used in their approach to most problems of administrative Law canons of statutory interpretation which have been intended not only to preserve the full amplitude of their jurisdiction over questions of vires but, also, to strike down in the realm of social policy changes in the direction the law ... Nor can one easily explain decisions like those in the *Taff Vale* case or in the *Osborne* case, or even in *Roberts v Hopwood*, except upon the assumption that the judges have the right to build, as it were, a framework within the boundaries of which Parliament must confine its social legislation. ... [T]he growth of administrative law is the outcome of a conscious judicial invasion of a sphere where novelty was intended by Parliament, and that the purpose of the invasion was to limit to the narrowest possible compass any novelty the judges might dislike.

In truth, Dicey was not arguing for a constitutional primacy for the courts in matters of liberty, as Hickman (2005: p. 322) has suggested. Instead he was recognising a constitutional fact that much protection of liberty could be traced to judicial decisions. Nevertheless, statutes might improve on case-law protections: Dicey (1982: p. 131) notes that the Habeas Corpus Acts, 'are treated, and (for practical purposes) rightly treated, as the basis on which rests an Englishman's security for the enjoyment of his personal freedom', in that they put right the defects in the judge-made remedy of the writ of habeas corpus.

So, how in all of this could Dicey (1982: p. 314) say that Parliamentary Sovereignty provided the 'form' and the supremacy of law provided the 'substance' of the constitution? With the modern preoccupation with constitutional review and human rights, it is easy to focus on the relationship between the rule of law and Parliamentary Sovereignty, and thus conclude that, if the latter trumps the former, then the former is the weaker and less important principle. The reality is that officials will daily meet the limits of their authority. Police officers will not be able to search without showing sufficient cause for a warrant. Tax inspectors cannot demand private documents without legal authorisation. Traffic wardens must prove illegal parking and not just assert. The rule of law is vital to the citizen's life as a *subject* of state power. Parliamentary Sovereignty seldom impinges on the citizen/subject's experience – it is the bedrock, and we do not see the bedrock for all of the grass, trees, rivers and bushes; but the whole landscape would be different if it were shaped differently. If Parliament were not sovereign but subject to constitutional review on an American model, we would see the possibilities of politics restrained by judicial power – there would be forbidding wastelands created by constitutional prohibitions that would grow and contract through judicial action. The importance of Parliamentary Sovereignty is not that it stands ready, like a tyrant, threatening to remove liberty and property if expedient, but rather for the strikingly different landscape that would exist without the freedom of action that it gives to the legislature. As subjects, it is the law that we encounter and rely upon; and we as citizens may seek to influence the law through our potential participation.

The rule of law is inherently of a more pervasive importance than the theoretical maximum of Parliament's power. It is ultimately through the law that Parliament's statutes are enforced (*R (Cart) v Upper Tribunal* [2009] EWHC 3052 (Admin); [2010] 2 WLR 1012 [38]). Parliament can overcome the Diceyan requirement of laws being enforced in the ordinary courts by overseeing its own legislation, as Jennings (1941: pp. 385–386) argued in respect of the wartime Emergency Powers Acts. That however was an extreme case, and hardly capable of being followed generally. Outside such rare exceptions, insofar as Parliament's laws are the commands of the sovereign, the absence of a definitive interpreter and enforcer will make such commands voluntary, and allow those receiving Parliament's commands to define their own obligations.

The dominance of party and the 'elective dictatorship' thesis

A common argument against putting trust in the 'political constitution', and in favour of increased judicial power in the constitution is that legislatures no longer effectively perform their 'legislative, scrutiny and accountability' roles (Tierney, 2013: p. 2187). In the context of the functioning of the British Constitution, this translates into a common concern as to 'the effective dominance of Parliament by the Executive' (Kavanagh, 2009: p. 376). Such concerns are typically grouped under Lord Hailsham's (1978: pp. 9–11) phrase 'elective dictatorship'.

Citations of Lord Hailsham's argument, or at least this headline point abound. When setting out his argument as to the 'unsettlement' of the British Constitution, Neil Walker (2014: p. 539) invoked 'Lord Hailsham in 1976 railing against the "elective dictatorship" of contemporary executive-dominated and ideologically committed Party government'. The late Sir John Baker (2013: p. 6) took Lord Hailsham's coining of the phrase as a starting point for concerns about executive dominance. Lord Steyn (2005b: pp. 346–347; 2006: pp. 246–247) would similarly treat Lord Hailsham as a starting point in two important articles in 2005 and 2006. Francesca Klug (2007: p. 704) reminds us that John Smith MP, the late Labour leader, proposed a British Bill of Rights because 'what we have in this country at the moment is not real democracy; it is elective dictatorship'. C.J.S. Knight (2009: p. 365) argued that the judges have stepped into the House of Commons' role as a check on executive power as 'a pragmatic development to counter Lord Hailsham's fear of an "elective dictatorship"'. From a republican perspective focused on the electorate's power within the constitution as constituted (as opposed to the electorate's constitutive power), the legitimacy of this 'pragmatic' development is dependent on the existence of undominated popular counter-control against judicial power.

We thus come to a central issue in the functioning of the British Constitution: whether the power of the executive *in* Parliament is a good or a bad thing.

The modern concerns are in contrast to many older commentators, who observed a similar relationship between the executive and the legislature, but saw it as advantageous. A classic statement of this view is given by Bagehot (2007: pp. 10–11):

> The efficient secret of the English Constitution may be described as the close union, the nearly complete fusion, of the executive and legislative powers. No doubt by the traditional theory, as it exists in all the books, the goodness of our constitution consists in the entire separation of the legislative and executive authorities, but in truth its merit consists in their singular approximation. The connecting link is *the cabinet.*
>
> [Emphasis in original]

The government is the government because the party (or, occasionally, parties) that form the government possess a majority of MPs in the House of Commons: 'because the Government controls the majority it may insist on the votes of the majority' (Jennings, 1966: p. 83). In this view, the 'efficient secret' of the 'near fusion' of executive and legislature makes for efficient government and effective accountability to the people.

A study of the classical sextet suggests that questions of executive and party dominance do not represent a recent 'unsettling' of the constitution, to use Neil Walker's (2014) phrase, but a long-term feature. Beatson (2010: p. 50) correctly ascribes the putative 'elective dictatorship' problem to 'the near fusion' of executive and Parliament which Bagehot described.

There is nothing new about concerns that party power can disconnect the legislature from public opinion. Remembering Dicey's (2008; pp. 8–9) second and third requirements for a connection between law and public opinion, the party system carried the means for frustrating the changes of the law demanded by public opinion, and ensuring that legislation was guided by some non-public opinion enforced by the influence of the party leaders. With the House of Lords no longer having the power to force important legislation to wait until public opinion was established, a more direct link with public opinion was required (Weill, 2003: pp. 479–480). A straight line can be drawn from Dicey's (1982: pp. lxxiii–lxxiv, cxiii–cxix) reservations about the 'party machine' controlling politics and Adam Tomkins's (2005: p. 138) call for 'the removal of party and party loyalty from the working of Parliament', a step he argued would improve the republican credentials of the British Constitution.

Bagehot and Jennings, in contrast, saw the narrowness of the gap between government and Parliament not as an accountability problem for Parliament holding the government responsible, but instead as being important to the accountability of the government to the electorate. For Bagehot (2008: pp. 98–99), the 'near fusion' was at the heart of the 'come-at-able' nature of the British Constitution when viewed from an elector's perspective. Likewise, the party system is not of itself a distortion in the constitution but the means by which electors throughout the country know what they are voting for, and how to express displeasure in a government (Jennings, 1966: pp. 17–18).

The classic constitution thus answers to Dahl and Lindblom's (1953: p. 314) description of polyarchy in that 'opportunities for political action are kept open to a representative section of the adult population', and therefore 'specific policies will rarely violate highly ranked, intense, stable, and relatively broad preferences of the greater number for a longer period than about the interval between elections'. Dicey's (1982: p. cxvii) description of the ability of the government to 'defy' public opinion with 'the arts of modern parliamentary warfare' will not assist it at a general election. As Jennings (1966: p. 86) said, '[t]he axe will fall upon those who lose touch with public opinion'. Furthermore, in the view of Bagehot (2007: pp. 139–144), Jennings (1966: pp. 16–17) and Laski (1951: p. 37), it follows that the party system does not create a distortion in the majoritarian system through internal party discipline. A different point arises if the established parties themselves present a united front by forming on particular issues a political cartel that fails to compete for the support of the electorate, as we considered in Chapter 4 ('Schumpeter and classic realism'), above. Providing there are competitor parties in a position to take advantage of popular discontent, the political system will continue to be 'adapted' to turn public opinion into legislative action even if the current well-whipped governing party chooses to ignore the wishes of the electorate. The connection with political opinion breaks down in the medium-to-long term only when the major parties maintain a common front, requiring a new party to 'break the mould', as the Labour Party did in the early twentieth-century. As Harold Laski (1951: pp. 16–24) noted, the reason why executive control of Parliament was weak for much of the Victorian period was the absence of great difference between the parties, and the social uniformity of Conservative and Liberal politicians, making the shifting of loyalties easier than when the competition for power changed to being between a substantially working class Labour Party and a still fairly aristocratic Conservative Party. If parties give real choice to electors, then the difference between the parties makes it harder for MPs to rebel, as to do so risks giving advantage to opposing parties, which, by definition they have less in common with than nineteenth-century Tories and Liberals had in common with each other.

Tomkins (2005: pp. 136–139) may see the ability of the government to command a majority in the House of Commands as a constitutional malfunction, but Bagehot (2007: p. 130) saw this as a function of the House of Commons central role in the constitution: 'The House of Commons is an electoral chamber; it is the assembly which chooses our president'. But unlike the US Electoral College, the role of the British Parliament in making a choice is a continuing one (Bagehot, 2007: pp. 130–132). US Presidents, once elected, are responsible to no one for their continuation in office for the next four years; British prime ministers are responsible to Parliament. The result for Bagehot (2007: p. 132) is that: 'The whole life of English politics is the action and reaction between the Ministry and the Parliament. The appointees strive to guide, and the appointers surge under the guidance'.

Bagehot (2007: p. 140) took the view that 'the fundamental – almost unasked question – [was] how the House of Commons comes to be able to govern at all'. Bagehot's point was that the House of Commons (then) had 657 MPs, who would be incapable of appointing and then maintaining a government in power unless those MPs were subject to genuine restraints of obedience to their leaders. Leadership necessitates party, in Bagehot's (2007: pp. 141–142) view:

> [T]he principle of Parliament is obedience to leaders ... The penalty for not doing so, is the penalty of impotence. It is not that you will not be able to do any good, but you will not be able to do anything at all. If

> everybody does what he thinks right, there will 657 amendments to every mention, and none of them will be carried or the motion either.
>
> The moment, indeed, that we distinctly conceive that the House of Commons is mainly and above all things an elective assembly, we at once perceive that party is its essence.

It is thus the purpose of party leaderships – and the cabinet provides the leadership of the majority party or coalition – to do much of the reasoning on behalf of their MPs. The leaders are chosen for that purpose. It means that the MPs ought to be presented with well-formed policies that will usually be in line with party philosophy, instead of each MP being left to reason through each matter of Commons business. On such a view, the lack of parliamentary defeats for the government, or the apparent subordination of Parliament to the executive, do not represent the system malfunctioning, but simply the system no longer functioning as it did in the nineteenth century (Hiebert, 2012: pp. 43–44).

Parliament deliberates and votes, and it is the ability of the ministry to lead its followers that decides the outcome. The ministry must be understood as a committee of the legislature. The ministry is not an 'expert group' to whom Parliament delegates its deliberating, but rather something formed out of the majority of Parliament. They are all part of the same 'select group' deliberation, not independent forces.

And it is as parties that legislators and ministers are accountable together to the electorate: the mechanism that links 'select group' deliberation to 'public deliberation' does not separate out a legislative and executive role.

The elective dictatorship refocused – loss of power for ministers and legislators

When addressing the executive dominance of Parliament, the 'elective dictatorship' hypothesis set out above is not therefore an objective conclusion, but a value-laden opinion as to how the government of the United Kingdom ought to be reconstituted. As such, it is a matter on which jurists and academics may participate in public deliberation, but in a polyarchy their views are ultimately worth no more than the votes of any other individual.

What we argue in this section is that the true problem is an absence of time to scrutinise the vast business of modern government which makes it difficult for Parliament to hold ministers accountable.

Classic theory of accountability to Parliament

The ideal of our constitutional theory is that ministers have authority over their departments, and they are responsible for their departments. Whatever is done by a department can be the business of Parliament. It can be taken up by an MP, and government inaction on electorally sensitive issues is an opportunity for the opposition (Bagehot 2007: pp. 182–183): 'The opposition have the unrestricted selection of the point of attack, and they seldom choose a case in which the department, upon the surface of the matter, seems to be right'.

One of the functions of the Commons is to transmit complaints to the government. If such a complaint relates to the policies of a ministry, then the minister will be obliged to investigate and explain. If no ostensibly respectable explanation can be found, the minister will be obliged to reform or risk looking ridiculous. Every policy reached without any reference, or with little reference, to the minister may become an embarrassment to the government. Such embarrassment may spell ruin for the career prospects of a minister who fails to take a grip of the situation. Responsibility of each minister and the government as a whole to the legislature exposes the mistakes of those who rule, and the individual weaknesses of those who comprise the government. Even if party loyalties mean that the votes are still won in the House, such victories are liable to be somewhat Pyrrhic from the greater electoral perspective when unjustifiable action has suffered public ridicule. The following description is striking (Pettit, 1997: pp. 236–237):

> The idea of a legislative assembly, and the idea of making those in government responsible to such an assembly, points us towards a set of arrangements that ought to boost a suitable economy of regard. For where there is such an assembly there will usually be a well-established sense of relevant standards, there will be systematic channels of information and publicity, and there will be a culture of forthrightness in criticism and commendation of members. The general assembly and various cross-party subcommittees, then, are forums where members may expect to suffer or flourish in the regard stakes, as it is made clear both what is expected and what has been achieved. And these arrangements for mobilizing regard should be reinforced in a culture where the doings of parliament quickly come to public attention, and quickly attract commendation or censure, through media coverage and commentary.

Those words, 130 years after Bagehot, came from Philip Pettit writing about how 'responsible government' may promote republican government. In Pettit's view as encapsulated above, the ideal *republican* system of responsible government will operate much as Bagehot described the British system working. There is select-group deliberation in that legislators will have to defend their positions and call on others to make such a defence. Being made in public, the select-group deliberation is exposed to the public and may become part of public deliberation. The ability to govern is not an assertion of a dominating, hegemonic authority held by any individuals, but is always precarious on what the public makes of the spectacle. Not everything is taken up into public deliberation, but anything *might be*. So every policy and law is subject to Parliament's invigilation, and, beyond that, invigilation by the electorate.

Such is the ideal, but the viability of it in the modern age is strained by the amount of business deserving of parliamentary enquiry.

The true elective dictatorship problem that we wish to set out starts with a tension within critiques supportive of greater judicial power. Lord Neuberger (2015a: [48]), as we noted earlier, argued that the executive domination of Parliament was a reason for increasing judicial oversight of legislation. But this argument that Parliament has become a rubber stamp for the executive is at odds with the increased judicial tendency to emphasise the need for explicit parliamentary authorisation (*Simms* 132; *Morgan Grenfell*). Yet, if we take the executive to genuinely dictate the law to Parliament, then the only thing that would be achieved by asking the executive to seek a more closely worded statute is to delay the inevitable. There is little point in requiring that executive action is specifically considered by Parliament if we hypothesise Parliament to be unreflective servant of the executive. The principle expounded in the *Simms* case is thus either a reassertion of a dogmatic insistence on the formal separation of powers when all substance is lacking, or it is a recognition that the 'fusion' of Parliament and executive is, after all, only 'near perfect'. Government and Parliament are, as Amery (1964: p. 28) said, 'closely intertwined and harmonized', but they 'are still separate and independent functions'.

The British Constitution's actual 'elective dictatorship' problem is not derived from the absence of a 'House of Mavericks' (Tomkins, 2007), but rather the degree to which the business of government and legislation takes place outside the notice of the legislature. This problem of power devolving on 'professional advisers' exercising administrative independence was part of Hailsham's (1978: p. 126) original 'elective dictatorship' complaint, but literature has naturally concentrated on complaints as to the authority of Parliament as against the executive. The check and balance described by Bagehot (2007: pp. 182–183), that anything may become a cause célèbre in Parliament, and that opposition may keep the government and administration honest by being able to choose its line of attack, becomes less effective as the business of government grows. The opposition may probe for weaknesses, but parliamentary time has not expanded at the same rate as the business of government, so the potential for uncovering the errors of ministers and officials and bringing them to public attention through parliamentary scrutiny alone is greatly reduced. This is all the more so as the House of Commons cannot carry out its role if it lacks information (Laski, 1951: pp. 86–87), and it is difficult for MPs to keep themselves informed on all matters when the business of government is so broad (the same, of course, is true of the ability of electors to meaningfully participate). The elective dictatorship is that ministers, often in truth acting as proxies for officials (Clayton, 2004: p. 40), will formally take many decisions, which they do not meaningfully oversee. The growth of autonomous departments and agencies creates a particular risk that the state can gain the ability to act autonomously from the society that it is supposed to represent. Government agencies can de facto take the role of pure expert decision makers, and be wholly independent of political control (Taylor, 1995: p. 1070).

The effect of common-law decisions such as *Simms* is that the government is put in a position where it must not just raise the issue concerned in Parliament, but do so on a background where parliamentary opposition will have been informed by the critique of the measure thrown up by the litigation.

The same dynamic is offered by the Human Rights Act – assuming that the elegant balance was more than the preservation of the façade of Parliamentary Sovereignty.

Behaviour within the constitution – electoral and select-group decision-making

Anthony King illustrated the classic constitution with two useful concepts: 'the line of authority', and 'come-at-ability'.

The line of authority was taken from Herman Finer's dictum from 1960, where he described the simplicity of the British Constitution in these terms (Finer, 1960: p. 67, cited King, 2007: p. 59): 'The line of authority between people and Government rises singly and directly; the line of responsibility of Cabinet and Parliament to the people descends singly and directly'. Bagehot (2007: pp. 98–99, see also King, 2007: pp. 58–60) emphasised that the nature of the constitution meant that those who governed were 'come-at-able' by those who were governed. These are two figures of speech which neatly sum up the central features of the classic constitution: that having authority for everything, Parliament is accountable for everything to the electorate in a single act of voting; and as the executive is largely fused with Parliament, the government and its MPs in Parliament cannot with credibility blame each other for failure of what is throughout a joint enterprise. As Bagehot (2007: pp. 17–23) pointed out, responsibility for the direction of the United States government is often unclear when President and Congress are pulling in different directions, and who should be held to account may likewise be unclear. British prime ministers may feel like blaming unruly backbenchers for failures, but as they, their fellow ministers, and the backbenchers represent a united package to be presented to the electorate, this would be somewhat futile.

Without leadership, no one is responsible for failure, nor for how apparently good ideas might upset the big picture. Bagehot (2007: pp. 136–137) quoted an anonymous financier as saying: 'If you want a certain cheer in the House of Commons, make a general panegyric on economy; if you want to invite a sure defeat, propose a particular saving'. The point is that, left to itself, an assembly of 650 MPs will adopt contradictory but individually popular policies, but it will be hard for the electorate to pick out who are truly responsible should the ship of state run aground; but a government that does the same will be plainly in the line of fire should its populism turn sour. And, which is even more important, any blame attaching to the government attaches to each and every MP of the party of government. Without the guidance of identified leaders, success will have too many fathers to know the paternity, and failure will be an orphan. That is what is meant by come-at-ability or Finer's line of authority and responsibility. There is no hiding place for those who have shared in commanding the power of Parliament, and disappointed the electorate. This is particularly the case given that Parliamentary Sovereignty means that a lack of authority is never an excuse – unless it is the electorate itself that denied authority to a single party by electing a hung Parliament.

So, when Beetham (1999: p. 42) says that elections 'cast a long shadow', and when we consider the interventional and inhibitory control exerted by the electorate over politicians due to the existence of elections, we can see the position of domination that the electorate can exert. The executive only exercises power because it has a willing majority in the Commons. The Commons' willingness to follow the executive is conditioned by its estimation of the public's response. The executive makes its own estimate of public opinion. The result is described by Jennings (1966: pp. 56–57): 'All Governments become unpopular in the end …; all Governments try to resist the inevitable unpopularity; and the result is a remarkably close correspondence between the actions of Government, viewed over a short term of years, and public opinion'.

A view must be taken on whether a measure may lose votes, gain votes, or be treated with indifference. As Bagehot (2007: p. 131) put it: 'The House only goes where it thinks in the end the nation will follow; but it takes its chance of the nation following or not following: it assumes the initiative, and acts upon its discretion or caprice'.

Voting is the link between public opinion and policy, and cannot be seen in isolation as Schumpeter does.

Whilst Tomkins (2007) may wish to see MPs exercising independent judgement over their party leaderships, Jennings (1966: pp. 16–17) argues with considerable force that this will defeat the expectations of the electorate itself: constituency electorates are more interested in that Mr Jones or Mrs Smith were candidates for the Conservative or Labour Parties than they were interested in anything particular about Mr Jones or Mrs Smith.

The effect of this is that there was no special place for the intellectual elite in determining what is best (Bagehot, 2007: pp. 171–172):[1]

> I maintain that Parliament ought to embody the public opinion of the English nation. … The 'too clever by half' people who live in 'Bohemia' ought to have no more influence in Parliament than they have in England, and they can scarcely have less.

1 A point truer now, in days of universal suffrage, than in mid-Victorian England.

Ultimately, the classic constitution entrusted power to the deliberation and voting of a 'select group', the largely fused legislature and executive – and that group was selected by the voting and deliberation of the public at large.

It is for this reason that Dicey (1982: pp. 26–29, 285) argued that the legal sovereignty of Parliament was subject to the political sovereignty of the electorate – the decision-making through 'select-group deliberation' is linked to public opinion arising out of 'public deliberation'. The authority of MPs to control the sovereignty of Parliament rests on their election and re-election. Dicey (2008: pp. 45–50) divided the nineteenth century into (a) the Period of Old Toryism or Legislative Quiescence, (b) the Period of Benthamism or Individualism, and (c) the Period of Collectivism. In each period, the direction of Parliament and the limits of that direction was ultimately determined by the outlook of the electorate.

With the political sovereignty held by the electorate when choosing a House of Commons, which in turn operates the legal sovereignty of Parliament, there is no place for uncontrolled expert/elite decision-making. All rules that are set by experts may be re-set by the legislators. Experts with official functions may be held to account by a Parliament exercising its right as a despot with infinite curiosity to exercise 'tyranny over public offices' (Bagehot, 2007: pp. 181, 183).

Conclusion

We can now see the classic constitution take shape. The electorate have a dominant position over Parliament in that it is the electorate that chooses the MPs that make up the House of Commons, which has a dominant position over the executive: it chooses the country's 'president', as Bagehot (2007: pp. 130–131) put it, and he (i.e. the prime minister) appoints his cabinet and other ministers, but any who lose the support of the Commons must resign. That is the theory of responsibility, but then there is the practicality of authority: the executive will lead the Commons; the Commons – with the Queen and the Lords falling into line – will vote for taxes to be levied on the population, and legislate for laws binding on the country as a whole. The executive has authority over the Commons, and the Commons has authority over the country. If the executive uses its authority badly in the eyes of the Commons, then the government will be held to account in the Commons; if the government and the Commons together use their authority badly in the eyes of the people; then they together will be held to account by the electorate at the next election.

This is what Bagehot (2007: pp. 98–99) described as the government of the country being 'come-at-able'. Jennings (1938: p. 139) explains that Parliament cannot be seen as a single sovereign person, but in terms of the wishes and ambitions of the MPs who temporarily comprise it:

> Since, if [MPs] wish for re-election, they may be called upon to give an account of their actions, they must consider in their actions what the general opinion about them may be. Parliament passes many laws which many people do not want. *But it never passes any laws which any substantial section of the population violently dislikes.*
>
> [Emphasis added]

It is a statement with resonances of Dahl and Lindblom's (1953: p. 314) view that representative democracy properly functioning 'will rarely violate highly ranked, intense, stable, and relatively broad preferences of the greater number for a longer period than about the interval between elections'.

The line of responsibility runs, as Finer said, in a clear way from the summit of the executive down to the electorate as a whole. The prime minister may appoint the cabinet, but is vulnerable if he loses its confidence; the executive as a whole (and each individual) must account to Parliament, and may be embarrassed by facing a cogent opposition sinking its teeth into a real grievance; and, at a general election, the government and its MPs stand to be judged together, as do the opposition and its MPs.

Hence, the only ground for 'coming-at' any part of the state by way of court action is that the particular part of the state has acted illegally. Dicey (2008: p. 260) stated the orthodoxy when saying that '[t]he duty of a Court, in short, is not to remedy a particular grievance, but to determine whether an alleged grievance is one for which the law supplies a remedy'. It is illegality rather than free-standing injustice that concerned the courts, and such illegality may be committed by the lowest official, the Secretary of State for the Home Department (*Entick v Carrington* (1765) 2 Wils. KB 275), or even by the House of Commons acting against an individual in excess of its legally recognised privileges (*Stockdale and Hansard* (1840) 11 Adolphus and Ellis 1).

The citizen could not, however, come-at an Act of Parliament by way of the courts as Parliamentary Sovereignty meant that such an Act could never be illegal. The citizen might be able to procure a ruling that will frustrate the meaning of a particular statute, as happened with legislation that empowered trade unions (Griffiths, 1997: pp. 63–84). However, the best efforts of judges reading down trade union rights legislation by reason of common-law rights of freedom of contract was not a litigation strategy that could win in the long term – that victory could only come from a political victory in Parliament (Griffiths, 1997: pp. 84–98). If a reformer desired that a particular bill be brought forward or shelved, then no help could be sought from the courts. The courts could not determine that legislation should follow a laissez-faire agenda, or determine that a collectivist path should be trod, even though courts may have a tendency to interpret legislation and develop 'common law' principles in either direction. Such victories would be very specific and often temporary. And, therefore, it is unsurprising that reformers such as Bentham came-at Parliament in order to change the law (Dicey,

2008: pp. 117–119). And, as the constitution is attuned to convert public opinion into political action, coming-at Parliament is most securely done by winning the battle for public opinion.

Despite the openness of the British Constitution to operate as a polyarchy, particularly its clear lines of come-at-ability, and of authority and responsibility, a substantial difficulty in accountability emerges with the size of the state. This is the real 'elective dictatorship' problem, set out above: the difficulty of effective oversight by legislators *and* ministers over administrators and officials when the business of government grows. Foreshadowing a theme of the next chapter, there is a potential for constitutional review under the Human Rights Act to place concerns directly onto Parliament's agenda, forcing democratic consideration of issues that might otherwise be resolved purely by officials.

7 Human Rights Act and democracy

Introduction

This and subsequent chapters turn their attention directly to the Human Rights Act. Certain propositions will become clear along the way. As a matter of formal structure, the Human Rights Act is capable of boosting contestation without restricting popular control – it may thus serve to promote the tendency of the constitution towards polyarchy where the electorate avoids elite-domination by having an effective and unconditioned means to assert equality with the individuals of the elite. The formal structure created by the Human Rights Act is equally capable of being operated so as to limit contestation and popular control; it may tend towards a hegemony centred on judicial power. The difference will depend on how the Act is in fact operated in the real world, and the extent to which the electorate may hold legislators to account for complying with the Human Rights Act. If a duty to comply with a judicial decision under the Act is seen by voters as representing a complete explanation by legislators (and their parties) for a course of conduct, then the link between public opinion and legislative action is restricted. Legislators cannot be seen as accountable by the public insofar as they are also seen by the public as having no constitutional choice. Democracy is predicated on the availability of a choice for electors to participate so as to hold elected representatives account for all legislative acts and omissions.

What we shall see emerge is the need for a theory of 'legitimate breach', which is to say an understanding on the part of electorate and legislators alike that non-compliance with the Act will not represent a constitutional or international crisis. A democratic reconciliation of constitutional review will need to be rooted in the belief that the existence of the Human Rights Act represents an ongoing constitutive decision that the Act should exist, and that decision is rooted in public opinion, the public being the constitutive power. However, such a reconciliation must acknowledge that public opinion may regard individual decisions under the Act as not being for the common good, and that such public opinion must be capable of directing legislative change on those issues. For it to be otherwise would tend to place the judiciary in a hegemonic position, and tend to thwart the free participation of the electorate. However, for the Act to balance democracy and rights protection, the manner in which democracy is practised must not itself create an existential crisis for the Act in terms of its ability to protect rights.

This chapter will seek to establish how the Act is designed to be capable of operating as a polyarchy. It will be shown that the Human Rights Act is designed so that participation by way of constitutional review litigation could operate as a route into ordinary political participation, rather than as a means of bypassing the political process altogether.

Structure of the Act

We may say that in striking a balance between rights protection and democracy, the provisions of the Human Rights Act can be categorised as follows.

Firstly, there are *interpretative* features. As noted in Chapter 5, the scope of a bill of rights may be set by provisions as to 'textual rules on interpretation' and 'textual rules on justification', and the judicial approaches for the same. We need not concern ourselves with sections 12 and 13, on freedom of expression and freedom of conscience and religion, as these have had no obvious effect on the Act's substantive requirements (*Cream Holdings*). Section 2 is the principal provision on interpretation and justification requiring the British courts to 'take into account' various sources (most importantly ECtHR decisions) when interpreting and applying the Convention rights incorporated in British law.

Although the question of what is meant by the British courts 'taking into account' decisions of the ECtHR are of vital adjudicative importance, it does not of itself answer the question of whether a broad or narrow approach will be taken to interpreting the scope and application of the protected rights. The approach, to date, has been to largely mirror ECtHR jurisprudence as to the scope of rights and their application: 'The duty of national courts is to keep pace with the Strasbourg jurisprudence as it evolves over time: no more, but certainly no less' (*R (Ullah) v Special Adjudicator* [2004] UKHL 26; [2004] 2 AC 323 [20]). Section 2 may lead to broad or narrow approaches, depending on how the ECtHR has decided the cases that need to be mirrored. However, British courts have begun taking an increasingly independent role as regards issues of justification insofar as Strasbourg has ruled a measure to be compatible by reason of being within a state's margin of appreciation (*Nicklinson* [70]–[76]).

Secondly, there are *enforcement* provisions, i.e. the remedies under the Act, and their limits. Sections 6–8 require public bodies to act in compliance with the Human Rights Act, and provide for damages and other judicial remedies for actions made unlawful by the Act. Whereas the Diceyan rule of law allows for specific remedies for breaching specific laws, the Human Rights Act regime provides for general principles under which officials, from police to tax inspectors, will meet the limits of their authority. It might be argued that much of this is now achieved independently by the courts by way of reading-in reasonableness requirements into statutory discretions, and reading-down the scope of broadly worded statutory powers (Sales, 2009: p. 607; Ahmed and Perry, 2014: pp. 515–521). A recent case on solitary confinement in prison is an example of the courts developing common-law powers so as to eclipse arguments based on Convention rights (*R (Bourgass) v Secretary of State for Justice* [2015] UKSC 54). However, it is always the case that statutory interpretation is the first port of call for interpreting statutory powers and determining the limits of statutory discretions (Bamforth and Craig, 2001: pp. 764–765). Thus the Human Rights Act reaches further than the rule of law under the classic constitution (even in the extended approach to the principles of legality expounded in *Simms*, see Chapter 2, 'Political costs'), and also gives a legislatively mandated basis for general court oversight of the use of official power in respect of rights of liberty and property.

Section 3 allows for legislation to be read whenever possible in compliance with the Convention rights incorporated into British law by the Human Rights Act, but cannot affect the validity of primary legislation, nor of secondary legislation whose incompatibility clearly derives from the terms of the parent legislation. Section 4 allows the courts to issue declarations of incompatibility against offending primary legislation which cannot be reconciled with the protected Convention rights. This provision itself directly leads to section 10, which allows for a fast-track procedure for legislating to resolve incompatibility issues – a procedure that also applies where there has been an adverse finding by the ECtHR (section 10(1)(b)). This provision received significant attention when the Human Rights Bill was presented to Parliament in that it would allow the government to present remedial legislation without the full parliamentary scrutiny requirements given to primary legislation, which was seen in some quarters as a significant departure from ordinary constitutional practice (HL Debate, 1997a: cc. 1236–7; 1997b: cc.541–545). However, the remedial legislation still requires approval by both Houses of Parliament (Schedule 2, paragraph 2(a)), and section 10(2) states that this approach should only be used if there are compelling reasons. This upholds majoritarianism, and reduces the prospects of minority obstruction by reducing the 'veto points', that is, the number of procedural steps where remedial legislation may be lost.

Thirdly, there are *entrenchment* provisions, or rather provisions that avoid entrenchment. Indeed, the interplay of sections 3 and 4 means that the Act cannot even be seen as immune to implied repeal as a constitutional statute (*Thoburn* [60]–[67]; *HS2* [208]); a future statute that is plainly contrary to the Act would prevail.

Fourthly, we must note the *internationalising* effect of many of the provisions. Most obviously, the Act implements 'Convention rights', meaning the Convention 'as it has effect for the time being in the United Kingdom' (sections 1 and 21). This means, as per its preamble, that the Act 'gives further effect to the rights and freedoms guaranteed under the European Convention on Human Rights', as opposed to creating something genuinely domestic (*Quark Fishing Ltd v Secretary of State for the Foreign and Commonwealth Office* [2005] UKHL 57; [2006] 1 AC 529 [33]). The 'mirror principle' derived from section 2 of the Human Rights Act ensures that the Act's meaning will normally be one and the same as the meaning of the Convention as found by the ECtHR. This is of great importance as to the existence of any duty (or sense of duty) for Parliament to comply with the decisions that domestic courts make under the Act.

Fifthly, and finally, there are provisions which are designed to *promote deliberation* rather than have any counter-majoritarian effect. The most important of these is section 19, which requires a minister promoting a bill to make a statement of compatibility, or a request to proceed absent such a statement. The official approach is this (DCMS, 2002: [9]):

> [A] 'statement of compatibility' … should be made only if it is more likely than not that the Bill's provisions would withstand a legal challenge on human rights grounds in both the domestic courts and the European Court of Human Rights.

When considering making a statement of incompatibility under section 19, ministers are posed with three related questions: a) are the proposals compatible with the Human Rights Act, b) if not, can they be redesigned so as to be compatible, and, c) if the proposals cannot be redesigned to be compatible, does the government wish to proceed with the bill regardless? The provision is silent on the important issue as to whether the statement of incompatibility represents a positive wish that the provisions should take priority over the Human Rights Act, or whether the future of the provisions would be determined by whether they are ultimately found to be compatible or not. Hence, in the only example of a government Bill presented *and passed* with a request to proceed without a statement of compatibility, the minister presenting the Communications Bill 2003 was clear that the government hoped that the provisions restricting political advertising would be upheld, and that matters would be revisited were they held to be incompatible (HL Debate, 2003a: cc. 658–659). As Lynch (2007: p. 309 fn. 25) pointed out, such provisions flag up non-compliance and may serve to increase the prospect of political costs arising from non-compliance.

Reconciliation and judicial deference

As noted in Chapter 2 ('Deference and the scope of counter-majoritarianism'), the literature on the relationship between the Human Rights Act and democracy/Parliamentary Sovereignty has much to say on 'judicial deference'. The debate concerns itself with when judges should restrain themselves from asserting their views on matters arising under the proportionality test, such as whether a 'less intrusive means' was available or on whether the advantages of a law were too small to justify the law's impact on rights. What should be plain from the republican analysis set out in Chapter 3 is that how judges might choose to exercise their power in respect of justification will not of itself affect any dominant position enjoyed by the judiciary, although it might affect the extent to which such domination is felt. Alien control does not disappear because the person or body with the power to dominate chooses not to interfere in particular cases.

To take the institutional competence approach to judicial deference, what Jeffrey Jowell (2003: p. 598) argued is instructive:

> [I]t is quite appropriate for courts modestly to acknowledge a practical appreciation of their own institutional limitations. There will be occasions where other bodies, whether Parliament, the executive or a non-departmental public body containing specialist expertise, will be better equipped to decide certain questions. The extent and degree of concession of course depends upon context and the right and interest involved.

For Jowell, it is the judges' assessment of their competence that matters. Judicial initiative is also found in the alternative approaches such as Lord Hoffmann's (2002) 'separation of powers' model, which depends on the judicial view of the proper division of functions, and in the 'justificatory model' where the judiciary may require impractical burdens of proof (Arden (2013: pp. 508–511; *Aguilar Quila*).

Canadian Chief Justice McLachlin (2006) argued that deference was a means of judicial accountability to the public. However, questions of whether judges should choose to defer or not to the judgement of the legislature on policy issues arising in constitutional review litigation can be better seen as decisions by the judiciary to create (or not) such counter-majoritarian effect as the particular bill of rights mandates. Any accountability of the judges to the public will be in the form of any response to the judges by way of democratic process. Far from judicial deference being a means of judicial accountability to the public, its constitutional importance presupposes a judicial position of dominance in being able to reduce legislators' and electors' ability to choose freely, if not to actually remove choices altogether. Indeed, Lord Hoffmann (2002: [8]) made it clear when setting out his 'separation of powers' argument that the absence of a realistic prospect of correction was at the heart of his concerns if judges were too proactive in ruling on issues of justification.

The unsurprising conclusion that must flow from the republican theory of government is that the reconciliation of rights protection and democracy must be rooted in popular control, not the forbearance of an elite, however benevolent. Individualised, unconditioned and efficacious political participation cannot exist if it is in fact conditional on the choices of a judicial elite, however disinclined that elite might currently be to use expansively its power in setting the scope of a bill of rights or in determining its approach to rules of justification.

Argument for reconciliation

The principal and simple argument in favour of reconciliation is that the Human Rights Act does not prevent Parliament from legislating contrary to judicial findings by the United Kingdom or Strasbourg Courts. The Act's design explicitly contemplates that the government might bring forward, and Parliament might pass, incompatible legislation – see section 19. The Act contemplates that that any remedial legislation ought to be undertaken by a full Act of Parliament unless there are compelling reasons to adopt the simplified approach. The judicial power cannot be seen as a dominating power because it is subject to counter-control by Parliament as part of the structure of the Act. This is not in any way similar to what Anthony King (2007: pp. 345–346) rightly describes as the 'vacuous' argument reconciling Parliamentary Sovereignty with membership of the European Union by reference to the right to repeal the European Communities Act 1972: an ability to secede from an organisation does not make membership of that organisation compatible with sovereignty as membership cannot co-exist with secession. In the case of the Human Rights Act, non-compliance by way of primary legislation is contemplated as co-existing with the general application of the Act. There is thus no (domestic) legal reason why any party should not campaign on the basis of a programme including elements which would be held to be incompatible with the Human Rights Act.

The Human Rights Act was deliberately structured so as to be compatible with Parliamentary Sovereignty. Although after (but not during) the debates on the then Human Rights Bill, Lord Lester (1998: p. 668) would talk in terms of the Human Rights Act retaining the 'ceremonial forms' of Parliamentary Sovereignty, in the Bill's debates Lord Scarman (HL Debates, 1997a: col. 1256) said the Bill had 'stood up for parliamentary sovereignty', and it was the latter that was more in keeping with the language of the Bill's supporters. What did retaining Parliamentary Sovereignty mean? As we saw in Chapters 2 ('Aspiration to uphold democracy') and 6 ('Behaviour within the constitution – electoral and select-group decision-making'), in classic constitutional theory, Parliamentary Sovereignty is the legal embodiment of popular sovereignty (Dicey, 1982: pp. 26–29, 285; Weill, 2003). The effect of Parliamentary Sovereignty, combined with Bagehot's (2007: pp. 10–11) near fusion of the executive and legislature, is that no would-be legislators can justify omitting a policy from their manifesto on the basis of a want of authority should they form part of a post-election majority. Legal authority remains with Parliament to make and unmake any law whatsoever, and with the authority of Parliament at the effective command of a government commanding a majority, the line of authority and responsibility was ostensibly kept as clear as Finer (1960: p. 67, cited King, 2007: p. 59) had argued in the early 1960s. As we saw in Chapter 2 ('Aspiration to uphold democracy'), this view is reflected in the words of Baroness Hale explaining why in her view a declaration of incompatibility as to the law on assisted suicide did not shift responsibility away from Parliament (*Nicklinson* [300]). As Lord Neuberger (2015b: [62]) recently said, after recommending the advantages of judicial decision-making in human rights: '[O]f course, if the unelected judges reach a decision which the elected MPs do not like, they can overrule it by statute'.

We can only join with Lord Neuberger in defending constitutional review on the basis that Parliament can simply overturn any unwanted decisions, or say that Parliament is the *only* 'forum' in which the issue would be 'decided' (as per Baroness Hale in Nicklinson [300]), if Parliament's choice is not subject to alien control. This means (Pettit, 2008: pp. 106–107), Parliament's choice must not be subject to the reduction, removal or replacement of options.[1] Legally, it is of course as Baroness Hale says: a declaration of incompatibility would not remove authority from Parliament, nor remove responsibility from legislators. Beyond that legal form, to avoid alien control from either the judiciary or those responsible for creating the Act in the first place, the legislature will need to remain at all times accountable to the electorate for its choices including exercising the choice to comply. To use Bagehot's (2007: pp. 98–99) expression, all laws remain 'come-at-able' by the electorate through Parliament, and no less so because of any relevant human rights decisions.

Improved contestation

Democracy is maximised through increases both of 'public contestation' and 'the right to participate in elections and office' (Dahl, 1971a: p. 6). If we accept the above analysis without qualification, then constitutional review under the Human Rights Act provides a forum for public contestation without altering the right to participate in elections or office. It is true that the range of subjects that can be meaningfully contested by way of constitutional review is limited. As a means of participation, it is neither 'individualised' nor 'unconditional', as decisions are taken by a higher authority following its expert deliberation, and not every aim can be encompassed within constitutional review. If an individual wishes to campaign for tougher sentences and stricter immigration control, or wishes to abolish grammar schools or give trade unions greater ability to organise, then the Human Rights Act will offer that individual nothing by way of contestation. Nonetheless, it may still be said, and said correctly, that the Human Rights Act provides a means to contest many potentially oppressive or unjustifiable laws and policies which might otherwise go unnoticed. In the words of

1 Chapter 3 'The axioms' (second axiom).

Lord Scott (*Belmarsh* [145]), a declaration of incompatibility 'provides, of course, ammunition to those who disapprove of the [relevant legislation] and desire to agitate for its amendment or repeal'. Constitutional review can give 'an added channel for participation' (Kavanagh, 2009: pp. 401–402). The suggestion of Lord Scott in *Belmarsh* and Lady Hale in *Nicklinson* [300] is that this should be seen as a channel directly into the select-group deliberation phase of legislative decision-making. It does not bypass public deliberation nor the virtual, inhibitory and interventional control exercised by the electorate over those it elects: any issue placed by constitutional review on the agenda of the legislature may be made a matter of public debate. The Act protects at least some of those liable to be unfairly overlooked, but it does not prevent issues being appraised and dismissed in political process. The Act 'nurtures' deliberation (Hilbink, 2008: p. 234), it does not impose outcomes.

A thorough consideration of declarations of incompatibility and their parliamentary responses up to 2013 has been made by Christopher Crawford (2013). A striking point as regards the list of declarations of incompatibility made under the Human Rights Act is that some relate to issues which were uncontested, there being no appetite to uphold the measure.

McR's Application for Judicial Review [2002] NIQB 58 held it to be incompatible with human rights for buggery continuing to be an offence between men and women in Northern Ireland regardless of consent.

Following *Blood v Human Fertilisation and Embryology Authority* [1997] 2 WLR 806, Mrs Blood was allowed to use the frozen sperm of her deceased husband to conceive their child. However, the law did not permit the father to be registered as such on the birth certificate. No legislation was brought forward to remedy the anomaly. After it was conceded that the present state of the law had no justification, Mrs Blood gained a declaration of incompatibility in the High Court in *Blood and Tarbuck v Secretary of State for Health* (unreported, 28 February 2003).

D v Secretary of State for the Home Department [2002] EWHC 2805 (Admin) concerned the right of discretionary life sentence prisoners for a review of their imprisonment after serving their tariff. There was no dispute as to what should be achieved by way of practical result: the dispute was whether a judicially reviewable policy of always referring cases to the parole board was sufficient or whether there had to be a legally enforceable right to a referral. Such a narrow dispute went no further than the Queen's Bench Division.

In *R (M) v Secretary of State for Health* [2003] EWHC 1094, the problem was that section 26 of the Mental Health Act 1983 allowed no flexibility as to who was the 'nearest living relative' having the right to represent the patient in various matters. There was no dispute that this was a violation of Article 8 of the Convention ('family life'), the problem being revealed by a case where the adoptive father was accused of abusing the patient as a child.

The above cases are not the stuff of great constitutional cases, but they might be said to be the bread and butter of a human rights culture. Similar to Jeremy Bentham's programme of seeking the reason for rules and the repeal of rules for which no reason can be found (Dicey, 2008: pp. 91–92), the Human Rights Act's requirement that infringements of rights be justified can expose the unjustifiable, and – which Bentham could not do – place such issues directly on the legislative agenda.

The Human Rights Act thus provides a route of participation where the ordinary route of democracy may be blocked by the relative unimportance of issues to legislators and the general public. We have argued that the exercise of legislative power in a democracy is non-dominating because the citizen who persuades a majority of his or her viewpoint will 'over-time' prevail. Yet a law that is oppressive may survive for no other reason than that those with immediate decision-making power do not see it as important enough to give their time. Time, as Beetham (1993: p. 64) noted, is a limit to participation. A bill requires parliamentary time, drafting time, ministerial time to present the bill (or the support of a private member bringing a bill), and civil-service time to manage the bill. It may be that every Member of Parliament would agree with Mrs Blood's request, but absent the Human Rights Act such agreement might never turn into action. In a world of direct democracy, remedies for minor oppressions might find their way to a ballot paper; in a representative democracy, responsiveness may in practice be restricted to recognising 'highly ranked, intense, stable, and relatively broad preferences' (Dahl and Lindblom, 1953: p. 314) or those to which a large section of the electorate are 'violently opposed' (Jennings, 1938: pp. 46–47). Minor oppressions may have little leverage in terms of inhibitory and interventional control within a representative democracy, and may flounder at the bottom of the in-tray of legislative priorities. As we argued in Chapter 6 ('Behaviour within the constitution – electoral and select-group decision-making'), the real elective dictatorship problem in the British Constitution is the lack of time for those who are elected to deal with the business of government and legislation.

Christopher Crawford (2013: pp. 86–87) is correct to say that there is no constitutional dialogue between Parliament and the courts when remedial legislation is either underway before the judicial decision or, as in the case of *D v Home Office*, made no difference in practice. However, this does not exclude the possibility that the existence of constitutional review can stimulate analysis and interest. Aileen Kavanagh (2009: p. 341) argued that the Human Rights Act provides 'some leverage on the centres of political power [to the] de facto politically disenfranchised'. The same point has been made by others, for example Helena Wray (2013: p. 860), in respect of immigrants. Kavanagh (2009: p. 344; see also pp. 341–343) argues that 'part of the justification of constitutional review is that it empowers and benefits individuals … by enabling [them] to demand an 'individualised explanation' and justification of the alleged infringement from the government'. Hunt,

Hooper and Yowell (2012: p. 39) argue that the Act provides Parliamentarians with material to challenge the executive as regards rights violations, particularly when armed with analysis from the Parliament's own Joint Committee on Human Rights. Viewed in these terms, the Human Rights Act promotes the come-at-ability of the executive on matters of human rights.

However, if the right to demand an explanation is 'individualised', that still leaves the question as to whether constitutional review is also a means for 'unconditional', and 'efficacious' participation (Pettit, 2012: pp. 279, 302). The answer must be, no. An individualised route to require an explanation is not the same as an individualised means of participating in the exercise of political power: human rights claimants ask a question; voters should be equals in providing answers. As we considered earlier, participation by way of constitutional review is for many a dead-end – whether it be through the scope of the Human Rights Act protections or their case-law interpretations, the Act may offer nothing. Many individuals will have concerns which fall outside the conditions for the Act having an impact. It is as Bellamy (2011: p. 92) notes: '[C]ompared to legislatures, courts fail to offer to all citizens as equal [sic] a chance for each and every one of their views and concerns about the collective provision and protection of rights to be counted, weighed, and challenged'.

In constitutional review, as in all subjects that come as questions for adjudication before the courts, not every claim for political consideration has a claim for legal consideration; even less are such claims equal. That is the nature of law.

Taking these limitations into account, a reconciliation argument would be as follows: the Human Rights Act may stimulate the ordinary political, democratic process, and, even though it cannot help all who are aggrieved, it represents an improvement to that process. The counter-argument would be that findings of incompatibility under the Human Rights Act (whatever the theory) are determinative, and thus the Act replaces the admittedly rough and ready link between public opinion and legislation found in the classic British Constitution. The difference is whether constitutional review supplements or supplants the 'come-at-ability' of legislative decisions by way of Parliament.

For the reconciliation argument to work, and for the elegant balance to be a real balance and not just a manoeuvre to preserve the façade of Parliamentary Sovereignty, the Human Rights Act must not give a de facto remedy in terms of law change, but instead provide a route by which the concerns of at least some of the unpopular are brought into the ordinary political process. The 'elegant balance' hypothesis depends on participation via the Human Rights Act not being 'effective' in that its results must not guarantee legislative change. The Act should operate as a way into participation in the ordinary political process, without rendering that process any less 'individualised, unconditioned and efficacious'. The political process by way of Acts of Parliament outranks constitutional review under the Human Rights Act, and the electorate, should they engage themselves on an issue, outrank the politicians who from time to time make up Parliament.

As we saw in Chapter 2, Masterman (2011: pp. 58–59) argued that the prediction that '[a] declaration [of incompatibility ... will almost certainly prompt the government and Parliament to change the law' had been vindicated, but that legislating incompatibly remained possible, although it would be necessary to 'articulate carefully considered reasons for so doing' in order to avoid the political costs. Such a dynamic is not necessarily undemocratic – if it simply means that certain courses of action face a hurdle of public scepticism. As Downs (1957: pp. 141–142) argued, voters typically rely on ideological shortcuts when deciding how to participate. Commenting years later on Downs's analysis, Samuel Popkin (1995: pp. 19–20) argued that it is the 'bottom line' that electors look to when gauging if a government is doing well or badly. It is not that the electorate will never pay close attention; just that at most times only a very small minority of 'activists and news junkies' will be doing so. The Human Rights Act may thus serve as one of those 'shortcuts'. In most cases, the Act may operate on public opinion by raising a 'bottom line' issue, e.g. is there compliance with the Act or not? This is just as different electors may be generally inclined to support free trade or free health care at the point of delivery, and only seldom engage with arguments relating to the acceptability of particular economic costs of such policies in particular circumstances. Likewise, electors may have a working assumption that Human Rights Act compliance is the best option for the common good. Providing judicial decisions do not provoke the electorate to consider supporting a legislative override, the Act will provide a stable restraint on politicians and administrators. But the electorate is always free to participate if enough citizens abandon their usual shortcuts and take a closer interest.

The Act favouring the legislature over ministers

Cases such as *McR*, *Blood and Tarbuck*, *D* and *M* are clear examples of constitutional review giving the legislature a welcome 'reminder' of rights issues (Kavanagh, 2009: pp353–354, 363; Young, 2009: p. 138). It is not so much constitutional dialogue, but rather the Human Rights Act provides the means to lay before Parliament the practical consequences of statutes. Absent the Human Rights Act, there would be no means for court challenge against an Act of Parliament. It addresses the problem of where the law creates acute difficulty for a small minority (in the case of *Blood and Tarbuck*, a very small minority), and is maintained by the indolence rather than the tyranny of the majority. There is no great exchange of views as there is either no difference in opinion once the issue is raised (*McR*, *Blood and Tarbuck* and *M*) or a difference only as to method (*D*).

In terms of their impact on the popular control of legislation, cases such as these originate in legislation passed beneath the notice of the electorate.

The offending statutes concerned doubtless were ones where legislation had been guided by expert deliberation. *Blood and Tarbuck*, *M* and *D* are not cases where the original legislation would have been greatly influenced by public deliberation. As Jowell (2004: p. 248) argued, there are statutes where the 'the full implications of their unqualified meaning may have passed unnoticed in the democratic process', and the Human Rights Act serves to highlight those implications and the injustices caused. The bringing of constitutional review may have had the effect of stimulating public opinion, particularly if legislators were seen to ignore a declaration of incompatibility. It is possible to hypothesise a political cost arising out of an uncorrected Human Rights Act infringement and levied by the disillusionment of electors causing a loss of votes. Such political costs may represent inhibitory control by the public if politicians' belief in the existence of electoral costs matches public opinion. But this is not the case if politicians come to *wrongly* believe in such costs – as may be the case in Canada, where an opinion poll in 2006 commissioned on behalf of a conference celebrating the Charter found that only 17% of citizens believed that the notwithstanding clause should be obsolete (Levant, 2007), notwithstanding conventional wisdom amongst politicians that legislative override of the Charter is anathema (Manfredi, 2001: pp. 186–188). A common understanding between citizens and politicans of the general importance to the electorate of Human Rights Act compliance is important, and likewise a common understanding of the relative importance of the particular policies at hand. Inhibitory control requires a meeting of minds between inhibitor and inhibited.

A theme of the Human Rights Act is that it brings decisions affecting rights directly to the legislature's attention, with the publicity generating potential political costs for non-compliance. Hence, unless expressly sanctioned by an Act of Parliament, any executive action from the use of the Royal Prerogative to the promulgation of secondary legislation will be invalid if incompatible with the Human Rights Act. The only means by which such action can be continued is by passing an Act of Parliament and traversing all of the veto points and stumbling blocks that that entails. From being a matter that slips past the notice of legislators, let alone electors, the matter is now one of importance. Remembering what Bagehot (2007: pp. 182–183) noted as the opposition having a free hand to choose its line of attack against governmental failures, the conduct of the government towards incompatible legislation provides an obvious point of attack. The accusation of human rights incompatibility may be a major stick with which to beat a government, unless the electorate sees non-compliance as justified.

Purposive interpretation

Under section 3 of the Human Rights Act, the courts must interpret primary legislation, 'so far as it is possible', in line with their interpretation of the Act's requirements. The result is that the courts will often reach non-natural interpretations of legislation but ones that go (in the judges' view) with the grain of the legislation (Phillips, 2010: pp. 34–38). Presenting the Human Rights Bill in the House of Commons, Jack Straw MP (HC Deb, 1998a: col. 778) said: 'We expect that, in almost all cases, the courts will be able to interpret legislation compatibly with the Convention'.

Subsequently at the committee stage (HC Deb, 1998b, cols.421–422), Mr Straw explained:

> [W]e want the courts to strive to find an interpretation of legislation that is consistent with Convention rights, so far as the plain words of the legislation allow, and only in the last resort to conclude that the legislation is simply incompatible with them ... I do not think that the courts will need to apply themselves to the words that I am about to use, but, for the avoidance of doubt, I will say that it is not our intention that the courts, in applying [section 3] should contort the meaning of words to produce implausible or incredible meanings.

What section 3 creates is the equivalent of what Lord Justice Laws expounded in *Thoburn*, and what we find in cases such as *Simms.*[2] Legislation is to be presumed not to contradict the Human Rights Act, which has been said provides a 'semi-entrenched' form of rights protection (Prebble, 2005: p. 318). More precisely, when we separate the related concepts of entrenchment and enforcement we find that such strongly purposive interpretations are better seen as a form of 'enforcement' that allows the setting aside of the natural and often intended meaning of statutes. It does not prevent legislation which is clearly incompatible, nor the express setting aside of an unwanted decision.

The expectation expressed by Jack Straw (in 1998) and others was that in the vast majority of cases legislation could be read in line with the Convention. Lord Irvine (HL Debate, 1998: col. 840) anticipated that this would happen in 99 percent of cases. The dividing line is illustrated by the cases of *Ghaidan v Godin-Mendoza* [2004] UKHL 30; [2004] 2 AC 557, and *Bellinger v Bellinger* [2003] UKHL 21; [2003] 2 AC 467. In the former case, living 'as his or her wife or husband' for the purposes of the Rent Act 1977 was purposively read to include same-sex relationships of equivalent closeness, even though being married was then legally impossible for the couple. In the latter case, being 'female' for the purposes of section 11(c) of the Matrimonial Causes Act 1973 was held not to be capable of being re-interpreted to include transsexuals, notwithstanding that the ECtHR had held in *Goodwin v United Kingdom* (2002) 35 EHRR 18 that it was necessary under Articles 8 and 12 of the Convention ('right to privacy and family life' and 'freedom to marry') to recognise transsexuals as belonging to their

2 Chapter 2 'Political costs'.

reassigned gender. There are in this area always questions as to the elasticity of language, and, as was the case in *Bellinger*, the difficulty of a court intervening to determine when precisely gender should be held to be reassigned – see Lord Nicholls (*Bellinger* [28]–[32]).

Section 3 creates a rights-compliant status quo. It strikes down non-compliant meanings of statutes, which can then only be restored by primary legislation. After the purposive interpretation given, it is necessary for Parliament to make a positive decision to overturn a decision such as *Ghaidan*. By contrast, where a declaration of incompatibility is made, the legislation to bring UK law into line with the Human Rights Act must traverse various veto points in Parliament. It is for these reasons, no doubt, that Lord Lester (HL Debate, 1997a: col. 535) made it clear that he 'would cease to be a friend' of the then Human Rights Bill if the scope for purposive interpretations was narrowed. For similar reasons Lord Lester preferred the fast-track approach to remedial legislation following declarations of incompatibility as there would be fewer stages where the legislation might fail (HL Deb, 2012: col. 886).

The counter-argument is that given by Michael Pinto-Duschinsky (2011: p. 72), whose recommendations on reconciling human rights and parliamentary democracy included that both the purposive interpretation and the 'fast-track' remedial legislation provisions should be repealed. Pinto-Duschinsky (p. 61) argued that section 3 interpretations involve, 'in practice, altering existing legislation without first making recourse to Parliament', and that the fast-track remedial process gives ministers 'an opportunity to bypass Parliament' (p. 10).

In the republican analysis, there is no necessary reason why the operation of section 3 (or the operation of the fast-track procedure) should promote the domination of either judicial or political elites over legislation. Taken at face value, section 3 invites the judiciary into a process of co-reasoning, and is subject to counter-control in the form of remedial legislation. Unless an interpretative power is operated to make the passing of certain laws impossible, as Laski (1951: pp. 44–45) once accused the judiciary of doing to trade union rights legislation, then section 3 cannot place the judiciary in a dominant position. Pettit (2008: pp. 114–116) contemplated, as a form of non-alien control, a co-reasoner who may delay action, but not prevent it.[3] Section 3 formalises the role of judicial opinion, described by Dicey (2008: p. 263), as a potentially influential cross-current of opinion acting on public and legislative opinion. The position of the courts is not one of domination: Parliament can attain the clarity required to close off section 3 interpretations or even expressly disapply the Human Rights Act to the case at hand. The same applies with the fast-track process: decisions are made by way of a single

3 Although this overlooks the cases where 'effectiveness [of a measure] depends upon its being passed without delay' (Dicey, 1982: p. xlii).

vote as opposed to three readings and a committee stage in no way prevents democratic accountability.

Importantly, we must remember that democracy cannot be considered as a process between legislature, executive and judiciary. It is about the relationship between public opinion and legislation. It is about the effectiveness of the routes for popular participation in the legislative process, and that participation should give the public a power of domination, even if such power will be in practice a reserve power (Pettit, 2012: pp. 230, 268–269).

Given that in a representative democracy the electorate is usually fairly passive, valuing the right to participate rather than the actual use of the right (Dahl, 2000), there is nothing undemocratic in the constitutive power (in this case Parliament passing the Human Rights Act in 1998 as promised in the recently elected government's manifesto) setting the rules of governance so that courts invigilate the results of select group and/or expert deliberation for compatibility with the Act. Underlying this analysis is a default assumption on the part of politicians that there will be political (electoral) costs for non-compliance; but section 4 opens the door to the assertion of public opinion to the contrary releasing politicians from those costs and enabling them to legislate incompatibly. The Act does not prevent the electorate's other 'highly ranked, intense, stable, and relatively broad preferences' (Dahl and Lindblom 1953: p. 314) asserting themselves against the results of constitutional review. But it is not undemocratic for judges to *de facto* determine outcomes when the electorate is too uninterested to participate. Inactivity may be evidence of contentment (Jennings, 1966: p. 211). Inaction due to contentment is consistent with virtual control, where the contours of state power are attributable to not in fact having infringed the tolerance of public opinion (Pettit, 2004: p. 62).

Disgruntled legislators might well say that they lack the parliamentary time to overturn all Human Rights Act decisions with which they disagree. It is, however, public opinion that is the starting point of democracy. Legislators could not be excused from legislating in those few matters where the electorate takes a firm and constant view. It is those matters where the electorate would wish to hold legislators to account that are truly important for a representative democracy – as such demands by the electorate represent the outcome of public deliberation, including what we saw in Chapter 4 ('Public deliberation') described as 'everyday talk' (Mansbridge, 1999: p. 225). Beyond the often notional potential for the electorate to take an interest (Dahl, 2000: p. 39), democracy is less interested in the actual choices of legislators and officials made through isolated select group or expert deliberation.

In short, the difference between sections 3 and 4 (i.e. the need to be proactive in overturning a decision) cannot be a shield for legislators who submit to the new status quo. That is, unless the electorate view compliance with the HRA as a full justification for otherwise unpopular legislation.

Legislative rights review under the Act

Hunt, Hooper and Yowell (2012) argued that the Human Rights Act empowers Parliament to (p. 3) 'play a more active role in the protection and realisation of human rights' – which we saw in Chapter 2 ('Legislative rights review') in the analysis of 'legislative rights review'. They approached the question of 'redressing the democratic deficit' created by the Human Rights Act by analysing the influence of the JCHR. Their hypothesis was very much that the influence of a parliamentary committee in promoting human rights protection was a democratisation of human rights.

Lord Lester (HL Debate, 2012: col. 885), a member of the JCHR, described the dynamic thus in respect of *F and Thompson*:

> The Joint Committee on Human Rights has the special role of scrutinising draft remedial orders and reporting to both Houses and to the Government as to whether there has been proper compliance. What has happened in this case is extremely welcome. In our first report, we were critical of the first draft remedial order, as my noble friend the Minister acknowledged. Then, the Government responded by listening, and by giving effect to all of our main recommendations. In other words, the work of our committee – an all-party committee, and a beyond-party committee, since it is not controlled by the Government – influenced the Government in reshaping the order which is now before the House for approval today. If one reads the most recent government response to what we have done, dated March 2012, one finds each of our points identified, responded to, and heeded. That is a sign of mature Government, acting in a responsible way, being accountable to Parliament through this watchdog committee, and now in this debate, in both Houses, by affirmative resolution …

Hunt, Hooper and Yowell (2012: p. 39) cite Bridget Prentice MP, that the JCHR empowers legislators to be involved in human rights debates:

> She observed that '[h]uman rights matters are sometimes perceived as arguments that are best left to lawyers and judges and are dealt with more commonly in the House of Lords, but added that amendments proposed by JCHR members in the Commons 'put human rights on the agenda of the elected House – where they belong, at the heart of our democratic process'.

This creates the sort of accountability that Lord Lester anticipated, above, and was seen by Murray, Hooper and Yowell (2012: p. 39) as a reply to those who say that the JCHR creates 'democratic debilitation' by issuing legalistic reports which frame deliberation in terms outside the competence of ordinary legislators. The point that Murray, Hooper and Yowell were making is that, even if the government saw the JCHR as being just another source of legal advice (Tham, 2010: p. 102), it would nevertheless empower legislators to participate in debates and challenge the executive.

The 'democratic debilitation' argument to which Hunt, Hooper and Yowell were replying was that put by Joo-Cheong Tham (2010: pp. 101–102):

> By privileging legal expertise, there is a grave risk that a Queen's Counsel opinion will become a pre-requisite for making effective human rights arguments. If so, the terrain of public debate will be further tilted in favour of lawyers and those groups wealthy enough to afford expensive legal opinions, such as governmental bodies. In other words, the legalisation of human rights debates brings about 'democratic debilitation'.

It was once notably claimed by the then Home Secretary, Jack Straw, that 'human rights' would become the language needed to win debates (Parekh, 2000: [7.16]). Tham's point is that this translation of political issues into human rights terms creates an elitist state of affairs. As we noted in Chapter 2 ('Legislative rights review'), the approach of Hunt, Hooper and Yowell is focused on empowering Parliament as against the executive in order to achieve rights-compliant ends – and so it does not address the core of the counter-majoritarian objection to constitutional review under the Act. Even if the JCHR helps Parliamentarians to challenge government, this can be seen as a committee with expert legal advice arming those inclined to make challenges from a particular direction. It creates an institutional disadvantage for those who believe that a derogation from conditional rights would be in the common good in particular circumstances.

Mechanism of compliance

We have seen that the Human Rights Act may bring issues into the glare of publicity and onto the floor of Parliament. We have seen in *F and Thompson* that the Act can enhance the role of Parliament in bringing legislation into line with human rights as interpreted by the judiciary. But these points relate to cases where the taking of remedial action had been accepted, albeit grudgingly in the case of *F and Thompson*. The issue remains as to whether the choice to comply was a free one. Did the results of constitutional review change the opinion of legislators? Did they affect public opinion on the issue concerned so as to exercise control over the action of legislators? Or did they act as a hindrance on the 'we can do that' hypothesis for legislators and/or electors in respect of legislative and policy choices held to be incompatible? Domination does not require the imposition of a single choice, but the ability of one agent to invigilate choices of another so as to remove, replace or reduce the availability of one or more options. There are those who argue that choice is maintained providing the political process has a choice as to how to comply with constitutional review decisions (Hogg and Bushell, 1999: p. 536; Van Bueren, 2002: pp. 464–466), but such a choice is not undominated. Domination, however, does not exist where the putatively interfering agent influences choices through persuasion, through what Philip Pettit described as 'co-reasoning', and which Dicey (2008: p. 263) described in terms of cross-currents of opinion affecting public and legislative opinion.

Empirically, excluding the single case of prisoner voting, the legislature has acted no differently than if compliance with Human Rights Act decisions had been a legal duty. Since the Act came into force, ministers have presented only two bills to Parliament without a 'statement of compatibility' – one of which was the abortive House of Lords Reform Bill, whose incompatibility arose solely out of the broader ongoing non-compliance with the *Hirst* decision on prisoner voting (House of Commons, 2012: [272]–[278]). By way of contrast, in New Zealand, from the enactment of its Human Rights Act 1990 until 2011, 22 laws had been presented to the national Parliament with an Attorney General's report of inconsistency, and 18 of those have been passed without amendment (Geddis, 2011: p. 98); and, as of 2005, seventeen private members bills had been prevented without a statement of consistency (Hiebert, 2005a: p. 90). The sole United Kingdom example of a bill passed without a statement of compatibility was the Communications Bill 2003, which maintained the ban on political advertising on television, and was potentially incompatible with the European Court's decision in *VGT v Switzerland* (2002) 34 EHRR 4.

Most cases concerning the constitutional review of statutes under the Human Rights Act that have gone against the government have involved purposive interpretations under section 3 of the Act altering the normal meaning of provisions to give them a compatible interpretation. It follows from the near-complete absence of bills presented to Parliament without a statement of compatibility that no legislation has been brought forward to reverse such decisions so as to re-impose the originally intended meanings.

There is only one example of non-compliance with a declaration of incompatibility. This is in the famous prisoner voting controversy. Following the ECtHR decision in *Hirst*, the Court of Session issued a declaration of incompatibility in the case of *Smith v Scott*. However, the example of prisoner voting is a difficult one for demonstrating the absence of a sense of a duty to comply with decisions under the ECHR or the Human Rights Act. In *Smith v Scott* [51] the government argued against a declaration of incompatibility on the grounds that remedial legislation would be enacted in response to *Hirst*. It remains a work in progress, with the government accepting that something must be done (although it disagrees with the decision), and Parliament refusing to do something in debates that only occasionally deal with the merits of prisoner voting, as opposed to the constitutional questions of Parliament's relationship with the Convention (HC Debate, 2012: cc.745–762; HC Debate, 2011a: cc.493–584).

Establishing a course of conduct does not of itself establish that a rule of conduct exists. Absent a strict domestic legal rule demanding compliance, which the Human Rights Act deliberately avoids creating, the questions can be framed in terms of Ivor Jennings's analysis of constitutional conventions. Jennings's (1938: pp. 129–131) classic analysis was that a constitutional convention required, (a) precedent for the relevant conduct, (b) the conduct to arise from a sense of obligation, and (c) a reason for that obligation. If the operative obligation is owed by legislators to electors, with the 'political costs' being a loss of support in the competition for votes, then the case for the reconciliation between rights and democracy looks strong. If we remember our hypothetical example from Chapter 3 ('Republicanism and domination') of Cicero and Tiro, there were many good reasons why Cicero might choose not to sell Tiro, but those reasons could not include Cicero not being entitled to sell his slave. A steady course of conduct will arise for a reason. The questions that arise are as to whether the reason arises out of an obligation, and who owes that obligation to whom?

So, to place this into Pettit's analysis of domination: (a) Parliament makes choice-x to enact the Human Rights Act; (b) subsequently, Parliament believes choice-y is correct to deal with a certain issue in criminal justice, but choice-y is held contrary to the Human Rights Act; then (c) the relevant judicial decision has replaced choice-y with the now encumbered choice-y*, meaning 'y plus the estimated costs of going against the Human Rights Act'. Setting aside internationalisation issues under the Convention, the position under the Human Rights Act is that there is no external agency to ensure that choice-x and choice-y become mutually incompatible, as would be the case with the European Union membership and a decision not to comply with EU law.[4] Under the Human Rights Act, the possibility of being overridden is ostensibly an inherent part of the legal order created under the Act. As regards the Human Rights Act, *taken in isolation*, it is in Parliament's gift to choose choice-x (Human Rights Act to exist) and choice-y (non-compliance with the Human Rights Act) at the same time. The question is the nature of the '*' that now burdens choice-y. If the costs of taking choice-y from the perspective of politicians derive from the electorate, then the existence of '*' will be a function of public opinion on the question of whether the choice should be taken. However, this does not rule out the possibility that choice-y is burdened (or seen as being burdened) from the perspective of the electorate as well.

Parliament is directed by the House of Commons, by 650 MPs who are in competition for votes. They are also citizens who will be affected by wrong decisions. They will frequently be interested in their place in history. But the

4 In the European Union, an EU law 'cannot be judicially contradicted by an internal law, whatever it might be, without losing their Community character and without undermining the legal basis of the Community' (*Costa* 456).

most fundamental costs that can be paid by legislators is not to be elected or re-elected, or to find themselves moving from the government to the opposition benches. So we see that choice-y* has a different nature for politicians and electors:

- Choice-y* (politicians) = choice-y encumbered in the eyes of politicians with the electoral risks of infringing the Human Rights Act.
- Choice-y* (electors) = choice-y encumbered in the eyes of electors with their estimation of the harm caused by infringing the Human Rights Act.
- Choice-y* (politicians) should be closely aligned to the resolution of choice-y* (electors). If the political costs to politicians come from electoral consequences, it should be possible for electors to participate so that their support for choice-y* greatly reduces or even removes the encumbrance '*' on politicians taking choice-y.
- If Choice-y* politicians are not closely aligned to the resolution of choice-y* (electors), then the link between legislative opinion and public opinion will be reduced or even removed. Legislative opinion would be directed by a force outside of public opinion on the issue.

This analysis gives a possible answer to a central paradox regarding the Human Rights Act: how could it be the electorate who exact the political costs that underpin compliance with the Act, if the Act exists to restrain the same electorate from being tyrannical (Ely, 1980: pp. 7–8)? The constitutive choice (as in the United Kingdom) to have a representative democracy without institutionalised referenda for ordinary legislation represents a constitutive choice for government to be accountable on a long-term record. The power of the electorate is greatest insofar as it holds 'highly ranked, intense, stable, and relatively broad preferences' (Dahl and Lindblom, 1953: p. 314). If we hypothesise that support for the Human Rights Act is one of those strong and stable preferences, MPs will know that there is an electoral cost to be paid for infringing the Act unless it is in respect of a stronger preference running in the opposite direction. If MPs were to follow 'every epidemical phrensy of the people', to use Burke's (1808: pp. 287–288, cited Dicey, 1982: p. 35) expression, then they would find that following a highly ranked, basically stable (if temporarily shaken) preference (such as the Human Rights Act) will gain greater long-term reward than reflecting every fashion of opinion for the short time that it lasted. It is not just, as Kyritsis (2012: p. 314) says, that 'a legislator who slavishly follows her constituents fails her role in a very important respect', but that such a legislator would be viewed as failing by those same constituents should the outcomes prove disappointing.

This approach explains why it is possible for the same electors and the same politicians to simultaneously support a law yet oppose steps that would make the law constitutionally permissible. The preference not to make constitutional change is greater than the preference for the measures concerned.[5] It would take the communication of an even higher ranked, stable preference for legislators to feel safe to act incompatibly. The above analysis might also explain an oddity in Canada. As we saw in Chapter 5 ('The linking of issues – constitutional review as a rights-protection pact'), legislative opinion has acted on the basis that overriding the Canadian Charter was illegitimate (Manfredi, 2001: pp. 186–188). However, an opinion poll commissioned by a conference friendly to the Charter showed 68% of Canadians open to the possibility of using a notwithstanding clause to override the Charter (Levant, 2007). An explanation might be that the public being open to the possibility of override is consistent with the general rule being that electoral costs will follow the actual use of override. This is because, unless it is clear when the electorate can be predicted to maintain support for particular acts of legislative override in the cold light of day, when passions have waned and election-day comes, it is rational for politicians to avoid the risk. We shall return to this when considering suggestions as to which issues might justify non-compliance with the Human Rights Act.

If we look to Pettit's dual-aspect approach to democracy: the electorate makes a constitutive decision that it wants the Human Rights Act, this constitutive decision wins out over the ordinary legislative preferences of the same electorate. However, the electorate is not dominated. The non-entrenched nature of the Human Rights Act means that the Act is subject to deliberate change by reason of Parliamentary Sovereignty no less than any other law. The significance of a 'constitutional statute' is always substantially determined by the potential for popular participation and the patterns of such participation. The Act does not hamper the ordinary routes of participation in terms of the public opinion being brought to bear in favour of a particular policy, because the legislation to implement that policy would itself counter-control any judicial decision as to the content and requirements of the Human Rights Act – in the language of Pettit's (2008: pp. 108–109, see Chapter 3, 'The axioms') third axiom, the electorate 'comes to be able to control what [the judiciary] does'. The Act is far from being an entrenched constitutional provision extrapolated by judicial activism which can only be challenged by special constitutional process. Even on the *Thoburn* analysis a constitutional statute is in the final analysis entrenched only by the legislative opinion, which, as Dicey (2008) argued, is ultimately determined by reference to public opinion. In the system of constitutional review created by the Human Rights Act, the force of constitutional review decisions is much like the extent of democracy in Robert Dahl's theory of polyarchy set out in Chapter 4 ('Polyarchy'), determined by the participation of the electorate.

5 For example, such a dynamic can be seen in the United States where support for banning the burning of the national flag does not lead to support for a constitutional amendment to create an exception to the First Amendments ('Freedom of Speech') to constitutionally permit such a ban (Sinnot Armstrong, 2003: p. 387).

The Human Rights Act provides a 'resistance norm' in the form of a wakeup call as to what is being done, and to force the question of whether it can be justified. As the due process of democracy is unhindered, it does not provide the sort of 'invalidation norm' that we considered in Chapter 2 on the passive virtues. Indeed, far from being hindered, the link between public and select-group deliberation may be galvanised.

And here lies perhaps the highpoint of the 'reconciliation' between rights and democracy. The effect of statutes not being set aside is that Parliament is continually confronted with the question of whether a particular constitutional review decision is sufficiently unpopular, disagreeable or demonstrably wrong as to lead to the acceptance of an argument Parliament should follow its own instincts on the particular decision at hand. Insofar as constitutional review is respected, such conduct (and thus any apparent rule to that effect) is continuously generated by the results of select-group and public deliberation. The constitutive power level of the two aspects of democracy identified by Pettit is not just notionally capable of stirring into life, but is constantly prompted by declarations of incompatibility and purposive interpretations; and each new act of parliamentary obedience and electoral acceptance represents a renewal of the original constitutive decision to enact the Human Rights Act.

Do bills of rights formalise pre-existing costs for rights violations?

At the heart of the above analysis is what we described in Chapter 5 ('The linking of issues') as bill of rights representing a mutual protection pact for different issues of liberty and civil rights. Having chosen the approach as regards entrenchment and enforcement, the constituting power must then chose the subject matter of the pact, i.e. what rights are to be protected. If one right is diluted, then all are diluted. Liberty (2011: [128]) commented thus on media attacks on human rights jurisprudence on privacy and the free press:

> [I]t is bitterly ironic that instead of seeking parliamentary clarification of the Article 8/10 balance, some newspapers have resorted to trashing an Act which provides the first legally enforceable right to free speech in British law.

The point Liberty makes is important: if an individual wants the protection of their human rights to be guaranteed by the Act, they cannot make enforcement purely optional. If the newspapers wish to take their disagreement with the cases on the Article 8/10 balance as far as legislating, then they risk losing protections that they themselves enjoy (Liberty, 2011: [41]–[42]). It is why, as we noted in Chapter 5 ('The linking of issues'), Canadian legislators have seen it as anathema to use a notwithstanding clause to overrule or pre-empt court decisions, lest the Charter loses its power to restrain objectionable legislation.[6] The point is essentially that made in strong terms by Keir Starmer MP (2015) as regards proposals to replace the Human Rights Act with a British Bill of Rights: 'A proposal that deprives people of their rights, divides nations abroad … is a grossly disproportionate reaction to one or two adverse rulings from Strasbourg'.

In respect of some rights issues, the linkage would apply regardless of the existence of formal linkage through a bill of rights. A principle once breached may be a principle in retreat. The shift charted by Dicey (2008: pp. 45–50) of public opinion moving from 'old Toryism or legislative quiescence' to 'individualism' to 'collectivism' occurred because exceptions to established principles grew up until an entirely new principle could be identified from what started life as exceptions. To give an example: Jones currently takes an absolutist Millian stance towards free speech (Mill, 1998: pp. 20–82). Jones considers the merits of choice-y, a law against Holocaust denial. Any choice as regards a particular application of free speech is inherently encumbered by a broader effect on the right of free speech: for Jones, taking choice-y would be encumbered by the risk that categories of prohibited speech would expand out of control. That is an example from within a single right; the same might apply between rights when seen as part of broader claims to freedom – violations of freedom inherently create risks larger than the immediate question. This can be taken to an extreme. As noted in Chapter 5 ('The linking of issues'), the United Nations High Commissioner for Human Rights (UNHCR 2015) argues that all human rights are 'interrelated, interdependent and indivisible'. Similarly, Andreas Dimopoulos (2015: p. 82) recently argued in the context of disabled rights that 'human dignity … can be regarded as the bedrock of human rights and the ECHR'. On those views, it is inherent that an attack on one right diminishes all rights regardless of the formal linkage through a bill of rights. This is a problematic assertion in practice. The problem is that many of the issues linked within a bill of rights (including those read into the instrument by the judiciary) will be remote from each other, and highly contestable. Dimopoulos admits the contested nature of 'human dignity', and many rights issues (such as abortion) have been answered in opposite directions by different courts (see *Roe*, and *BVerfGE 39*, 1, in the USA and Germany respectively). It is also problematic because disputes in human rights often arise out of rights which are not absolute. Talk of human rights being 'indivisible' is difficult if the question is as to whether a measure infringing a right serves a legitimate aim or could be achieved by a less intrusive means. To return to the 'rights-protection pact' concept, it is unrealistic to suppose that, on all issues covered, a bill of rights simply recognises the strength of pre-existing links: the creation of the pact will strengthen weak links and create links where none realistically existed. Creating a bill of rights inherently alters the nature of the decision-making. It

6 Chapter 5 'The linking of issues'.

'replaces' a simple decision on a particular issue with one that calls into question the general approach to rights protection, and thus encumbers that decision with concerns of broader importance.

The nature of the mutual protection pact in the Human Rights Act is thus not just to link rights which may or may not be 'interrelated, interdependent and indivisible', it represents a decision to resist shifts in opinion on a broad front by keeping tempting exceptions as derogations to a general rule and requiring justification as such.

Structural argument for duty of compliance with constitutional review

The high point of the reconciliation between democracy and the Human Rights Act offered in this thesis has already passed.

The principal difficulty in the reconciliation is that, in the overwhelming majority of contentious cases, what the pact represents is not a mutual protection of rights whose content has been defined by the constituting power. The content of the Human Rights Act is only in the first instance defined by the constituting power. Like any bill of rights, it is to a significant extent a pact to respect judicial decisions on the scope of those rights and on the proportionality of derogations. Insofar as the Act serves as a shortcut for citizens to identify when their political leaders are acting oppressively and unjustifiably, it must be recalled that such shortcuts operate as a means of allowing citizens to reach opinions without paying the costs of becoming well-informed (Downs, 1957: pp. 141–142). There is nothing unusual in electors' tracking the opinions of others: voters will use parties as a shortcut for identifying how to vote, and without necessarily analysing the content of what the party elites have promised (Popkin, 1995: pp. 22–27). Properly understood, the rights-protection pact represented by a bill of rights is substantially about loyalty to a judicial process for determining the scope of rights and the validity of justifications for infringing rights. The position with the Human Rights Act is that concurrent pacts have been made at the international level through the ECHR, and at the national level through the Human Rights Act. While the existence of the shortcut is contingent on public opinion, the content of shortcut is largely subject to judicial control. The logic of the position is as Kyritsis (2012: p. 301) says:

> Judges may get it wrong in a specific case, but our commitment to a procedure that gives them the power to decide will compete with our moral objections to the substance of that specific decision.
>
> [Emphasis in original]

We saw in Chapter 6 ('Behaviour within the constitution') Peter Mair's (2013: p. 98) view that we are entering an era when 'citizens stay at home while parties get on with governing'. A complete commitment to the

Human Rights Act procedures amounts to citizens staying at home while judges invigilate politicians and administrators on their behalf. The question is how far a citizen deciding that counter-control is justified in respect of a particular constitutional review decision represents either (a) a reduced commitment to the Act or (b) a counter-control decision entirely sanctioned by an Act that never hypothesised that citizens would just 'stay at home' and accept the results of constitutional review.

The logic of the situation is this, and to state it positively, (i) the Human Rights Act is essentially a rights-protection pact, (ii) a material part of that pact is the judicial role in determining disputes as to the scope of the rights brought into the pact by the constitutive power, and the application of those rights when the question of necessary derogations arise, (iii) it follows (*Belmarsh* [42]) that the judicial power has 'a very specific and wholly democratic mandate'; (iv) any decision to ignore or override a judicial finding of a rights violation will be an existential threat to the rights-protection pact because the protection provided by the pact would be shown to be unreliable; (v) so any suggestion to ignore or override the Act poses the question of whether the constitutive power wishes the Act to continue; and (vi) it follows that the power to ignore or override the Act should be seen not as something in play in ordinary legislative decisions, but rather as something to be used only *in extremis*, or, in the words of Jean Chretien in the context of statutes of overriding the Canadian Charter, as a 'safety valve', something to 'correct absurd situations' (Manfredi, 2001: p. 184).

On this view, applying the dual-aspect theory of democracy, a decision at the constitutional level to create the Human Rights Act means a constitutive decision that democracy should be limited at the level of ordinary legislative decisions (Weyland, 2002: pp. 6–7). The Human Rights Act is constituted so that the *constitutional* decision of whether this continues to be acceptable is made with the *ostensibly ordinary legislative* decision to deliberately pass incompatible legislation. If the incompatible measure is choice-y, then choice-y is encumbered as choice-y* with the '*' representing the potential for a major constitutional change.

This is what we shall we call the 'structural argument' for compliance: essentially that any decision to create a bill of rights is inherently one of creating the rights-protection pact. A decision to set aside that pact on any given occasion weakens that pact, and strikes at its very nature. There is no true balance struck, as after any breach a return to a point of equilibrium representing the putative 'elegant balance' is doubtful. Legislating incompatibly may be demystified or rendered routine. Alternatively, those responsible for the breach will rush to affirm theories as to why this exception is truly exceptional – as has occurred in the United Kingdom when senior Parliamentarians have proposed non-compliance in respect of prisoner voting and the *Hirst* decision (HC Debate, 2012: cc. 749–750, see Chapter 9, 'Illegitimate decisions'). On this view, little more than 'the ceremonial forms required by the English dogma of the sovereignty of Parliament' are retained (Lester, 1998:

p. 668) as anything more would be incompatible with the decision to create the Human Rights Act.

The reconciliation with democracy under the 'structural argument' for compliance exists very much at the level of a democratic choice at the level of the constitutive power, and not at the ordinary level of democratic decision-making and participation. As Steven Greer and Rosie Slowe (2015: p. 383) argue, it is the nature of constitutional review for there to be disappointment as to outcomes. They argue that, this being so:

> The best a mature, civilised and sophisticated liberal democracy can hope for is to learn to live with it, maintain a sense of proportion about it, and refrain from blaming the rules of the game when the side they favour 'loses'.

To take disagreement as far as proposing a legislative response to counter-control constitutional review is to propose changing 'the rules of the game', and thus inherently changing the constitutive choice. As Lord Mackay put it, 'if you set up a system that includes decisions by the courts, until you change that system you are bound by those judgments' (quoted, Miller, 2011: p. 11).

We must face the issue that Jean Jacques Rousseau (1988: p. 32) raised as to the difficulty of committing to support the will of someone else:

> The Sovereign may indeed say: 'I now will actually what this man wills, or at least what he says he wills'; but it cannot say: 'What he wills tomorrow, I too shall will' because it is absurd for the will to bind itself for the future, nor is it incumbent on any will to consent to anything that is not for the good of the being who wills.

Should a country's electorate commit itself to treating even unexpected and unwelcome judicial decisions as a definitive statement of what is required by its commitment to human rights, then it outsources its will in the manner that Rousseau condemned. Electors doubtless use ideological shortcuts as Downs (1957: pp. 141–142) described so they can say to themselves, e.g. 'I believe in jury trials; removing juries in fraud cases is therefore something I oppose'. The difference with a citizen using constitutional review as a shortcut for identifying whether to support or oppose a measure is that, normally, the citizen may redefine the limits of how they understand or apply the shortcut in particular cases, e.g. 'I do believe in jury trials; but with the complexity of fraud trials, neither the prosecution nor the defence can be confident of a fair hearing from a lay jury who cannot follow the issues'. If the shortcut is to follow the opinion of another (e.g. 'I believe in jury trials; the acceptability of exceptions I leave for judges'), then one must either have a rule of obedience ('submit'), at least until such a rule becomes irksome ('rebel'), or else craft an exception by reference to some procedural or substantive quality of the decision. While it lasts, a constitutive rule of obedience undoubtedly restricts popular sovereignty as exercised at the ordinary democratic level, the level at which the elegant balance of the Human Rights Act should operate. The approach may only be saved for the republican theory of government if the choice to constitute such an approach is itself democratically and freely taken *and* continuously retaken (albeit in the case of retaking decisions, this may be by way of virtual control if nothing else).

Under the dual-aspect theory of democracy, the argument as to whether the Human Rights Act should be entrenched ought to be resolved by open debate, not through trying to induce the electorate to treat a deliberately un-entrenched statute as if it were entrenched. If retention of Parliamentary Sovereignty is in substance limited, then the Act should not suggest otherwise. This is nothing more than the application of the *Simms* principle applied to an individual's freedom as citizen: limits should be plainly stated, so that any political costs of creating such limits must be faced.[7]

It must also be noted that this 'structural argument' can be fitted neatly into Jennings's analysis of constitutional conventions. A sense of obligation can be supported by 'the prevailing political philosophy' (Jennings, 1938: p. 131). If the prevailing political philosophy holds that constitutional review should exist, and the Human Rights Act is the legal embodiment of that philosophy, then that is the reason for compliance. This, of course, assumes that a convention in favour of compliance is the 'prevailing political philosophy' at the level of the electorate (Jennings, 1938, p. 131, see also Dicey, 1982: p. 301, and Chapter 8 'Constitutional conventions and constitutional review') – as opposed to being the philosophy of legislators and party elites, presented as a cartel to the electorate.

Conclusion

The argument set out in this chapter has been the positive case for the 'elegant balance'. It has looked beyond the headline statement that the courts lack the power to set aside statutes, to place the existence, reality and limits of judicial power under constitutional review within the context of popular participation. If the Act has general popular support (and the Human Rights Act can scarcely be legitimate if it does not), then the starting point for legislators is that legislating incompatibly with human rights decisions will carry a political cost in terms of public esteem and votes. It would nevertheless be possible for popular participation to make it clear that such a political cost will not be levied (much the opposite) where judicial decisions run contrary to strong preferences of public opinion. As representative democracy is typically only responsive to public opinion at the level of such 'highly ranked, intense, stable, and relatively broad preferences' (Dahl and Lindblom, 1953: p. 314), there is no loss in the ability

7 Chapter 2 'Political costs'.

of the electorate to direct legislation. Given that the electorate seldom participates to such a degree, the Act will serve to restrain politicians in respect of the vast majority of issues where public opinion does not meaningfully press on legislators – it will create inhibitory control as politicians will normally fear an adverse electoral response where they are non-compliant. Except on such matters of genuine importance to voters, the electorate (it can be predicted) will act according to the information shortcut that not complying with Human Rights Act decisions is a bad thing. The Act will mean that a judicial elite will act as a controlling force over a political elite on issues that democracy is unlikely to reach for want of public participation.

However, the Human Rights Act does not of itself create any filter as to when the electorate can both 'start paying attention' and ignore the usual shortcut in favour of complying with decisions.

The genius of this 'elegant' balance is that what would normally be a constitutional decision to amend or override a bill of rights is in form an ordinary legislative decision. The result of the un-entrenched nature of the Human Rights Act and the limits of its enforcement is that the Act positively admits that it can be overridden and yet remain effective. Ordinarily, decisions under the Act will be translated into legislation. This judicial interference will fall short of being alien control if it is subject to legislative counter-control whose use is itself controlled by the electorate, albeit most likely as a matter of virtual or inhibitory control rather than direct interventional control. It is public opinion alone that would release legislators from the fear of political costs for overriding the Act. Insofar as no such public opinion interventions are made, it may be inferred that the use of the judicial power is within the boundaries 'virtual control' exercised by the electorate.

The above reconciliation argument will, as we shall now see, face considerable difficulties. What we have seen in the opening chapters is that the effect of constitutional provisions and principles is substantially a matter of how electors, legislators and administrators participate within those provisions and principles. This gives rise to a central problem for citizens and legislators: would using their participatory rights to seek the overriding of the Human Rights Act actually be compatible with, or be seen as being compatible with, participation seeking that the Act should exist in the first place? This is the structural argument for compliance – that the retention of Parliamentary Sovereignty must be a mere 'façade' (Cooke, 1998: p. 49) if the Act itself is to be meaningful. Alongside this dynamic is the question of whether the participatory choices of legislators have tended to close off the potential for electoral participation seeking the override of human rights decisions. It may be that the electorate's freedom of choice has been reduced by the presentation of Human Rights Act decisions as compulsory, and that certain choices have been removed in that the major political parties have presented a united front in treating compliance as compulsory.

We return to the republican principle of equality, and the 'eyeball test' that ordinary electors should be able to see decision-makers as their equals and not their superiors (Pettit, 2012: pp. 84–87; Maynor, 2003: pp. 45–46). An absence of effective counter-control on matters of importance to the public will place the judges in a position of superiority. It is one thing to create a constitution where elected representatives must accept judicial decisions, but another thing where electors will limit their participatory choices in response to judicial decisions. This is to treat judges as superiors; to decide, as Rousseau (1988: p. 32) said, 'What he wills tomorrow, I too shall will'.

8 Reasons for compliance

Constitutional conventions, atrophication and internationalisation

Introduction

What we presented in the last chapter were practical theories as to how the Human Rights Act not only preserves the 'come-at-ability' of the British Constitution as described by Bagehot (2007: pp. 98–99) by allowing for the Act to be overridden through ordinary legislation, but that the Act may serve to stimulate deliberation and participation within the political process. Any counter-majoritarian effect would restrain majorities in the legislature, but would not hinder the freedom of choice that citizens have when exercising participatory rights to counter-control judicial decisions.

Such an approach represents how the Human Rights Act *could* work within the British Constitution. It would similarly represent how a British Bill of Rights could work if its schedule of rights took effect by similar mechanisms to that found in the body of the Human Rights Act – and it is unlikely that any such reform would involve a move to 'strong-form' constitutional reform where primary legislation could be set aside by judges.

We have assumed a lack of blocks to equal participation that might thwart the reconciliation of democracy with the broad judicial power to determine the scope and application of the Act. Matters of legislative controversy may variously involve questions of economics, morality, criminological theory, self-interest, resource allocation and the like. It is often difficult enough for interested citizens to participate in public deliberation, even if such participation just comprises informing themselves a little, reaching an opinion and casting their votes (Downs, 1957). If the same issue is transformed into a legal issue, and the correctness or reasonableness of that issue is made central to the debate on a legislative response, then effective participation is even more than usually reserved to those with the appropriate 'learned capacity' (Beetham, 1993: p. 64). To apply Beetham's (1999: p. 167) 29th criterion in the democratic audit (i.e. the ability for voters to participate in politics generally): it is difficult for all citizens to participate in political life if the questions of politics are translated into legal form. Dahl's conditions for polyarchy and Beetham's democratic audit both stress the importance of access to information. This was essentially Tham's (2010: pp. 101–102) criticism that a QC's opinion may become a condition for participation. Commentary from the JCHR may translate human rights law into something closer to layman's language, but for the purpose of equipping Parliamentarians to take up the side of the debate for the broadening the scope of rights, or restricting the possibility of derogations.

The last chapter demonstrated a steady course of conduct by which Parliament has complied with Human Rights Act decisions. We shall now examine deeper the possible reasons for that compliance. Ultimately, the last chapter only presented an argument that *the form* of the Human Rights Act is compatible with polyarchy existing alongside a process of constitutional review that has significant practical effect in protecting rights. It is necessary to look in greater detail – and to do this we shall analyse the position in terms of Jennings's analysis of constitutional conventions.

Constitutional conventions and constitutional review

As compliance with the Human Rights Act is as a matter of form voluntary, we need to scrutinise whether compliance is compulsory as a matter of substance. The obvious approach for considering whether a non-legal but binding obligation exists within the constitution is to ask whether there is a constitutional convention. We shall use the approach of Ivor Jennings (1938: pp. 129–131) to ascertain whether a convention exists to bring us closer to identifying the 'political costs', which are so often referred to as underlying compliance with judicially expounded human rights principles. As noted in Chapter 7 ('Mechanism of compliance'), the three criteria for a constitutional convention are:

i. Precedent for observance;
ii. Observance by reason of sense of obligation;
iii. Reason for obligation.

Dicey (2008: pp. 296–300) argued that constitutional conventions, whilst not themselves law, are often underpinned by legal concerns. Alternatively, a constitutional convention may be supported as representing 'the prevailing political philosophy' (Jennings, 1938: p. 131), what Dicey (1982: p. 301) calls 'the maintenance of political morality'.

The importance of closely examining the reasons for compliance when considering the existence of a constitutional convention is shown by considering another related theory for legislative compliance with constitutional review decisions: atrophication (Vermuele, 2012; Chandrachud, 2014: pp. 638–641).

We should first of all note that the possible role for a 'prevailing political philosophy' in maintaining a constitutional convention of Human Rights Act compliance has essentially already been considered in Chapter 7 ('Structural argument for duty of compliance with constitutional review') in the 'structural argument'. This argument was that, if public opinion strongly requires the continuation of the Human Rights Act as an effective form of constitutional review, then it may be said with force that the 'prevailing political philosophy' will be breached by *any* non-compliance. We shall see in 'Atrophication due to non-existence of historical data' in this chapter that there will be a particular difficulty for citizens considering whether to depart from this approach, given a lack of information as to the consequences of breach.

Atrophication and constitutional review

The argument as to atrophication of powers is based on the idea that powers can fall into such disuse as to become illegitimate. Adrian Vermeule (2012: p. 421) argues:

> When a power goes unexercised over some sufficiently long period, its use comes to seem illegitimate to boundedly informed publics. Such publics use a political precedent heuristic, according to which an attempt to revive the power at a later time amounts to an illegitimate attempt to change the rules of the political game.

Vermeule's focus is on demonstrable failures by citizens (and often commentators) to consider the full historical background for a power. A power is seen as illegitimate, he argues, because people use a 'simple political precedent heuristic for judging the competing claims of constitutional actors' (p. 426). This is 'low-information rationality' (p. 434), essentially the same as the idea of an 'information shortcut' that we have used extensively in this thesis (Downs, 1957; see also Hardin, 2004: pp. 79–80; Udehn, 2003: p. 141; Popkin, 1991: pp. 9–15). Hence, precedents have been overlooked when certain constitutional conduct was widely denounced as unprecedented and illegitimate, such as Franklin Roosevelt's court-packing legislation in 1936, the establishment of American military commissions in 2001, and the dismissal of US Attorneys in 2006 (p. 436). The argument is that the illegitimacy of using the power derives from its non-use (or perceived non-use), and that illegitimacy becomes of itself a complete reason for continued non-use. Vermuele (pp. 443–444) argues that occasional use of a power should be considered for the sake of preventing it atrophying. So, in respect of the Human Rights Act, 'Parliament should see that overriding a decision to which it does not object is a valuable institutional investment in long-run power'. The wisdom of this is doubtful: such a tactic would run counter to the idea that rights infringements are serious matters, requiring the sanction of meaningful public deliberation. Unless there was a cartel-like consensus amongst major parties, such an approach would give the opposition a valuable line of attack.

Whilst recognising that participation even by many elites is often ill-informed, an important difficulty with Vermuele's theory of atrophy is that it presupposes that participants are not open to meaningful deliberation on the issues at large. As a proposition, atrophication seems promising. We commonly see arguments put from national history which seek to persuade people that this or that course of conduct is contrary to national identity, and so (without consideration of the particular merits) ought not to be countenanced. The former Attorney General, Dominic Grieve (2014), linked compliance with the Convention to the 'national narrative' that 'has been so powerful that it has acted as a an almost mythic restraint on successive British governments trying to curb freedoms when tempted to do so by threats to public order or national security as we saw over 90 and 42 day pre-charge detention under the last Government'. Baroness Hale (2015: p. 18) similarly invoked this heritage, arguing that the UK Supreme Court carries out 'the role of a constitutional court to protect fundamental rights, within the framework of law and the constitution ... building upon centuries of law and jurisprudence which make up our national narrative'. Such arguments promote atrophication insofar as they aim to have a decision taken for reasons other than an analysis of present-day circumstances, but by reference to historical precedent (real or spurious).[1]

Vermeule's (2012: pp. 427–428) point is that non-use of a power may lead to assumptions that the use of the power is improper as arguments and precedents to the contrary fall out of public memory – there is a 'belief trap', which becomes 'self-immunizing'. Whether we talk in terms of 'information shortcuts' (Downs, 1957) or a 'simple political precedent heuristic for judging the competing claims of constitutional actors' (Vermeule, 2012: p. 426), such a dynamic whilst immensely plausibly is vulnerable to public engagement, and informed deliberation challenging orthodoxy.

The sense of illegitimacy invoked in the atrophication hypothesis would satisfy Jennings's second criterion of compliance with the precedent being out of obligation, but it does not satisfactorily address Jennings's third criterion for a constitutional convention, i.e. the reasons for compliance. Atrophy alone does not address the different dynamics that may support a Convention, principally, (1) breaking a Convention may, as Dicey (1982: pp. 296–300) stressed, lead to illegality further down the line; and (2) breaking a Convention may offend the 'prevailing political philosophy' (Jennings, 1938: p. 131) so as to lead to a political trial of strength which will predictably end in defeat for the 'offender', e.g. the House of Lords using its former legislative veto (Low, 1920: p. x), or the monarch making personal use of prerogatives which have long been used only on the advice of the elected government (Amery, 1964: pp. 6–7; 1952: p. 59). On any view, an

1 There are perhaps striking similarities between bringing forward such heritage arguments as relevant to modern political and ethical dilemmas, and Charles Taylor's (1999: p. 101) theory of 'unforced convergence', namely that adherence to human rights norms could be more effectively spread if those norms were linked to local history and traditions.

atrophied power would be most likely to stay moribund if, when its use is proposed, a real reason for the putative rule emerges and holds good. It really does not matter how badly 'eminent Canadian constitutional scholars' underestimated the use of the notwithstanding clause power (Vermuele, 2012: p. 428), if there were strong constitutional reasons for its non-use, nor should the scarcity of precedents matter if deliberation demonstrates good reasons to bring the power into common use. Atrophication of the sort described by Vermeule (2012: p. 427): a mere 'belief trap' without consideration of substantive reasons for an opinion enduring, will always be vulnerable to a shift of public opinion, which leads to people questioning why they do things. Even the oldest and most fixed beliefs (e.g. as to the nature of marriage) may eventually be asked to justify themselves, and the reasons be found wanting by public opinion.

The importance of underlying reasons is inadvertently shown by Jennings (1938: p. 82) writing in the 1930s: 'it is by convention and not by law that [the President of the United States] cannot be re-elected for a third term'. When President Roosevelt stood successfully for a third term in 1940, the reason for the 'convention' was shown to be nothing more than an opinion that standing a third time might be unpopular. There was a general opinion that it ought not to be done – as was shown when the 22nd Amendment was passed in 1951 limiting presidents to two terms – but it was not as strong as the opinion in 1940 that Roosevelt should be President rather than Wendell Wilkie. Unsurprisingly, after 1940 it was determined that the convention had never actually existed (Dyer, 1943: p. 320).

Applying Jennings's analysis of constitutional conventions, (1) as we saw in Chapter 7 ('Mechanism of compliance') there are overwhelming precedents for compliance with the Human Rights Act in terms of declarations of incompatibility being acted upon, purposive interpretations being accepted, and legislation never being put forward on the basis of maintaining it regardless of a declaration of incompatibility; and (2) as will be seen now, the legislature has treated itself as if subject to an obligation to comply. But ultimately the key part of Jennings's analysis is (3) why does Parliament comply? If we understood that, then we should be better placed to determine the limits of Parliament's obligations, for no sense of obligation can forever outrun its own underlying reasons.

Atrophication due to non-existence of historical data

A refinement on atrophication can be suggested: non-use can create a gap in knowledge such that there is no data to rationally consider whether a risk is present or worth taking. We have seen that there are substantial reasons why a citizen, especially one inclined to view the Human Rights Act as a useful restraint on government and administration, should see compliance with the Act as being prima facie obligatory. There are international law reasons, and there is the need to keep the Act credible as a 'rights protection pact'.

The basic atrophication point is that lengthy non-use creates a sense of obligatory non-use. It might be better to say that a lengthy period of abiding by a rule of Human Rights Act compliance will:

a) Generate information as to the consequences of compliance. People may see decisions favourably, or unfavourably;
b) Generate no information as to the consequences of limited non-compliance.

Hence, if citizens use Human Rights Act compliance as their starting point in terms of participation, they will gather information that may make them better or worse disposed towards the Human Rights Act. In contrast, if a country has always complied with constitutional review decisions, then citizens will have gathered no precedents to evaluate the long-term constitutional risks of non-compliance with future decisions. If someone is generally well-disposed to the effect of the Act, but opposed to a particular decision, they have no data on which to satisfactorily judge whether they can participate so as to simultaneously support the Human Rights Act and support a particular incompatible decision. To a considerable extent it would be a leap in the dark.

It is unsurprising therefore that the active debates on non-compliance with ECHR and Human Rights Act decisions, such as the Commons debates on prisoner voting (HC Debate, 2011a; 2012), have tended to focus on:

a) General satisfaction towards the Convention;
b) General dissatisfaction towards the Convention;
c) Theories that would permit legitimate breach in highly contained circumstances, which we shall consider in the next chapter.

Absent a positive theory as to the availability of legitimate breach, the power to wilfully enact or maintain non-compliant legislation will show every sign of atrophying. Debates will be around general satisfaction or dissatisfaction towards constitutional review, the continuation of the Human Rights Act, or membership of the Convention. If a citizen's 'prevailing political philosophy' is supportive of the Human Rights Act, taking the opportunities offered by retaining Parliamentary Sovereignty will be made ever more daunting due to an ever longer period for which no information is generated as to the reality of the risks that non-compliance would cause.

Legislative acceptance of obligation to comply

We saw in the last chapter the overwhelming course of conduct in favour of complying with the Human Rights Act. We turn now to whether this derives from a sense of obligations – the second part of Ivor Jennings's analysis of constitutional conventions.

The best evidence of the belief in an obligation for Parliament to maintain a Human Rights Act-compliant statute book is found in the responses to controversy. We noted in Chapter 7 ('Mechanism of compliance') that the response to the ECtHR's *Hirst* decision remains a work in progress, with the government accepting an obligation to comply. We shall consider in Chapter 9 ('Illegitimate decisions') the explanation offered in Parliament by back-benchers to justify non-compliance, and see that the argument amounts to acceptance that there should normally be an obligation for legislators to put aside misgivings of the effect of human rights decisions and comply.

The Communications Bill 2003

The only post-Human Rights Act example of an Act passed without a statement of compatibility concerned the Communications Bill 2003. This maintained the ban on political advertising on television, which was potentially incompatible with the European Court's decision in *VGT*. The Explanatory Note (DCMS, 2012: [12]) stated that the government would defer to the ECtHR:

> [I]f there were a successful challenge to the ban in the domestic courts the Government would reconsider the position, and would certainly propose to amend the legislation if the European Court of Human Rights found against the UK in any challenge specifically concerning the UK ban.

It is worth underlining the distinction drawn between the compliance obligation in respect of United Kingdom constitutional review decisions, and those made by the ECtHR. In the hierarchy of the strength of interference in the legislative process, a decision of the ECtHR is more powerful: the British Courts will cause the government to 'reconsider the position'; the ECtHR will be given obedience. The same position was taken by Baroness Blackstone on behalf of the government when presenting the Communications Bill to the House of Lords (HL Debate, 2003a: col. 659).

However, the point that we make in this section is that there is no suggestion that agreement with the reasons of the court (domestic or European) would have been a precondition for the legislature's compliance with the decisions.

F and Thompson

The case of *F and Thompson* concerned the Article 8 right to privacy and the proportionality of lifelong reporting obligations for those convicted of sexual offences and sentenced to more than 30 months in prison. It was held that these provisions were disproportionate 'because they make no provision for individual review of the requirements' (*F and Thompson* [58]). Lord Phillips said at [57]:

> I think that it is obvious that there must be some circumstances in which an appropriate tribunal could reliably conclude that the risk of an individual carrying out a further sexual offence can be discounted to the extent that continuance of notification requirements is unjustified.

This makes the case appear straightforward – and the legislation so wrong that it is a wonder that the issues needed any judicial help let alone the Supreme Court. But it calls to mind Lord Hoffmann's (2002: [8]) comment that whilst most House of Lords (now Supreme Court) cases could be decided in either direction, the judges would often adopt 'the usual polemical style which judges feel it necessary to adopt in order to persuade their colleagues and the public that no other answer is possible'. Lord Phillips, in fact, did not conclude that a tribunal would necessarily in real life ever identify that there is no risk of reoffending. He admitted in the preceding paragraph that the psychiatric literature does not presently allow for accurate diagnosis of the propensity (or lack thereof) of sexual offenders to reoffend. The court's conclusion rests on the notoriously intuitive issue of whether the 'precautionary principle' requires a particular action to minimise risk to greatest possible extent (*F and Thompson* [56]): 'If uncertainty exists can this render proportionate the imposition of notification requirements for life without review under the precautionary principle? I do not believe that it can'.

The application of the precautionary principle is an issue on which individuals may easily divide, often for reasons that are very human (e.g. particular aversion to particular harm, bias towards the status quo) (Sunstein, 2005: p. 39). There is no wholly rational way of measuring the steps that we should take, and the sacrifices that we should be willing to take, in order to avoid particular risks. The Supreme Court (and indeed all the judges who heard the case) were willing to take a greater risk than Parliament with sexual reoffending: they had faith in the ability of a tribunal to determine that a risk of reoffending was very low, and that the risk was worth taking to relieve the particular offenders of reporting duties. As Crawford (2013: p. 88) notes, there were 'perfectly valid reasons' for legislators to continue to believe that their way was better than following the court's decision.

F and Thompson involved a Conservative Home Secretary responding to a declaration of incompatibility made in respect of legislation passed under the previous Labour government (Section 82 of the Sexual Offences Act 2003). Instead of blaming the previous government, the Home Secretary was deeply hostile to the decision. Theresa May MP said that she was 'disappointed and appalled', and that the government would make 'the minimum possible changes to the law in order to comply with the ruling'. She added: 'I would far rather not have to stand here saying that we have to make a change to the sex offenders register, but we do have to make a change' (HC Debate, cc. 959 and 961).

Presenting the government's response to the House Lords, Baroness Neville Jones said (HL Deb, 2011: col. 714):

> The Government are appalled by this ruling, which places the rights of sex offenders above the right of the public to be protected from the risk of reoffending, but there is no possibility of further appeal. This Government are determined to do everything that we can to protect the public from predatory sex offenders and so we will make the minimum possible changes to the law in order to comply with this ruling.

Baroness Hale (2013: p. 17) contrasted the vehement government criticism of the Supreme Court decision in *F and Thompson* with the government's and Parliament's legislative acceptance of the decision. But this is to draw attention to the fact that legislators may hold wholly negative views of human rights decisions, and yet treat the same decision as definitive on what the law must or must not be.

It should be noted that when Baroness Neville Jones, above, said that 'there is no possibility of further appeal', she was right in form not substance. It would have been perfectly possible for the government to persist in the view that the legislation was compatible with the Convention, and so force a test case in Strasbourg. Although not formally a right of appeal from a domestic ruling as to the content of Convention rights under the Human Rights Act, it would have resolved whether any duty of compliance to the decision in *F and Thompson* was underpinned by important international obligations. What was said about appeal rights was the truth; but it was far from the whole truth. The government did have litigation choices other than compliance with *F and Thompson*: it just did not want the world to realise that.

The Belmarsh case

In *Belmarsh*, the House of Lords ruled by 8–1 that the detention without trial provisions of sections 21–23 of the Anti-terrorism, Crime and Security Act 2001 were contrary to the Human Rights Act. The legislation only applied to those who were subject to immigration control, and who had the option to leave the United Kingdom, although in practice would not choose to leave for the same reason that they could not be deported to their home country: the threat of torture. Seven of the majority held that the legislation was irrational and discriminatory, being subject to immigration control was unrelated to the danger posed by suspected terrorists.

The response to the decision was considered in detail by Christopher Crawford (2013: pp. 63–69). Lord Falconer, the Lord Chancellor, declared that the *Belmarsh* judgment had shown to him that the government had got the balance between rights and security wrong (quoted, Butler and James, 2005), but Charles Clarke, the Home Secretary took a quite different view. Whereas initially it appeared that the Home Secretary might reject the declaration of incompatibility if he thought it impossible to bring forward legislation to both comply with the *Belmarsh* judgment and protect the country from terrorism (quoted Blackman, 2004), he soon told the House of Commons that the government would comply. This was the case even though the Home Secretary believed that the powers condemned by the House of Lords had 'played an essential part in addressing the current public emergency, because they have been successful in containing the threat posed by those certified and detained under them' (HC Debate, 2005; cc. 305–309). Shortly afterwards, the Minister of State announced to the House of Lords (HL Debate, 2005: col. 1102):

> I accept that judgment, and therefore believe that it is important to address those concerns. We should not simply renew the current legislation, which the Law Lords so overwhelmingly regard as flawed. We should replace it – with strong measures that are fully compatible with the European convention on human rights, and applicable to both British and foreign nationals.

The position taken by the government was ultimately summarised by the then Prime Minister Tony Blair (2010: p. 575, cited Crawford, 2013: p. 66): 'Once the House of Lords made the ruling, we had to amend the law'.

Bellinger

A striking example of the sense of obligation to comply with Human Rights Act and ECtHR decisions is found in the House of Lords debate on the Gender Recognition Bill (HL Debate, 2003b). The legislation followed a declaration of incompatibility in the House of Lords in *Bellinger* as to transsexuals' right to marry, and the ECtHR decision in *Goodwin* on broader legal recognition of the reassigned gender. The Human Rights Act decision was thus underpinned by the international ECHR obligations. Unlike *F and Thompson* and *Belmarsh*, the government gave this Bill moral rather than grudging support, asserting: 'We should be legislating on the issue, irrespective of any ECHR judgment' (col. 1326).

What interests us is the positions taken by the Bishop of Winchester and Lord Carlile. The Bishop of Winchester was opposed to the idea of recognising gender reassignment. He argued that the judicial decisions were based on very limited expert opinion, and that the *Goodwin* decision was 'in parts a frankly shocking read in its unjudicial one-sidedness' (col. 1297). Lord Chan, a distinguished doctor, argued that the then balance of medical opinion did not support the step taken (cc. 1306–1308). However, despite setting out a detailed argument against the decisions, the Bishop conceded (col. 1301): 'I was not questioning the fact that we were bound by the cases, but the quality of that judgment by which we are bound'.

Lord Carlile QC, an eminent public lawyer and early campaigner for transsexual recognition, replied immediately (col. 1301):

> Our judges are appointed to interpret and apply our law. I say with the greatest respect to the right reverend Prelate that I do not think we dignify ourselves by saying that an issue decided by the courts is wrong because we happen to think that the judgment was not of sufficient quality.

The merits of the legislation and the decisions are not in issue for present purposes; we are interested in the acceptance of a duty to comply with the court decisions. We see that the Bishop set aside his criticisms of the proposed law as he believed that Parliament was 'bound' to enact it. And Lord Carlile appeared to think it undignified even to critique the judicial decision.

Conclusion on legislative acceptance of obligation to comply

The point of this review is to illustrate in the context of decisions taken under both the Labour government and the Conservative-led coalition, that compliance with the Human Rights Act has been treated as if it were a binding obligation despite disagreement. In respect of the Communications Bill 2003 and the ban on political advertising on television, the government was clear that it believed in the ban and that the ban was compatible, but would nevertheless comply with adverse decisions. In respect of both *F and Thompson* and *Belmarsh*, the government of the day stated a belief that existing legislation was justified and better than alternatives, but brought forward legislation solely to comply with the judicial finding of incompatibility. In *Bellinger*, the most vocal critics of law change explained their criticisms, but admitted that the merit of the matter was moot: compliance was compulsory.

Legal obligation to comply

The ability to 'come-at' the government is hindered if it can credibly claim an absence of choice. In the context of *F and Thompson*, Crawford (2013: p. 82) argued that the government complied because 'It is politically easier for the government to blame the judiciary and make minor changes to the legislation than it is to leave the legislation as it stands and provoke a constitutional crisis'. Instead of taking responsibility for the legislation it brings to a legislature where it commands a majority, the government presents itself as having no choice. The potential for governments blaming a duty of obedience to constitutional review is shown by the Canadian experience.

In Canada, politicians have gone as far as (a) giving legislation a title which places responsibility for remedial legislation on the judges,[2] and (b) boycotting sessions to pass the legislation, leaving the floor and the voting to a minority of genuinely supportive legislators (Ontario Deb, 1999). Even

2 The Amendments because of the Supreme Court of Canada Decision in M. v. H. Act.

when a politician's stated views shift, it may be unclear whether they had changed their minds or were avoiding conflict with its higher priority of rights compliance – Hiebert (2006: p. 20) gives the example of the rapid and unexplained conversion of Canadian Prime Minister Chretien away from a purely heterosexual definition of marriage following provincial court decisions.

The potential for smoke and mirrors – and the correctness of any claims that compliance is compulsory – can only be countered with an analysis of the reasons for compliance. If Finer's (1960: p. 67, cited King, 2007: p. 59) line of authority and responsibility is seen on certain matters as starting and ending with constitutional review decisions, then government is not come-at-able from the perspective of the electorate in respect of those matters and who thus cannot 'have confidence ... in their ability to influence [the political system]' as per Beetham's (1999: p. 167) 30th democratic audit criterion. If Parliamentary Sovereignty is preserved in substance, such a presentation by the government of its choices is a misrepresentation, and thus a manipulation of the electorate and legislators alike. A government that explains its choices by misrepresenting the nature of the choice will exercise alien control over the electorate – the reality of choice is undermined if the public are led to believe that no choice exists (Pettit, 2009: p. 41).

We shall now turn to the third part of Jennings's analysis of constitutional conventions: is there a reason for compliance? In line with the Diceyan hypothesis of constitutional conventions being underpinned by the law, we consider first the question of whether law underpins compliance.

Domestic legality

In the House of Lords debates on compliance with *F and Thompson*, Baroness Stowell presented the legislation for the government (HL Debate, 2012: col. 886), and said: 'The Government were disappointed with the UK Supreme Court's ruling, but we take our responsibility to uphold the law seriously, and that includes human rights law'.

This goes beyond any sense of political or moral obligation to bring forward remedial legislation; the obligation is said to be one of upholding the law. Lord Lester in the same debate also viewed compliance in terms of the rule of law – in his view 'the main benefit' of bringing forward compliant legislation after *F and Thompson* 'is to secure the rule of law' (HL Debate, 2012: col. 885). To Lord Lester, the decision was the law, and laws should be obeyed. Any good or bad done by the new position as regards sex-offender reporting requirements was of secondary importance to the overriding priority that, in a society of law, the law must be respected.

A fundamental part of the rule of law is congruence between the law as stated and its enforcement (Fuller, 1969: pp. 38–39). Plainly, non-compliance with the Human Rights Act opens up a gap between the law operating in the United Kingdom and the human rights protected by the

Act, as construed by the Act's lawful and definitive interpreters. Such non-compliance inevitably degrades any quality the Human Rights Act's decision might have as law. However, there is an obvious awkwardness in this approach: the Human Rights Act is deliberately structured so that declarations of incompatibility should not have the quality of law: compliance was not a legal obligation on Parliament.

It follows from this that, unless the 'elegant balance' is just a façade or so much lip service (Cooke, 1998: p. 49; Jowell, 2003: pp. 596–597), the invocations of the rule of law at a domestic level such as were made by Lord Lester or Baroness Stowell in *F and Thompson* can correctly be seen as interference with freedom of democratic choice by means of manipulation. Under Pettit's (2008: p. 100) 'first theorem' described in Chapter 3 ('The four theorems'), a party may exert alien control by 'credibly misinforming the agent about the blocks and burdens in place', e.g. informing the public that action is impossible, so there is no point in citizens participating to promote now unavailable ends. This may induce the sort of atrophication described by Vermeule (2012: p. 426), presenting the 'simple political precedent heuristic' that will over time become unchallengeable in the popular mind, even if arising out of error. In a matter of specialist knowledge, such as what is legal or not, non-specialists such as ordinary citizens will tend to believe what they are told by authoritative sources – and may become unwilling to countenance other possibilities.

International legality

As noted in Chapter 5, one of the issues that affects the extent of the counter-majoritarian effect of Bills of Rights is the extent to which they are 'internationalised', whereby issues cease to be the business of domestic governance alone. This dynamic applies significantly to the Human Rights Act, where section 2 requires the courts to 'take account of' the case law of the ECtHR. This means what is known as the 'mirror principle', which typically means copying Strasbourg case law (*Ullah* [20]). It may be at times that the British Courts do less than the Strasbourg's case law requires because they believe that the European Court has misunderstood the relevant United Kingdom law. Sometimes this leads to Strasbourg accepting its error, as in respect of certain matters relating to criminal law and hearsay (*R v Horncastle* [2009] UKSC 14; [2010] 2 AC 373; *Horncastle v United Kingdom* [2014] ECHR 1394); sometimes Strasbourg stands its ground, and the British Courts have fallen into line, as in respect of Article 8 protection for tenants (*Manchester City Council v Pinnock* [2011] UKSC 6; [2011] 2 AC 104).

What concerns us here is that the United Kingdom courts have also asserted independence to expand the effect of the ECHR from beyond the Strasbourg jurisprudence in matters of proportionality (*Nicklinson* [70]–[76]). The culturally sensitive margin of appreciation that Strasbourg gives in setting minimum standards across 47 contracting states is inappropriate to a national court addressing the affairs of its own country. It is the nature of human rights instruments that the courts have great latitude to determine their approach to the issues of 'justification' that are at the heart of the practical application of constitutional review. The approach suggested in cases such as *Nicklinson* is that the British Courts will take a more expansive view of their role than just mirroring Strasbourg's case law. This will increase the scope for the Human Rights Act to have a counter-majoritarian effect without any supporting internationalisation by way of the ECHR.

We can therefore see:

i) A national decision may be 'internationalised' insofar as there is an equivalent ECtHR decision. Whatever the national constitutional theory, non-compliance creates international costs. This leads us back to the questions considered earlier, and Danny Nicol's (2010: pp. 10–11) argument that subscribing to international governance may entrench policies, and Inger-Johanne Sand's (2007: p. 288) analysis that national constitutional forms for implementing such obligations may be of little relevance to the constitutional consquences.
ii) A national decision may be 'internationalised' insofar as, although there is no conclusive ECHR case law, the national court presents a persuasive argument that the case would be resolved the same way in Strasbourg. Crawford (2013: p. 84) believed that there was no prospect that *F and Thompson* would have been decided differently by the ECtHR, and that this was a factor in the government accepting the Supreme Court decision.
iii) A national decision may stand on its own insofar as it appears – and may even be admitted by the United Kingdom court – to go beyond what Strasbourg would require. In such a case internationalisation will not underpin the entirety of Act's jurisprudence – indeed, contrary international authority may provide a critique of national court decisions.

The invigilatory force of the ECHR is plain from the speech of Baroness Stowell presenting the remedial order following the decision in *F and Thompson* on the right to privacy and reporting obligations of sex offenders (HL Debate, 2012: col. 875):

> *Our constitutional arrangements* are such that when the highest court of the land identifies an incompatibility with the European Convention on Human Rights, the Government of the day, *whoever is in power*, take remedial action. This is for various reasons, not the least of which is to ensure that the Government are not left vulnerable to further legal proceedings, potentially involving millions of pounds of taxpayers' money.
>
> [Emphasis added]

The point was put differently in respect of the Communications Bill 2003, where the government statements suggested that a domestic defeat would lead to a reconsideration, whereas a defeat in Strasbourg would definitely lead to remedial action (DCMS, 2002 [12]; HL Debate, 2003a: col. 659). But whether the government sees a domestic defeat as conclusive of what would happen in Strasbourg or a persuasive indication of the same, it is clear that the impetus to comply with domestic Human Rights Act decisions is strengthened by the close association with the Act's requirements and international obligations.

In terms of non-compliance, put simply, a bill of rights will seek to replace choice-x with choice-(x+y), where in this case y represents the internationalised costs of taking choice-x. But this is inadequate for making an important qualitative distinction between where the political costs of non-compliance are contained, or where they represent a crisis for a particular arrangement or relationship. We shall call these respective costs 'little-y' and 'Big-Y'.

Little-y costs exist where non-compliance is to some extent legitimate or at least forgivable. For example, the Home Secretary could be seen as having broken the US–UK extradition treaty by refusing to extradite Gary McKinnon on human rights grounds that had been rejected by the courts (Home Office, 2012), but, whatever annoyance there might have been on the part of the United States government, the treaty remained in place. The structure of the Human Rights Act and the claims of the 'elegant balance' argument are that the costs ought to be very much in terms of a 'little-y' – not so little as to render the constitutional review decisions irrelevant, but neither such a 'big-Y' that Parliamentary Sovereignty is illusory if the Act is to survive. Legitimate breach of the Human Rights Act is built into the structure of the Act. Doubtless there is a level of non-compliance which would render the Act pointless but no individual action of non-compliance would of itself be illegitimate.

Big-Y costs exist where non-compliance represents at the very least an acute crisis for an arrangement or relationship. In the law of the European Convention, the ECtHR expects compliance: as is clear from the Court (*Greens* [115]) giving the United Kingdom six months to comply with *Hirst*. The question thus moves to a non-legal one given that ECHR law (unlike EU law) lacks direct effect and legal supremacy: even if the legal duty is strict as a matter of treaty law, can that duty go unenforced without a crisis in Convention membership? If breaches cannot be legitimate within the ECHR legal framework, are they in practice forgivable by the parties to that framework?

Forgivable breaches?

The major test for the enforceability of the legal duty of Convention compliance is that of prisoner voting. It has been held by Strasbourg that the United

Kingdom's present general ban on convicted prisoners voting is contrary to the Convention, (*Hirst*, *Greens*). This is accepted by the United Kingdom courts, although the only actual declaration of incompatibility comes from the Scottish Courts (*Smith v Scott*), the UK Supreme Court having recognised the incompatibility, but declined to make a declaration on account of the applicants themselves not being entitled to the benefit of the decision (*Chester*). Whilst Sophie Briant (2011) approached the question of compliance in terms of diplomacy and dialogue between the UK authorities and the ECtHR, the real question is as to whether the other contracting states will set a choice of *comply* or *denounce*. Mr Justice Sales argued extra-judicially that the courts should not proceed on the basis that there is any doubt as to the United Kingdom's compliance with ECtHR decisions: 'there is no doubt that the Council of Europe ... will stand behind judgments of the ECtHR and require them to be implemented' (Sales, 2012: p. 262). Against this, it was argued by Lord Irvine (2012: pp. 245–246) that departing from the ECHR was a state matter with no definite result. It is unremarkable that the ECtHR in *Greens* [115] should have proceeded on the basis that its orders must be complied with – the question is whether in reality, in the international law/relations context, the United Kingdom does have a choice which represents choice-(x+'little-y') (i.e. that it can disobey *Hirst* and then continue as a member of the Convention as if nothing has happened), or whether non-compliance must represent choice-(x+'Big-Y') (i.e. non-compliance represents a substantial threat to continued membership).

It may well be true that 'the Council of Europe will stand behind the judgments of the ECtHR', but what will the Council do to 'require them to be implemented' (Sales, 2012: p. 262)? The ECtHR has recently decided that all applications concerning the United Kingdom's prohibition against convicted prisoners from voting should be given summary judgment, and without an award of damages (*McHugh v United Kingdom* [2015] ECHR 155). Were this the European Union, such non-compliance would at the very least lead to an award of '*Frankovitch*' damages: a price would be put on non-compliance, and non-payment would pose an existential question to the nature of the European Union itself – any forgiven non-compliance would represent a retreat from the cardinal principle of European legal supremacy (*Costa*, 456). What the ECtHR has done is to make the issue now purely one of politics as to the enforcement of the right itself. The question for the Council of Europe is not clouded by any issue as to the need to enforce monetary awards, nor can it turn into the United Kingdom buying a right for non-compliance by meeting the damages as they arise.

Many would argue that the United Kingdom's approach in prisoner voting poses an existential crisis for the Convention – so the choice taken by non-compliance is one of choice-(x+'Big-Y'), e.g. a significant risk of ending the United Kingdom's membership of the Convention or destroying the authority of the Convention. This was the point continually made in the House of Common by opponents of the ban on convicted prisoners voting

(HC Debate, 2011a; HC Debate, 2012). It is also the argument Jonathan Fisher QC makes when saying that a necessary concomitant of a decision to be part of the ECHR is to accept compliance with the *Hirst* decision (Swinford, 2015).

As well as the consequences of non-compliance in terms of the United Kingdom's position in the Council of Europe, there are also wider issues as regards the effect of non-compliance on the operation of the Convention. What we noted in respect of democracy within a state is true of political systems created between states: participatory choices may be constitutive of the reality of the system. Entering into such a treaty has two consequences: to restrain other states, and to restrain one's own state. In terms of domestic constitutional law we are apt to look at the Convention in terms of its effect in the United Kingdom, but for many it is important to consider membership in terms of the benefits of membership to citizens of other countries. The argument that any assertion of a choice not to comply with an ECtHR decision must undermine the protection of the Convention was frequently made in debates on prisoner voting. Indeed, the internationalisation of human rights in the European Conventions means that the issue of the enfranchisement of convicted criminals in the United Kingdom is linked to the issues of human rights in Russia (HC Debate, 2011a: cc. 504, 508, 518, 528; Rycroft, 2008: p. 67) – a proposition which, absent the linking of the rights under the Convention, would appear absurd. As these rights have been linked by the Convention, it can be said in earnest that the United Kingdom has undermined fundamental rights internationally because (1) it has failed to enfranchise convicted prisoners serving less than three years in jail (*Scoppola v Italy (No 3)* (2013) 56 EHRR 19), although (2) had it extended disenfranchisement beyond the term of the sentence for more serious crimes, there would be no problem. And the reason for this ostensibly strange distinction is solely down to the contestable lines drawn by the ECtHR (*Hirst*; *Scoppola*; *Greens and MT v United Kingdom* (2011) 53 EHRR 21; *Anchugov and Gladkov v Russia* [2013] ECHR 638, *Söyler v Turkey* [2013] ECHR 821). In other words:

i) ECtHR chooses an interpretation that choice-x (e.g. disenfranchisement of all convicted prisoners) is contrary to the Convention;
ii) ECtHR has thus attached a hindrance to taking choice-x.

But all of this is to say that it is ultimately a matter of statecraft, just as Lord Irvine (2012: p. 246) argued, as to what will result from non-compliance with an international law obligation, and what importance the United Kingdom attaches to such compliance. It would also be a matter of statecraft if a state decides to renounce a single-issue treaty. The corresponding diplo-

3 Issues of links between Convention membership and EU membership (Pinto-Duschinsky, 2011: pp. 52–55; Arden, 2010: p. 157) are of diminished British significance.

matic task is on a grander scale with multilateral arrangements that link a broad range of subject matter. But it would still be a matter of statecraft to estimate the consequences, the possibility of such actions being condoned, or leading to a favourable renegotiation, or leading to a choice between 'comply or denounce'. For Lord Irvine (2012: pp. 245–246) to say that the consequences of British non-compliance with an ECtHR decision is a matter of statecraft is to say that expert deliberation by well-informed diplomats would be required in order to estimate: (a) the room for manoeuvre that other states will allow the United Kingdom,(b) the consequences that the non-compliance by the United Kingdom might have on human rights compliance in other states, and (c) how the such results should concern the United Kingdom. Whether the consequences are 'little-y' or 'Big-Y' is inherently not transparent, and difficult for electors to rationally gauge.

The consequence of saying that non-compliance is a matter of statecraft is not that the United Kingdom has an undominated choice to enact laws contrary to the European Convention. Accession to the Convention creates interference with legislative and executive choices – it creates a hindrance to taking certain choices. As we said earlier, there are two natural consequences and motives for entering into such a treaty which may be held to a greater or lesser extent: to restrain other states and to restrain one's own state. The choice to create such a constitutional scenario will bring to bear, to adopt Dicey's (2008: pp. 8–9) analysis of the link between public opinion and legislation, a body of external opinion that acts on legislative choice. This interference may amount to alien control if (1) it makes particular choices materially less likely by adding a penalty (or at least the appearance of one, if the actual sanctions of external opinion are unclear), and (2) the interference is neither a matter of co-reasoning nor, properly understood, subject to counter-control. The Convention is not a matter of co-reasoning because it does not include as part of its structure the forgiveness of infringements; and individual decisions are not subject to counter-control within the structure of the Convention as it is impossible to unilaterally change what the Convention has been held to mean by the ECtHR. It is not a cross-current of opinion in a Diceyan sense (Dicey, 2008: p. 263), as the authority of an international court is separate from its persuasive power, at least in the short to medium term. The only *established* counter-control mechanism in respect of the ECHR is that of renouncing the Convention itself, i.e. the step with the highest possible external political costs attached to it.[3]

The essential issue is this: there are no clear mechanisms to enforce ECtHR decisions. Article 46 of the Convention provides the 'Committee of Ministers' shall supervise the implementation of decisions, and may refer matters back to the Court – which ultimately goes round in a circle. Recent studies by Shai Dothan (2016) and Déborah Forst (2014) emphasise that reputational considerations and diplomatic pressure are the forces supporting compliance but Forst's final words (p. 43) underline the weakness and nebulous nature of ECtHR enforcement:

> Eventually, the Parliamentary Assembly could increase the pressure put on the national delegations through the adoption of sanctions, such as a temporarily suspension of voting rights, when national parliaments do not seriously oversee how their government have implemented the Court's judgments.

As with the Council of Europe's (2012) 'Brighton Declaration' which considered enforcement of judgements at length, it is difficult to find solid and reliable consequences for non-compliance. Enforcement measures from accusations to expulsion from the Council of Europe are ultimately in the hands of other countries, who will be mindful of general international ties with the state concerned (Dothan, 2016, p. 48). Certainly there is nothing equivalent to the long-term illegality that Dicey (2008: pp. 296–300) described as underpinning British constitutional conventions. Nevertheless, prompt compliance is overwhelmingly the rule (Forst, 2013: p. 7), so such reputational and diplomatic issues cannot simply be discounted.

The possibility of 'forgivable' breach is thus speculative. It is by definition dependent on the opinion of the other 46 Convention governments. Absent a rule for what will be forgiven, forgiveness is an act of power not of justice. Forgiveness is something which may be procured, but never expected. A choice dependent on the arbitrary will of another is the quintessential republican example of a relationship of domination as set out in Chapter 3.

There is one further reason why statecraft cannot be the means to uphold a country's citizen's right to invigilate their own laws. We now turn to the impact of internationalisation on the position of the electorate in terms of its ability to control the use of statecraft.

Internationalisation, statecraft and accountability

The relationship between statecraft and democracy is a difficult one. The difficulty is explained by Harold Nicolson, one of Britain's leading twentieth-century writers on diplomacy. Prima facie, all matters of foreign policy are subject to the same theory of democratic accountability that applies to other government actions (Nicolson, 1939: p. 82, quoted by Otte, 2001: p. 159): 'The diplomatist, being a member of the Cabinet, is subject to the majority in Parliament; and Parliament being but a representative Assembly, is subject to the will of the sovereign people'.

However, the nature of diplomacy means that the 'sovereign people' will lack the information about the choices that face a country. Diplomacy is a 'means' and a 'method' of an intricate nature for identifying whether agreements are possible (Nicolson, 1946: pp. 164–165). In the field of national security decisions, it is obvious that foreign policy decisions will be taken in the absence of publically available information (Colaresi, 2012: pp. 671–672). The same is frequently true of more peaceful decisions where foreign policy and domestic policy meet: secrecy of diplomacy creates asymmetries of information which permit foreign policy to be controlled and manipulated by the state (Alterman, 1996: pp. 25–26; Ripsmann, 2004/2005: p. 189). The result is that foreign policy is the most remote from democratic accountability (Knecht and Weatherford, 2006: p. 719). There is, Knecht and Weatherford argue, a considerable 'asymmetry between what leaders know and what the public knows'. A 'little-y' cost can be made to appear to the public like a more fundamental 'Big-Y' cost and vice versa.

Colaresi (2012) argues that accountability to the electorate in foreign affairs is very much a matter of 'retrospective oversight', in that often it will not be until after matters are resolved that the necessary information for public accountability will be available. Where there are genuine crises in world affairs, a government cannot avoid such 'retrospective oversight': whatever it does or does not do, the adequacy of its response may be called into question – in terms of domestic British politics, it will provide a line of attack in Parliament if nothing else (Bagehot: 2007: pp. 182–183). However, it would be difficult to hold a government to account for not vigorously seeking a compromise – the asymmetries of knowledge about whether the potential for compromise existed will make it hard for the opposition to find a 'line of attack' in Parliament. In matters of foreign policy there is the 'paradox, of national foreign policy often requiring the frameworks of multilateralism' (Hill, 2003: p. 248), which means that the existence of an opportunity in foreign policy will often require the consent of other states. Having not been party to the negotiations, it will be difficult for an opposition to stir up a cause célèbre on the grounds that a better deal was there for the taking.

To place the questions of 'statecraft', the ECHR, and public accountability into the context of the goals that the electorate might want achieved, we can see the following:

a) *To be a member of the Convention on present terms.* This is plainly a decision that is open to be taken, and there are no asymmetries of information obscuring public understanding of that decision. Viewed realistically, the availability of this decision is not contingent on the consent of foreign governments, as that consent is an established fact.
b) *To be a member of the Convention subject to a theory of legitimate breach.* As this will change a multilateral framework, it is contingent on external agreement (Hill, 2003: p. 248). The availability of any theory of legitimate breach is subject to alien control by other Council of Europe states, and identifying the possibility of such agreement to reform the Convention will be substantially a matter of diplomatic method. Information as to whether any such possibilities are available will be both specialist and, most probably, secret.
c) *To be a member of the Convention but be allowed to breach the Convention in a particular case.* There is no formal change of the framework, but the same comments apply. How far the other parties to a multilateral

framework 'stand behind' the agreement – to use Sales's (2012: p. 262) words – will be identified by (in the first instance) diplomatic method and (ultimately) by experience.

d) *Not to be a member of the Convention.* We return to a simple constitutive choice, one that can be readily understood by the public as much as any issue can be.

If we look at two basic alternatives to simple acceptance or denunciation of the Convention:

i) *Do something, but stay within the Convention*: Legislators and electors prefer flexible membership, either 'b' or 'c', but the 'bottom line' (Popkin, 1995: pp. 19–20) is that membership must be retained. The other Council of Europe states may invigilate choices 'b' and 'c', forcing a retreat.

ii) *Renegotiate, if possible; leave if not*: Legislators and electors prefer flexible membership, and should that be unavailable would prefer 'd', non-membership. The other Council of Europe states may invigilate the availability of choices 'b' and 'c', but the fundamental constitutive choice of membership or denunciation would be undominated.

If the two commands of public opinion in response to an unpopular ECtHR decision are 'do something' but nevertheless 'stay within the Convention', asymmetries of information provide an excellent opportunity for ministers and legislators to reconcile the commands through simulation of action for the benefit of a public which should by definition (1) be willing to accept failure in terms of not achieving the particular policy goal, and (2) be unlikely to have the expertise or attention span to evaluate the quality of the failure. As Rispmann (2004/2005: p. 189) suggests, deceiving the public about diplomatic (i.e. secret) talks is fairly easy. If Knecht and Weatherford (2006: pp. 705–706, 719) are correct that public engagement in foreign policy is substantially responsive to the existence of a crisis, then there is no incentive for a government to engage public attention too greatly in attempts to renegotiate. It will be rational for government to manage diplomatic attempts to identify opportunities for greater flexibility so that any failure will pass underneath the radarscope of the public's limited attention in non-crisis foreign affairs, or to trumpet success if hitherto barely noticed discussions yield success. The worst case scenario is to behave as if the country had freedom to legislate incompatibly, and then (having gained public attention through a crisis) back down due to the overriding constitutive preference to be a member of the Convention.

Until a state engages in diplomacy, it has no way of judging whether options 'b' and 'c' (see above) exist, and even then ministers, legislators and administrators will not know until the time comes for the other Convention states to either stand behind the Convention or consent. It is unlikely that the ordinary citizen will often have the confidence to engage at such a nuanced level, as opposed to the grand constitutive decision of whether membership is a good or bad thing. We may see a clear link with the atrophication issues discussed earlier. The ability of the electorate to participate as regards the decisions of seeking flexibility within the Convention is hindered by an absence of information on which the electorate could deliberate. Even assuming that the electorate was sufficiently interested to consider departing from its usual 'information shortcut' (which we assume to be the presently constituted position of full Convention membership), a mixture of diplomatic obscurity and lack of precedent will make the risks forbiddingly difficult to evaluate.

Conclusion on internationalisation, accountability and constitutional conventions

It follows that Lord Irvine is right (and Sir Philip Sales wrong) as to whether judges should assume that compliance with ECtHR decisions will be necessary. It is a matter of 'statecraft' and for diplomatic professionals. Judges cannot know whether it is possible or not. Nor can politicians or diplomats know until after they have tried. And thus ordinary voters cannot hope to realistically know what the position is – and with that ignorance any accountability for unwanted ECHR compliance must fail outside of crisis situations. If the acceptance of a major crisis in international affairs is the price to pay for achieving 'suitably individualized, unconditioned and efficacious' popular control of rights issues (Pettit, 2012: p. 302, see also p. 279), there will be a very substantial hindrance to taking that step. The electorate has such control in terms of the constitution-making part of the dual-aspect theory of the democracy: it may demand continuation or denunciation of Convention membership. The availability of any choices in-between is, by virtue of the multilateral nature of the Convention, a matter of both diplomatic speculation and counter-control by the other contracting states.

Human rights decisions and the quality of deliberation

We saw in Chapter 7 ('Improved contestation') that the Human Rights Act may improve participation and focus deliberation where it highlights denials of rights that no one wishes to defend, such as *Blood and Tarbuck*. Plainly, as in the case of prisoner voting, constitutional review may bring issues into renewed public deliberation. However, a question arises as to whether the Act necessarily promotes *reasoned* deliberation. As seen in Chapter 3 ('Republican freedom vs republican participation'), the reason democratic decision-making does not dominate citizens is the potential to persuade fellow citizens: 'We can do that if a majority of my fellow citizens can be convinced'. If the Human Rights Act promoted reasoned deliberation, then that would improve democracy.

Jeremy Waldron (2006: pp. 1349, 1384–5) argued that constitutional review can reduce the quality of debate of relevant moral issues. He has since illustrated this complaint with the British Parliament's debates on prisoner voting rights, the one example where Parliament has debated in earnest non-compliance with the Human Rights Act (admittedly in respect of a requirement originating very much in Strasbourg). Waldron argues that the quality of Parliamentary deliberation on rights issues after the Human Rights Act, has been poor in comparison to 1960s debates on capital punishment, homosexuality and abortion (JCHR, 2011: Q.50):

> I go back and read those glorious debates and they show a Chamber that appears to recognise what it is like to debate issues of rights, to take a right seriously, to be profoundly aware of the interests that may be at stake and the interests that it is inappropriate to put in play against rights …

The same point is made by the JCHR (2013 [232]). Parliamentary debates have centred on of the relationship between the United Kingdom and Europe, not on prisoner voting itself (see also, Hiebert (2013: pp. 2272–2273)).

Admittedly, both Jeremy Waldron and the JCHR are firmly in favour of prisoner voting, and this may skew their view of what counts as reasoned debate. However, a review of House of Commons (HC Debate, 2011a; 2012) debates show that closer attention was given on both sides to the obligation to comply with ECHR decisions than the merits of the particular issue. In the 2011 debate sponsored by David Davis and Jack Straw, it is not until Dennis McShane MP speaks (39 minutes into the debate), that an argument based on penal policy is put, and even then he veers almost immediately into his views on the good work of the Convention and how compliance supports that work (HC Debate, 2011a: cols.507–509). Without a reasonably clear understanding as to when non-compliance may be considered legitimate, and such understanding being centred on the merits of the issues at hand, it is inevitable that debate will be similarly side-tracked. For those supporting compliance, it is difficult not to emphasise a strong presumption in favour of Convention compliance, and the same would apply if we were looking at a non-internationalised decision arising out of the Human Rights Act. For those opposing the measure, an argument against such a presumption will be a natural focus, being a hindrance that must be cleared before their preferred policy (whether a prisoner voting ban or otherwise) can be meaningfully considered.

The House of Lords debate on the legislative response to *Bellinger* and *Goodwin* did include a detailed consideration of the pros and cons of the issue of transsexual recognition, whether such issues be humanitarian, medical, religious, practical, or ethical (HL Debate, 2003b). As a debate, it was more like the debates on legalising abortion and recognition that

Waldron commended for consideration of the issues at hand (JCHR, 2011: Q.50). The oddity of the debate was that the outcome was not in dispute: even those who regretted the judicial decisions on transsexual recognition agreed that the legislation needed to pass. The House of Lords was free to debate the nature of gender without the shadow of challenging the authority of the Convention. Hence, the Bishop of Winchester cogently presented theological and philosophical reasons for the immutability of gender: and promptly admitted that the Bill must pass to comply with the human rights decisions (HL Debate, 2003b: col. 1301).

It must therefore be queried whether, absent a theory of legitimate breach, the Human Rights Act (or indeed the Convention that it implements) can promote genuine undominated (and meaningful) public and select group deliberation.

Conclusion

This chapter has seen that, in terms of Jennings's analysis of a constitutional convention, Parliament frequently complies with declarations of incompatibility from a sense of obligation rather than agreement with the decision (*F and Thompson* and *Belmarsh*). We have also seen cross-bench critics of legislative change accept that their objections are moot because of the Human Rights Act and ECHR decisions (*Bellinger* and *Goodwin*).

However, in terms of a reason for compliance, there is no legal duty of compliance with the Human Rights Act, although there may be a simultaneous international law obligation under the Convention itself. There have been many examples of ministers and supporters of the Human Rights Act talking as if there were a domestic rule of law requirement to comply with the Act, but this can be seen as misrepresenting the available choices to the electorate. What was highlighted in Christopher Crawford's (2013: pp. 63–69) analysis of *Belmarsh* was the sense of enormity attached to non-compliance. Chris Mullin MP recalled the Attorney General saying, 'It will be a big thing, if we don't accept the judgment' (Crawford, 2013: p. 66, citing Mullin, 2009: pp. 731–732); the 'big thing' being, in many commentators' eyes, a full-blown constitutional crisis. However, the reasons why there should be a United Kingdom constitutional crisis are unclear – unless non-compliance with the Human Rights Act is, notwithstanding the limits of that Act, to be taken as such a crisis, i.e. the 'prevailing political morality' is that the Act should exist, and this requires strict compliance (see the 'structural argument' in Chapter 7, 'Structural argument for duty of compliance with constitutional review').

In contrast, the international law obligations are real enough. As we saw in Chapter 6, a consequence of Parliamentary Sovereignty is that the government could not avoid accountability by reference to a lack of power. As Jennings (1938: pp. 154–157) recognised, international law provides a practical restriction to Parliamentary Sovereignty. Unless the electorate supports the constitutive decision to denounce the Convention, then options are limited by the need to act within the multilateral framework of the Convention: a necessary concomitant of trying to achieve an end through foreign policy (Hill, 2003: p. 248). The electorate's participation is also restricted through the asymmetries of information that necessarily arise in respect of foreign diplomacy.

Legislators have, notwithstanding the retention of Parliamentary Sovereignty, used the Human Rights Act and Convention membership as a shield against being accountable for passing legislation that might otherwise be unpopular. This is in tension with the 'elegant balance' hypothesis of the Human Rights Act reconciling rights protection and democracy. However, in respect of the ECHR itself, such an argument flows naturally from the current constitutive choice to be party to the Convention as presently understood. Even if statecraft might secure forgiveness for an occasional breach (e.g. because other Council of Europe countries are not really concerned about prisoner voting) it would not amount to a general freedom to exercise Parliamentary Sovereignty. Lord Irvine (2012: pp. 245–246) was correct to say that the courts should not assume a particular outcome to any compliance controversy at the level of the Council of Europe – but (correctly) he also did not suggest that statecraft could reliably counter-control the authority of ECtHR decisions.

9 Legitimate breach

Introduction

All systems of constitutional review are counter-majoritarian. As we saw in Chapter 5, it is the purpose of constitutional review to act as a force to restrain the majority within legislatures. In Chapter 6, we saw that Parliamentary Sovereignty meant that no government could avoid accountability by blaming a lack of domestic authority. In Chapter 7 we argued that the counter-majoritarian effect could be seen as applying primarily to restraining the opinions of legislators and administrators, given that the inclination of electors to bring their opinions to bear on specific issues is for most issues somewhere between negligible to non-existent. In Chapter 8 we considered the question of whether legislators have complied with Human Rights Act decisions from a sense of obligation and, if so, what obligation? In this lies a fundamental challenge for the 'elegant balance' hypothesis: if the Human Rights Act has reconciled rights protection and democracy, the ability of the electorate to participate so as to dominate legislative opinion must remain an 'I/we-can-do-that' matter in terms of Pettit's (2008: pp. 104–106) alien-control analysis. Insofar as creating a system of constitutional review may at times cause legislation to be directed by judicial rather than public opinion, the balance achieved by the Human Rights Act would indeed be elegant if the effectiveness of such judicial opinion is underpinned by 'political costs' traceable to undominated public opinion.

Ostensibly, the Human Rights Act offers to achieve two goals necessary to the reconciliation described above. Firstly, the Act has the capacity to be overridden but remain intact. Secondly, in the preservation of Parliamentary Sovereignty, the Act keeps in the hands of elected representatives the same power that existed in the classic constitution to address any issue with any legislative means. This makes possible electoral accountability for all choices by legislators as to the use or non-use of that power.

However, the above describes the position as a matter of form – and form is often insufficient to describe the relationships of accountability between institutions, and between institutions and the public. However much the Human Rights Act respects the form of Parliamentary Sovereignty, we must consider how it can operate compatibly with the substance of electoral accountability between legislators and electors (such as it is). Such a reconciliation must not just allow for the fundamental democratic assumption of 'if I can convince a majority of electors that X is right, then we-over-time can do X' that we set out in Chapter 3 ('Republican freedom vs republican participation'), it must allow for the Human Rights Act to be overridden and yet remain intact as a counter-majoritarian force. A reconciliation, for example, based on the right to simply repeal the Act would be no reconciliation at all. Such a reconciliation would represent an acceptance that the Human Rights Act could not coexist with the electorate exercising 'individualised, unconditioned nor efficacious' control on rights issues.

The same applies as regards internationalisation. A reconciliation between democracy and rights protection under the ECHR cannot be based on the possibility of denouncing the Convention. Nor can a reconciliation be based on the speculative possibility of forgivable breaches, as the availability of such breaches cannot derive from an undominated choice of a country's citizens, as the availability of any such choice is subject to the alien control of foreign countries. That is the inevitable result of involving national human rights protection with foreign affairs (Hill, 2003; p. 248). There is a constitutive choice to accept or reject such alien control in its entirety, but a constitutive choice to permit individual breaches or create a theory of breach must be taken on the *international level* – so, undominated choice in terms of ordinary legislative power at the national level (i.e. the constituted people) is by definition impossible.

It follows that our proposed reconciliation argument applies best insofar as Human Rights Act decisions are not internationalised – and there will be an increasing number of such choices as the courts move away from the 'mirror principle' in favour of more detailed national scrutiny of proportionality issues (*Nicklinson* [70]–[76]). Nevertheless, arguments on the limits of legitimacy of constitutional review have in particular been raised in respect of the Convention and ECtHR judgments such as *Hirst* and *Othman (Abu Qatada) v United Kingdom* (2012) 55 EHRR 1 (see also Bratza, 2014: pp. 123–124) – it will be useful to draw on these arguments and consider their application in the national context.

Legitimate breach

What we argue here is that a genuine rights/democracy reconciliation requires a theory of legitimate breach, i.e. a common understanding within public and select-group deliberation as to when it is appropriate to legislate contrary to the Act. Without such a common understanding (a) it will be difficult for politicians to know when the (electoral) political costs for non-compliance are real or just assumed, (b) politicians can easily and convincingly present compliance with constitutional review as a complete explanation for otherwise unpopular laws or policies, (c) the perceived approach of politicians may make the costs of participating for the purpose of achieving an incompatible law prohibitive (or at least appear to do so), and (d) the 'we-can-do-that' assumption necessary for undominated choice by the electorate may be either (i) reduced through 'manipulation', 'powerful rhetoric' and credible misinformation (Pettit, 2009: p. 41; 2008: p. 110),[1] such as to believe that non-compliance is improper, or (ii) de facto removed because non-compliance is inherently incompatible with the higher constitutive choice to retain the Act.

A precondition for the 'elegant balance' is that the atmosphere for further deliberation after a declaration of incompatibility should follow the approach of Baroness Hale in *Nicklinson* [300], where she stressed without rhetoric or rancour that 'Parliament is then free to cure that incompatibility … or to do nothing'.

In contrast, we find the retired Lord Lloyd (2006: p. 93) expressing his view after the *Belmarsh Case* that disobedience would, quite independent of the merits and demerits of the legislation at hand, lead to a major constitutional crisis. But Lord Lloyd did not say what sort of crisis it would be. Crawford (2013: p. 67) noted that it was an election year:

> One can only imagine the hysteria that would have occurred if the government had been seen to 'go against' the judgment of the highest court in the land. The Opposition would have likely had a field day with the issue.

That seems a little unlikely, given that the government faced a Conservative opposition led by Michael Howard. Were a crisis feared due to electoral issues, then the 'political costs' would be traceable to the electorate. But that would still leave questions as to whether the political costs were real or assumed, and whether the costs were issue-sensitive according to public opinion or applicable to any attempt to violate any constitutional review decision.

The importance of the approach taken by Baroness Hale in *Nicklinson* [300] is that it denies the existence of any constitutional crisis whenever there is serious consideration of non-compliance with a declaration of incompatibility. Deliberation on the issues involved, notwithstanding the declaration of incompatibility, would be more than just to consider how to comply. There would be reasoned arguments as to the merits of the measure viewed in their own right. In context, there would be no constitutional conflict between the judiciary and the executive should Parliament be asked to not to comply with a declaration of incompatibility. Instead, as Lord Scott said (*Belmarsh* [145]), the declaration of incompatibility 'provides, of course, ammunition to those who disapprove of the [relevant legislation] and desire

1 Chapter 3, 'The framework approach' and 'Three axioms and four theorems'.

to agitate for its amendment or repeal'. The Act stimulates a process, and there is no crisis when the result is continued incompatibility.

On Hale's approach in *Nicklinson*, there is no doom-laden talk of unspecified constitutional crises, but continued discussion on the merits of the issue. Out would go any 'powerful rhetoric' (Pettit, 2009: p. 41) that asks an elected Parliament not to act as the system for translating public opinion into legislative change, but instead to see itself as the conduit for judicial opinion arising out of constitutional review. And nor would such rhetoric tell the electorate to treat itself as if it had no opinions of its own – or at least none that it would act on as the constituted people influencing ordinary legislative decisions.

Approaches to legitimate breach

The basic problem we have is that the reconciliation of rights and democracy requires that a genuine freedom to pass incompatible actions should coexist with a commitment to the Human Rights Act. As we noted in the Chapter 7 ('Structural argument for duty of compliance with constitutional review'), if obedience to constitutional-review decisions is a citizen's general rule (i.e. his or her 'shortcut' to take a position on world events), they must either submit to all decisions, rebel entirely at some point, or form a view on when this general principle need not apply. Such a theory of non-compliance could most obviously take two forms: firstly, a theory based on the legitimacy of the constitutional-review adjudication concerned; and, secondly, a theory based on the legitimacy of overruling the results of constitutional review.

What we shall see is that attempts have focused on restricting the scope of counter-control so as to either limit the area of conflict (extreme decisions, legally illegitimate decisions), or blame the conflict on the court responsible (again, legally illegitimate decisions). Such approaches do not amount to a general theory of the public deliberation being able to invigilate all constitutional-review decisions. Quite notably, they assume that a restriction of present-day legislative freedom is uncontroversial if constitutional-review decisions can be attributed to the constitutive choices of those who enacted or created the bill of rights concerned. Obviously, a constitutive choice outranks an ordinary legislative choice, but uncritically maintaining such a system means treating past generations of citizens as superior arbiters of today's common good. Total deference to original meaning is as much a form of alien control as total deference to judicial interpretation.

'Illegitimate decisions' as ground for legitimate counter-control

Perhaps the most obvious argument in favour of a political overriding of a human rights decision is that which states the judges have gone beyond their legitimate power. This 'illegitimate decision' approach has arisen in the ECtHR context, but it can be readily translated into the national context, subject to issues as regards the appropriateness of margins of appreciation and deference given by international and national human rights courts.

Jack Straw, who as Home Secretary piloted the Human Rights Bill through the House of Commons, forcefully made the 'illegitimate decision' point when proposing that Parliament should not enfranchise prisoners as required by the ECtHR's *Hirst* decision (HC Debate, 2012: cc. 749–750):

> Does the Justice Secretary accept that on matters of fundamental human rights, the United Kingdom, under successive Governments, has been impeccable in observing the judgments of the Strasbourg Court, even – for example, in respect of terrorist suspects – when it has disagreed profoundly with those decisions? Long may that continue. Given that we are talking about the rule of law, does the Justice Secretary also accept that – in breach of ideas of the rule of law that are based on consent – the Strasbourg Court has extended its jurisdiction from fundamental human rights to social and civic rights, for which we have not signed up? As Lord Hoffmann, the former Law Lord, has said, the Court 'lacks constitutional legitimacy' in respect of such matters, and 'has no mandate to unify the laws of Europe' on subjects of this kind.

Seconding the motion from the Conservative back benches, David Davis argued (HC Debate, 2012: col. 750): 'Every time the European Court goes beyond the remit set by the treaty, to which we did sign up, Parliament will reserve the right to correct it and put things back into proper law[.]'

Placed in these terms the argument is essentially a backward looking argument insofar as it is rooted in the nature of the mandate given. To recall the much quoted 'democratic mandate' argument raised by Lord Bingham (*Belmarsh* [42]), the argument is placed firmly in the legal history of the constitutive decision to create the bill of rights, in this case to create the Convention. This is clear from Lord Hoffmann's (2009: [24]) Judicial Studies Board Lecture which was quoted by Jack Straw, above:

> The fact that the 10 original Member States of the Council of Europe subscribed to a statement of human rights in the same terms did not mean that they had agreed to uniformity of the application of those abstract rights in each of their countries, still less in the 47 states which now belong. … The Strasbourg court, on the other hand, has no mandate to unify the laws of Europe on the many subjects which may arguably touch upon human rights … The proposition that the Convention is a 'living instrument' is the banner under which the Strasbourg court has assumed power to legislate what they consider to be required by European public order.

The above translates broadly, but not exactly, into the context of the Human Rights Act. The question will arise as to whether the United Kingdom's

Supreme Court possesses a mandate to develop human rights jurisprudence into areas where the same decisions by Strasbourg would lack legitimacy. The question can be avoided as long as the United Kingdom's judiciary observed the 'mirror principle' that '[t]he duty of national courts is to keep pace with the Strasbourg jurisprudence as it evolves over time: no more, but certainly no less' (*Ullah* [20]). As long as the principal explanation for any Human Rights Act decision is that the United Kingdom courts have reflected Strasbourg case law, then any illegitimacy in the Strasbourg Court's decisions caused by unmandated activism will contaminate the United Kingdom courts that dutifully reflect such illegitimate decisions. But, equally, the force of internationalism will underpin compliance. In a purely domestic context, the same argument will apply, save that a national court may have a longer (but not infinite) rein when applying the Convention to national circumstances (Hoffmann, 2009: [14]; *Nicklinson* [74]). As Richard Bellamy (2011: p. 97) has pointed out, anchoring United Kingdom jurisprudence to that of Strasbourg 'creates a brake on [domestic] judicial activism'.

In terms of our analysis on the counter-majoritarian effect of constitutional review, the 'illegitimate decision' approach amounts to an assertion that the judicial approach to interpretation was beyond what could be supported by the scope of the text or any stated rules on interpretation. This, it is argued, releases countries from their ordinary sense of duty to respect the ECtHR decision.

Sir Nicholas Bratza (2014: pp. 123–124), the British judge in the ECtHR, linked this approach to a feeling that:

> [T]he Court has not only reached the limits of what can be regarded as legitimate treaty interpretation but has crossed the boundary and entered the forbidden territory of legal policy-making or at least has stretched the Convention rights beyond what the language of the instrument can support. The judgments in two cases against the United Kingdom – *Hirst*, concerning the right of serving prisoners to vote and *Abu Qatada [(2012) 55 E.H.R.R.]*, relating to the deportation of a militant Islamic cleric to Jordan – have led critics of the Court in this country to argue strongly that this has happened and that measures are necessary to reverse this trend.

It should be noted that Bratza did not accept that judicial overstretch would entitle Convention States to override ECtHR decisions. He was rather seeking to meet the argument as to legitimacy in its own terms.

Bratza's riposte raises the difficulty in the 'illegitimate decision' approach of Jack Straw and David Davis as to identifying judicial overreach in terms of legal adjudication (HC Debate, 2012: cc. 749–750), or that of Pinto-Duschinsky (2011: p. 72), who similarly argued that the European Court should set out clear rules on the margin of appreciation in order to identify 'core human rights'. Whilst *Abu Qatada* probably stretched the Convention beyond its natural meaning by requiring foreign governments to exercise an exclusionary rule in respect of evidence obtained through torture as a precondition to extradition, it is difficult to see how prisoner voting rights do not engage issues at the core of the right to vote (*Hirst*). The question in *Hirst* was one of justification, and one of the principle advantages that the Convention brings to the political process is precisely that it can expose laws and procedures which (even if not the weightiest human rights issues) lack any justification that the government or legislators can defend. In the view of the ECtHR majority in *Hirst*, the court did give the United Kingdom a broad margin of appreciation – but believed the law was still unjustified.

Furthermore, this 'illegitimate decision' approach is a very minimalist approach to when counter-control against constitutional-review adjudication is legitimate. It does not provide a theory of how to address a gap between the requirements of public opinion and judicial opinion, and which of them should guide legislation. Judicial decisions under the Human Rights Act/ECHR would be free from counter-control unless they went beyond the legitimate range of choices as to the Convention's scope and application that the wording of the Convention can support. This approach, as Bratza argued, would apply to very few ECtHR decisions, if any. Indeed, Jack Straw (HC Debate, 2012: cc. 749–750) expressly talked down the range of subjects where his arguments might support non-compliance by praising compliance with controversial ECtHR terrorism decisions.

Bratza's response demonstrates that the 'illegitimate interpretation' approach also fails from the point of view of equality of citizens in that it offers an approach to political accountability which is essentially legalistic. Bratza (2014: pp. 123–124) asserts an approach to interpretation that he believes to be correct in legal principle, and explains how the decisions in cases such as *Hirst* and *Abu Qatada* are wholly defensible within that approach. However, the complaint that citizens might make is not against judicial activism viewed in terms of jurisprudential theory, but rather that their range of participatory choices as citizens has been reduced by the judges' adjudicatory choices: there has been invasive interference by the process of constitutional-review adjudication. The judges choose a result, and the citizens are expected to restrict their participatory choices accordingly unless the decision by the most authoritative court can be comprehensively refuted as a matter of legal logic. The citizens, if engaged with the issues, may want to exercise counter-control if they disagree with the result as a matter of their own reasoning, not because they have found an error of law.

A similar disjuncture is found in Tom Southerden's (2014: pp. 257–259) comments on how the government argued differently on immigration issues arising from Article 8 of the Convention ('family life') depending on whether addressing the court or the public. Southerden argued that the courtroom arguments of government lawyers 'had become so distorted that they flatly contradicted Theresa May's response to a Parliamentary question on that very subject'. But the arguments required to win any case in court are constrained by legal precedent and an estimate of judicial behaviour (Cohen, 1935: pp. 845–846). There is an inherent problem in having to justify oneself, simultaneously, politically to the electorate and legally to the judiciary (Dyzenhaus, 2015: pp. 425–426). If questions of justification under the Human Rights Act are questions of law to be resolved by legal reasoning, then what is relevant to determine expert deliberation by the judiciary will differ (perhaps drastically) from what rises to the fore in public deliberation dealing with citizens' concerns for their own personal good – their own good being part of that common good. It is an inevitable result of requiring parties to speak the language of human rights jurisprudence, as they must do in court, that people do not necessarily say as litigants what they really think as citizens. This does not mean lying about facts, but what is highly relevant in the political forum may be irrelevant (or at least materially less relevant) in judicial reasoning and vice versa. As we saw in Chapter 3 ('Republican freedom vs republican participation'), if the terms of debate are restricted to what an elite analyses as reasonable, then the expression of the public's view of the common-good interests, *as translated* into a form acceptable to the elite, will part company from the public's actual opinions. One must often either be disingenuous before the elite, or stay silent as a citizen.

Southerden (2014: p. 260) argued that 'scare tactics, falsehoods and the knowing misrepresentation of the judiciary's position were used widely by ministers seeking to defend and promote their policy'. But there is a failure (by both Southerden and the ministers concerned) to recognise that elite deliberation and public/select-group deliberation are capable of reaching different results, correct in their own terms. The government was implicitly accepting that it is not sufficient in passing a particular immigration rule that select-group (i.e. ministers and legislators) opinion coincides with public deliberation – it must be further compatible with the Human Rights Act. The government could have employed Parliamentary Sovereignty to get its own way if it believed that Human Rights Act decisions harmed the ability of immigration law to promote the common good. Instead, the reality (not the form) of adjudication and legislation under the Human Rights Act seems to have meant that the government did not feel able to say that, whatever the legal merits of past decisions, the policy merits were different, and then go on to invoke Parliamentary Sovereignty on that basis. It was as if traducing the correctness and legitimacy of previous judicial decisions was a precondition to legislative action. Behind the 'dysfunctional dialogue' that Southerden describes, there was an unwillingness by the government to use Parliamentary Sovereignty in order to assert an unconditional dominance of public opinion.

The 'illegitimate decision' approach is essentially elitist. It does not ask the question that is properly addressed to the constituting people (i.e. is this the sort of decision that you wish to be taken by judges?), nor the one addressed to the constituted people (i.e. does this decision legally promote a law you wish to exist?) It asks a jurisprudential question as to whether the decision is supportable, which becomes a filter to being entitled to consider the legislative proposal on its overall merits.

Those arguing for a more domestic model of constitutional review have frequently implicitly bought into this elitism. The expectation is that British Courts will be more restrained – or at least more culturally appropriate in their interpretation and application of human rights (Hoffmann, 2009: [38]–[39]) – and thus the counter-majoritarian effect created by British judges is acceptable because they are an elite to which we can safely defer. At times, the same can be seen in reverse: the government sought elite validation from abroad when challenging the domestic courts' approach to Article 8 ('right to family life') in the context of immigration. The government legislated to redirect the British case law towards the ECtHR case law, where the margin of appreciation offered by that international court seemed to the government to be more favourable to its goals (Southerden, 2014: pp. 258–259). In other words, the British government implicitly looked to the Strasbourg elite for validation in its difficulties with the British judicial elite. However much the particular policy may be a response to public opinion, the link between public opinion and legislative action was contingent on, and limited by, the availability of *ostensible* elite validation.

To translate this into the terms of Pettit's alien-control analysis set out in Chapter 2, if a finding of judicial activism removed the duty to comply with a relevant decision holding choice-x to be incompatible, freedom of choice would then be restored. Assuming that the finding of judicial activism was uncontroversial, there would now be no political costs attached to taking choice-x. The problem is that reaching this position of restored freedom is itself encumbered by the need to establish that the judicial decision was itself improper – only then would the republican hypothesis of 'if I can convince a majority that choice-x is correct, then (over time) choice-x will be taken' be restored.

We may doubt the ability of the electorate to engage in issues of judicial activism – if we are to suppose that public opinion will only release the government from the political costs of non-compliance in cases where it has been demonstrated that the judiciary have overstepped their legitimate role. Dahl (2000: pp. 39–40) argued that citizens would only participate if they were able to 'possess some idea of plausible remedies and solutions'. The difficulty of making a finding of judicial activism a precondition of participation, with the object of overruling a decision, is that most citizens are ill-qualified to come to such a view, and will instinctively look to see what trusted experts make of the issue (Popkin, 1995: pp. 19–22); and the higher judiciary are precisely the people who citizens would naturally see as the experts on what the law means. It is difficult for the ordinary citizen to have confidence that judges are wrong in law. Criterion 29 of the democratic audit (Beetham, 1999: p. 167) asked whether electors were equipped to participate in political life – if aspects of political participation are translated into the legal question, 'are the highest judges wrong in their views of the law?', then most citizens will be ill-equipped. Doubtless, citizens may take sides in fundamental constitutive questions, such as the judicial restraint/dynamic interpretation gulf that opened up in American jurisprudence in the 1970s (Ely, 1991: pp. 842–854). However, such issues are constitutive questions going to the very existence of the system of the constitutional review in its present form. We are considering the 'elegant balance' hypothesis that the Human Rights Act reconciles rights protection and democracy, and, as we have argued, this requires (a) that the political costs for non-compliance with the Human Rights Act are imposed on politicians by electors, and (b) that *on particular issues* the same electors may have a 'highly ranked, intense, stable' preference for non-compliance (Dahl and Lindblom, 1953: p. 314). Doubtless some citizens are lawyers and would have the confidence to reach a firm view that *this time* the judges are wrong. Doubtless many citizens will have a selection bias towards a finding of judicial activism when the particular subject matter is dear to their hearts – although this is to collapse 'judicial activism' as a criterion for (and thus limit to) legislative override into the perceived merits of the law. Maybe, occasionally, there are decisions so wrong that an ordinary citizen will be able to appreciate it. But for average citizens, judicial activism is not something on which they can hold a rational view.

It follows that any workable theory of non-compliance ought to be political rather than legal in its nature. A legal test will threaten to make counter-control contingent on a supportive legal opinion, as well as carving out a broad area where counter-control is seen as unwarranted interference by public opinion with a legally appropriate decision. If a person must attack a decision of a competent court as being legally wrong en route to making a case for legislative counter-control, then it is liable to be thought 'undignified', as Lord Carlile described the Bishop of Winchester's critique of the ECtHR's decision in *Goodwin* (HL Debate, 2003b: col. 1301). There is thus a considerable hindrance to the freedom-of-choice hypothesis that is necessary for citizens to be free from domination in terms of 'individualised, unconditioned and efficacious' control of legislation.

We return to the *Nicklinson* point. The elegant balance requires overrule without rancour. It means that it is possible for any legislator or citizen to say: the courts have made their decision, and that is their role; we may consider how to respond, including whether to respond, and that is our role.

'Exceptional cases' as ground for legitimate counter-control

Legitimacy for statutory override need not be conditional on a finding of judicial overreach. There are suggestions in the literature of exceptional issues which may justify the legislature overriding judicial decisions without agonising about judicial activism. Commitment to Human Rights Act compliance may be challenged by stronger preferences.

In respect of when it might be realistic to overrule a judicial human rights decision, Jack Straw suggested that declarations of incompatibility that condemned abortion rights might be overridden, even though he believed that such a decision would be a legitimate interpretation of the Act (HC Debate, 1998c, col. 1301). Francesca Klug and Amy Williams (2012: [4.6]) mentioned the following as areas that Jack Straw could have added: 'advertising restrictions, gun controls and election expenditure limits'. This begs the question of whether there is a common theme in these examples, e.g. degree of certainty that the court was wrong, strength of policy disagreement, importance of the issue? We might say that these are matters of great public importance on which there has been a strong long-term, cross-party and public consensus.

This might be the start of a principle that Human Rights Act decisions are vulnerable if there is a consensus against the measure. Alternatively, the examples given by Straw, Klug and Williams could be taken as statements by leading proponents of the Act as to what issues might stretch their own loyalty too far. It is frequently said that proponents of constitutional review are those who expect to be pleased by its results. Ginsberg and Versteeg's (2013) conclusion that bills of rights are usually put forward to promote particular policy ends against the risks of electoral defeat. Morton and Knopff's (2000) 'court party' hypothesis was precisely that the strongest supporters of judicial power under the Canadian Charter were those who expected to gain politically from judicial interpretation. Hogg and Bushell (1997: pp. 77–78) noted that the American theorists who supported the judicial activism of the 1950s–70s were politically sympathetic to its results. If we conclude from this, to quote Costas Douzinas (2000: p. 95), that to some degree 'human rights is politics by other means' and 'a Bill of Rights [is] more than any party programme a political manifesto', then perhaps all Jack Straw, and Francesca Klug and Amy Williams were saying is that their strength of opposition to some outcomes under the Human Rights Act would be greater than their default position of supporting the Act's enforcement.

We might hypothesise two things: (1) as suggested above, that a strong consensus against a decision might lead to non-compliance by Parliament; and, (2) less principled, but perhaps quite practical, that Human Rights Act decisions will be vulnerable when its strongest supporters are disaffected. All of the issues raised by Straw, Klug and Williams are plausible candidates for issues where the electorate has 'highly ranked, intense, stable, and relatively broad preferences' (Dahl and Lindblom, 1953: p. 314). We return to a deceptively simplistic point: a strong preference for a particular policy might perhaps outweigh the usual preference for HRA compatibility. We say 'deceptively', as politicians will need to separate out short-term populism (for which the populace may punish them), and genuinely strongly held opinions. Also, as a theory of legitimate breach it is somewhat wanting – all it says is that if the public want it hard enough then it should happen, and that the rights/democracy balance will be set by the public's reluctance to think beyond a 'bottom line' attachment to Human Rights Act compliance. As a theory of legitimate breach, this 'only when important enough to be done' approach suffers from being somewhat circular and somewhat trite, and it fails to provide anything useful for deliberation.

We want something more than just citizens suggesting their personal candidates for issues where legislative override might be needed as a 'safety valve' to 'correct absurd situations' (Manfredi, 2001: p. 184). Ideally, we want an approach to legitimate breach that can help frame reasoned deliberation by citizens concerned for the common good – it is difficult to deliberate over strengths of feeling. This would help reassure those who support Convention compliance as a total or near-total rule that the decision is not a matter of a tyrannical majority, but a reasoned view on the common good.

Back to republican basics – the common good

A theory of 'legitimate breach' founded on co-reasoning may properly honour the citizens' right to be the dominant power in the state, whilst using constitutional review to promote rights protection. As explained in Chapter 4, public deliberation and select-group deliberation should be closely related, as politicians and ordinary citizens engage in a wide national debate. As we saw in Chapter 2 ('Deference and the scope of counter-majoritarianism'), any issues of importance would be subject to broad public debate before any set-piece Parliamentary deliberation (Laski, 1951: p. 31; *Chester* [132], [136]). Where the question of legislating incompatibly arises, the judicial decision will take the role of co-reasoning in that it will inform public deliberation, but it should be accepted that there is nothing illegitimate in any legislator or citizen trying to demonstrate to others that, insofar as such-and-such an issue of the common good arises, a judicial decision will not promote the common good.

We must return to the basics of republican theory: that the people are the best and supreme judges of their own common good. The nature of constitutional review under the Human Rights Act involves answering many questions of the common good as questions of law, and the presentation of the answers of those questions of law as if they were authoritative definitions of the common good such that the people should act upon them. If laws should be 'framed by every private man unto no other end (or they may think themselves) than to protect the liberty of everyman' (Skinner, 2008: p. 87, quoting Harrington, *Oceana*), and the citizen's participation in the making of the laws should be aimed at achieving the 'common good' (Sellers, 2003: p. 1), then a rule of compliance with constitutional review will invite citizens not to 'think themselves'; citizens would be invited to assume that the common good will be maximised by uncritically accepting that judicial findings will better promote the common good than anything that might be achieved by the citizens having a dominant invigilatory power over legislation.

Herein lies a central enigma with the proportionality test. To recite the factors in full (*Huang* [19], *Oakes* 139):

i) the legislative objective is sufficiently important to justify limiting a fundamental right;
ii) the measures designed to meet the legislative objective are rationally connected to it;
iii) the means used to impair the right or freedom are no more than is necessary to accomplish the objective;
iv) the need to balance the interests of society with those of individuals and groups.

It should be asked how, in applying these tests, does the artificial reasoning of law depart from the natural reasoning of ordinary legislators, ministers and electors? Doubtless, public decision makers will typically not structure their thinking formally in that way – and it will often be unnatural for them to force issues into such a structure, *Miss Behavin'* [13]. If we recall from Chapter 3 ('Republican freedom vs republican participation') our premise of non-domination in republican governmental theory, it is that a citizen can think rightly that, if they can convince a majority of their fellow citizens of a particular policy, they will 'over-time' get their way. Such a premise is dependent on an openness to argument. If we look at the proportionality criterion, we can see that any civically well-motivated citizens who are open to deliberation would change their minds if they came to believe that any of the proportionality factors were against a measure. It is fairly plain that if any decision maker (or citizen) believed that a measure affecting liberty was for an unimportant purpose, or failed to achieve the purpose, or could be done better, or was simply a sledgehammer to crack a nut, then they themselves would think that the measure was a bad idea.

In other words, if a finding of incompatibility is (as it overwhelmingly is) based on the proportionality of the statute, then opponents of the measure should be able to say a lot more against the law than simply that the judges found it incompatible. The reasons for the finding of incompatibility should themselves be a strong case against the statute. As the opposition may choose any line of attack against the government (Bagehot, 2007: pp. 182–183), a judicial finding of disproportionality should provide a compelling route to demonstrate the government's unreasonableness if it persists with a law that lacked a reasonable objective or could have been done in a less intrusive manner, etc. However, if the judges confine themselves to law not morality, as Sir John Laws (1998: p. 257) suggests, then the judicial reasoning will not provide an answer to moral concerns that may motivate citizens' participatory choices. The decision might challenge citizens to reconsider, or to ask themselves how firmly they desired an outcome, but it will not purport to tell citizens what is right or wrong.

If the questions decided by the court on matters of proportionality are, as Tony Baldry MP said following the *Belmarsh Case*, not a matter of 'ethical, moral or philosophical judgment', but 'legal judgment' (Crawford, 2013: p. 63; Nicol, 2006b: p. 722), then a public which asks essentially the same questions on its own ethical, moral, philosophical or (for that matter) political basis ought not to be surprised if it comes up with a different answer. Nor ought such an electorate to regard its conclusions as inferior to those of judges. As we saw in Chapter 2 ('Legislative-rights review'), Dyzenhaus (2015: pp. 425–426) is right that constitutional review simultaneously asks legislators to provide legal and political justifications, but the participatory choices of citizens need not depend on being satisfied that the legal justifications were correct. It may be that judges and other lawyers have an advantage in terms of appreciating how far moral questions can be solved by law, and when it is best not to try – what Lawrence Friedman (2009: p. 1164) describes as a better appreciation of 'structural variables' such as the difficulty in drawing lines in subjects like pornography regulation and prayer in state schools under the US First Amendment. But, in defining the common good, it does not follow that judicial opinion on the difficulty of reducing a policy aspiration to effective legal form should be determinative as to whether a legislative experiment should not be attempted to maximise the common good.

In asserting their views as to what they would like the law to become (i.e. legislative change), electors who wanted a Human Rights Act decision to be overruled would not be saying that the judges were wrong in law. Citizens should feel free to use their participatory rights to overrule judges because the judges had answered a legal question. Citizens will typically defer to judges as to what the law is, and could continue to do so. They would simply be asserting their superior and inalienable position to define their own, common good.

The common good within proportionality

We may see the above in one of the most controversial areas of human rights jurisprudence, that of immigration and Article 8 ('family life'). In 2007, the House of Lords held unanimously in *Huang* that those who have no entitlement to stay in the United Kingdom under the Immigration Rules could nevertheless argue denial of their family life as an overriding reason for being allowed to stay, above and beyond the way in which family life and depth of connection to the United Kingdom are factored into the Immigration Rules. The countervailing factors recognised by the Law Lords related to the rule-of-law considerations that rules should be predictable and enforced (*Huang*, [16]):

> There will, in almost any case, be certain general considerations to bear in mind: the general administrative desirability of applying known rules if a system of immigration control is to be workable, predictable, consistent and fair as between one applicant and another; the damage to good administration and effective control if a system is perceived by applicants internationally to be unduly porous, unpredictable or perfunctory; the

> need to discourage non-nationals admitted to the country temporarily from believing that they can commit serious crimes and yet be allowed to remain; the need to discourage fraud, deception and deliberate breaches of the law; and so on.

The resultant numbers allowed to stay under the principle would not of itself be relevant to the proportionality test, although the 'expectation' was that it would be 'a very small minority'. However, this expectation did not give rise to 'a legal test' (*Huang* [20]). Regularity in the application of the Immigration Rules was key to the strength of the justification for rejecting the Article 8 claims of family life to stay in the United Kingdom, and the extent to which the courts' approach created in practice an exception to the Immigration Rules (measured in hard numbers) was neither here nor there.

It might be thought that the effect on numbers is precisely the sort of area where legislators and citizens may feel that departing from judicial approach is not to violate the Convention itself, but rather taking a different view to the judges on justification issues under the Convention. They would be asserting the relevance of a factor that to many is not just relevant to the common good, but at the heart of immigration policy, whether one desires more or less, i.e.: numbers. The effect of a law is something that is intrinsically difficult for judges to opine upon; but the consequences of a law are an intrinsically valid concern, as Sir Stephen Sedley (1995: p. 392) accepted: 'There is nothing wrong with the argument that if this is the due result there is something wrong with the principles or the process that have produced it'.

It is an inherent flaw from a republican and democratic perspective in constitutional review that the good of the public is defined by an expert/expert group (i.e. the judges) and not by the public themselves. The result of not seeing the public's view of its own good as something separate from the legal questions arising for expert deliberation by judges promises the unseemly rancour that in 'Illegitimate decisions' in this chapter we saw Southerden (2014: pp. 256–260) chronicle.

A principal advantage of constitutional review is the independence of the judiciary (Kyritsis, 2012: p. 321), which is 'instrumentally valuable, in the sense that it delivers the requisite distance from the legislature and, thus, makes courts pro tanto better at reviewing it'. However, it must be questioned whether 'distance' is not a quality that works best when applied to objective rather than subjective factors. To give an example from *Belmarsh*:[2] it is objectively undeniable that detention without trial is as draconian for non-citizens as for citizens (*Belmarsh* [83]), and likewise objectively irrefutable that nationality is no guide to the threat a terrorist poses ([32]).

2 Noting that in *Belmarsh* there was a higher than usual hurdle of justification in that the relevant Article 15 of the Convention required the measure to be 'strictly required by the exigencies of the situation'.

However, factors such as the threat to 'community cohesion' that the government saw in interning citizens ([64]) are inherently subjective. It is subjective in terms of evaluating a risk which is inherently qualitative; and, even were the risk capable of quantitative analysis, the willingness to take a particular type of risk may itself be subjective (Sunstein, 2005: p. 39). However much the detachment of the judiciary may persuade citizens that it is appropriate to establish constitutional review in order to put into effect a shortcut favouring judges over politicians in issues of important freedoms, it does not follow that citizens should defer to judges on such subjective issues. Whether 'distance' means standing above 'phrensies' of public opinion, or an elite complacently underestimating problems (Burke, 1808: pp. 287–288; cited Dicey, 1982: p. 35), or any step in-between, is not something for which there is a general rule. Even if the starting point is that a rights-sensitive subjective judgment of a judge is likely to be superior to that of politicians, it is nevertheless the case that citizens, as both the ultimate arbiters of the common good and as the people whose 'good' comprises the 'common good', may conclude that the politicians are right in particular cases and freely exercise their participatory rights accordingly. Of course, citizens might well conclude, as Lord Falconer did after the *Bemarsh* decision, that the judges had the better arguments (quoted, Butler and James, 2005).[3] The point is that citizens' ultimate participatory choices should flow from their opinion of the common good, not the deference shown by Tony Blair (2010: p. 575, cited Crawford, 2013: p. 66) in saying: 'Once the House of Lords made the ruling, we had to amend the law'.

Weighting a balance

In its submission on a British Bill of Rights, Liberty (2011: [124]) argued that the Home Office was wrong to suggest that Article 8 jurisprudence failed to 'reflect a balance between Article 8 rights and the wider public interest in controlling immigration'. Balancing those concerns, Liberty argued, was precisely what the court did: the balance is a careful one and all relevant factors must be taken into consideration. To say that Article 8 is a qualified right was 'a restatement of the bleeding obvious', as Southerden (2014: pp. 259–260) quoted Peter Wishart MP.

However, the same criticisms as regards 'numbers' applies here. Saying that the courts strike a balance does not exclude the possibility of the electorate wishing that a different balance be struck. For example, a quite different balance is struck in respect of the public interest in removing people for extradition as opposed to deportation in the context of immigration control, as held in *HH v Deputy Prosecutor of Genoa* [2012] UKSC 25; [2013] 1 AC 338 [28]:

3 Chapter 8, 'The Belmarsh case'.

> 'Expulsion and deportation are matters only of domestic policy' (para 62), in which 'the striking of reasonable balances is an inherent feature of the policy itself' (para 63); whereas 'extradition promotes a universal public benefit (para 62), which is 'systematically served by the extradition's being carried into effect' (para 63). An even stronger view was taken by Silber J ... when he stated that 'It is clear that the approach of the courts to Article 8 rights has to be ***radically different*** in extradition cases ... because of the very important obligation of the state to ensure that those who are to be investigated, prosecuted or imprisoned for criminal offences are returned to those countries' (emphasis added).
>
> [Emphasis in original]

In extradition there is a 'categorical assumption about the importance of extradition in general' (*Norris v United States* (No. 2) [2010] UKSC 9; [2010] 2 AC 487 [55]) but this is absent in immigration. It is clear why on legal reasoning a court would make the distinction. It is harder to see why legislators and the public could not assert in particular places in particular circumstances that they believed that immigration control was of comparable importance.

It is doubtless correct that extradition between civilised, law-abiding states is an important common good (Scott Baker, 2011: [2.3]). We do not desist from trying suspects because to do so will cause hardship without the guarantee that they are guilty, so why should it be very much different because the trial – like at least an element of the crime, normally speaking – were abroad? Such powerful arguments do not apply in immigration, where humanitarian and hardship considerations will naturally go to the issue of whether someone should be allowed to settle or not. However, it does not follow that citizens should respect judicial estimates of the common good as regards the imperatives in respect of immigration or any other area of public policy – any more than they should have respected the courts' approach to the imperatives of freedom of contract that Laski (1951: pp. 44–45) and Griffiths (1997: pp. 63–84) deplored. The imperatives for extradition are at a constant high and readily explicable from a legal point of view, as they go directly to the questions of legality, i.e. the congruence between law and its enforcement. But the imperatives of immigration control rise and fall. From a rule-of-law perspective, immigration rules may typically allow for flexibility and discretion. But from a common-good perspective, flexibility may at different times and in different places be highly welcome or gravely suspect. Andrew Le Sueur (2011: pp. 3–4), for example, argued that the application of the proportionality test in immigration may tighten where local circumstances demand tighter control (in his example, the context of migration into the small island of Jersey).

We have been examining the fourth limb of the proportionality test, i.e. the need to balance the interests of society with those of individuals and groups. In any matter where the court decides that a law or rule represented a sledgehammer to crack a nut (*Aguilar Quila* [58]), it must be open for legislators and electors alike to say that the judges have underestimated the nature of the nut and the magnitude of its effect on public interest.

Conclusion on the common good and proportionality

What we have seen as regards proportionality is that findings of incompatibility will turn on issues for which there is no reason why electors should feel incapable of engaging their reason and coming to a different conclusion than the judges on pivotal issues. If this right is not absolute, then the question of whether to apply the right or not is one of definition of the public interest, i.e. the weight put to the popular conception of that interest, and the willingness to risk putative 'less-drastic means'. Remembering that the state ought to track the people's view of their own interests (Pettit, 1997: p. 56) and that the people cannot but be dominated if they do not communicate their interests (Maynor, 2003: p. 115), citizens must be willing to assert their own views of the particular issues that comprise the calculation of the public interest. If Parliament uncritically translates constitutional-review decisions into legislative change, the consequential and inevitable acceptance of the results of the proportionality test as applied by the judges would mean that the judiciary's conception of common good would be tracked instead of that of the citizens.

As qualified rights are not absolute rights, their infringement is an accepted part of the Human Rights Act's structure. When considering the overturning of proportionality decisions, the question is one of allegiance to process and whether judicial decisions as to the application of the Human Rights Act should be uncritically accepted. Such an acceptance would be the acceptance of domination. It is to say, 'What he wills tomorrow, I too shall will', (Rousseau, 1988: p. 32). With uncritical acceptance, there would be no invigilation of the process where the citizens may exercise power as equals; judicial power would be institutionally hegemonic in that it ought to survive any foreseeable attempts by the electorate to exercise their participatory rights. This is something that can only be done if we suppose that the decision makers concerned (i.e. the judiciary) should have a superior role, such that the body of citizens should not have individualised, unconditioned, nor efficacious control over the relevant issues. This may be the case in a highly divided society, where different groups of citizens do not trust other groups with certain decisions – a clear-cut example being Canada's original constitution, and the protection for minority denominational schools (Greene, 1989: p. 15). Otherwise, such deference represents a belief in the superiority of decision makers (judicial or otherwise) that must fail Petit's eyeball test for equality between citizens (Pettit, 2012: pp. 84–87; Maynor, 2003: pp. 45–46).

We thus come full circle: either electors may think, 'we-over-time can do that if a majority of fellow citizens agree', or they cannot. If the reason for not being able to think that is because the electors accept a duty by reason of a judicial decision *not* to bring their opinions into public deliberation and voting decisions, then one of these applies:

a) The citizens are accepting the judge as a superior reasoner by virtue of office;
b) There is a lack of belief in the good faith of a portion of citizens within a materially divided society;
c) If the decision is attributable to the wording of the bill of rights rather than judicial interpretation, then the citizens who acted as the constitutive power when enacting the bill of rights are seen as superior judges of today's common good than today's citizens;
d) Allegiance to the constitutional-review process is seen as coming first for the greater common good.

Whichever is the case, popular control is subject to domination by virtue that legislators will have an almost irrebuttable presumption against responding to Human Rights Act – incompatible public opinion on particular issues (however broad and stable such opinion might be), and the public would have accepted that there should be no accountability for legislators conducting themselves thus. This may be a sensible use of the constitutive power – but it cannot represent a reconciliation of rights and democracy at the ordinary legislative level that the Human Rights Act was said to achieve.

By centring our theory of 'legitimate breach' on a deliberative process to answer issues raised in constitutional review that overlap with the 'common good', the objectivity of the judicial decision remains instrumentally valuable (Kyritsis, 2012: p. 321). It is just that the judiciary are an instrument for framing public deliberation, not for restraining it.

One final point must be made as to the judicial role in 'nurturing a polity-wide constitutional dialogue' (Hilbink, 2008: p. 234). Judges will not nurture the dialogue if they engage in what Lord Hoffmann (2002: [8]) described as the 'the usual polemical style which judges feel it necessary to adopt in order to persuade their colleagues and the public that no other answer is possible'. In making human rights decisions on proportionality, judges will often be required to rule on issues of the common good, such as the application of the precautionary principle (*F and Thompson* [56]). Deliberation throughout the polity will be nurtured by acknowledging, rather than glossing with rhetoric, the essential subjectivity of such issues. In constitutional review, judges must make legal rulings as to the nature of the common good, but they can nurture deliberation by acknowledging in their judgments that there are counter-arguments that could legitimately be considered should the subject matter of the decision be taken up into public deliberation. For example, Lord Wilson's contention that 'a court will be of maximum assistance to Parliament in this regard if it not only identifies the factors which precipitate the infringement but articulates options for its elimination' is instructive (*Nicklinson* [204]). Such an approach will not just serve as a discipline to the judiciary not to overstep the limits of adjudication, but will allow legislators and citizens to better identify whether they should or should not accept the results of constitutional review as a matter of elite or expert authority.

The common good and absolute rights

The argument set out above as to 'legitimate breach' is simplest to apply as above within the structure of the proportionality test. But what about non-derogable rights such as the freedom from torture or degrading treatment under Article 3 of the Convention? It is not possible to adequately explore such a difficult and emotive issue here, but a few thoughts will be given.

The application of the Human Rights Act and the Convention may often test 'our commitment to a procedure' against 'our moral objections to the substance of [a] particular decision' (Kyritsis, 2012: p. 301). A decision to disapply Article 3 is indisputably a constitutive choice. It would change the nature of Article 3, which is incorporated as an absolute standard by the Human Rights Act. However, section 4 of the Act admits of the possibility of this being done, but clearly signals the nature of the decision.

The nature of the Human Rights Act therefore allows the commitment to Article 3 to be continually retaken, at least if the nature of that commitment is understood as nothing more than a particularly firm view as to where the common good lies. Such a commitment, entered into freely and with proper information, will represent an ongoing constitutive choice. The availability of the choice to remake the decision prevents the issues lapsing into dogma.

Conclusion

We have seen that compliance with the Human Rights Act may meet Jennings's criteria for a constitutional convention insofar as they are either underpinned by ultimate questions of legality (Dicey (2008: pp. 296–300), or by the 'prevailing political philosophy' (Jennings, 1938: p. 131). However, compliance with the Act is only supported by questions of legality insofar as the decisions are internationalised by concurrent ECHR obligations – which will normally be the case, but increasingly decisions will be attributable to the independent approach of the United Kingdom courts. As regards the 'prevailing political philosophy', it may be the case that the commitment to the Human Rights Act necessarily means a commitment to compliance with the Act, the 'structural argument', particularly when a lack of data on the consequences of non-compliance inhibits decision-making. But this structural argument asserts a position quite different to that expressly set out in the Act, and that explained by those behind the Act when the constitutive decision was taken to enact a system of weak-form constitutional review in the United Kingdom.

The reasons for compliance fail to set out any theory by which the electorate can consider whether non-compliance with the Act should lead to political (electoral) costs being exacted on the responsible legislators. Insofar as the internationalisation and structural arguments for compliance apply, they logically purport to be absolute. There is no decision to be made: non-compliance should always lead to heavy political costs. In the case of internationalisation, such costs will include costs exacted by international rather than electoral opinion, assuming that other Council of Europe states demand compliance with the Convention.

What we have argued in this chapter is that a theory of non-compliance cannot be based on the legitimacy of the court's decision as a matter of legal reasoning – the approach raised in the House of Commons 'prisoner voting' debates (HC Debate, 2012: cc. 749–750). Such an approach would both be of very restrictive scope, as Judge Bratza (2014: pp. 123–124) has demonstrated, and the legal questions involved would be hard to process in meaningful public deliberation. Similarly, we are looking for more than intuitive assertions that particular issues might fall into the category of exceptional cases, e.g. abortion, advertising restrictions, gun controls and election expenditure limits (HC Debate, 1998c, col. 1301; Klug and Williams 2012: [4.6]). Such lists amount to unstructured special pleading. If the Act both guards against majority tyranny and respects democracy, then we should look for how it can promote deliberation, particularly when citizens consider overruling the Act.

What we have suggested instead is that a theory of 'legitimate breach' should focus on the issues of the common good that are represented in judicial decisions. The elements of the judicial proportionality test map precisely onto issues that will be determinative of ordinary, non-legal reasoning. No one will support a measure if it has no legitimate aim, is not rationally connected to that aim, goes further than is necessary, or is simply a sledgehammer to crack a nut. Demonstrating the legitimacy of legislative overrule should be structured so as to address how the judicial reasoning departs from citizens' own conception of their own common good – something that citizens are inherently the ultimate arbiters.

This 'common good' approach must be acknowledged at the constitutive level, albeit, like the 'republican government' clause of the US constitution, injusticiable.

This approach should avoid the creation of a 'court party' that seeks to maximise judicial power for political gain (Morton and Knopff, 2000). Although much could still be gained from litigation in terms of challenging the government to justify laws – the results of constitutional review will be determinative unless genuine controversy arose in public deliberation. However, gaps between public and judicial opinion could never open up too far without legislative correction. A theory of non-compliance rooted in public opinion and public engagement would create a check on the extent to which it was possible to win important rights-related legislative change through victory in court. A theory of legitimate breach would serve to remove the 'structural argument' from the field of ordinary legislative decisions to that of constitutive choice.

10 Conclusions

Introduction

The final chapter will set out the conclusions from the arguments made so far. The conclusions, like the book, are addressed in particular to the Human Rights Act as existing at the time of writing. However, whatever happens in respect of the Act in the future by reason of the present 'British Bill of Rights' debate, the points are of general application to any system of 'weak-form' constitutional review. Unless the United Kingdom was to change the Human Rights Act for constitutionally entrenched constitutional review enforceable against primary legislation, the central argument as to viewing the availability of legislative override from the perspective of actual popular participation will remain. A British Bill of Rights will not change the reality that in the British Constitution, as with representative democracies in general, the electorate are marginally engaged on most issues but expect clear, stable, majority public opinions to prevail on matters of sufficient importance to affect voting intentions.

The first conclusion is that upholding Parliamentary Sovereignty is not determinative of upholding democracy. Democracy is not achieved by formal constitutional provisions but to a greater or lesser extent may be achieved by participation within that structure.[1] If the elegant balance between rights and protection and democracy is to be achieved by the Human Rights Act, it will be because compliance with the Act is a choice to be taken by Parliament in every legislative decision following a judicial decision under the Act. What separates closed hegemony from polyarchy is the ability of ordinary citizens to participate as equals and displace the usual advantage of elites – such participation being as of right, and the exercise of which requires no justification to a higher power.[2] Whatever the formal structures permitting popular participation, the reality is that there will always be greater practical participation for those with the 'time' or 'learned capacity' to become closely

1 Chapter 4 'Polyarchy' and 'The democratic audit'.
2 Chapters 3 'Republican freedom vs republican participation' and 4 'Polyarchy'.

involved.[3] Nevertheless, a polyarchy will have the potential for all laws to be subject to control by a process where all citizens are equal – a potential which is no less valued by citizens for being largely ignored by most citizens most of the time.[4] Such a process will be 'individualised, unconditioned and effective' in that citizens can dominate any area of law and legislation through their participatory choices and demands.[5]

The concept of the 'elegant balance' rests on the concept of legitimate breach of the Human Rights Act within the ongoing structure of the Act. This is to say, popular participation must be capable of dominating the making of legislation, even if this means controlling the results required by constitutional review under the Act. The British Constitution in matters affected by the Human Rights Act will only constitute a polyarchy, and thus be capable of operating democratically, if electors who choose to participate so as to support a non-compliant measure are not thwarted by one of: (a) the concept that others, namely judges, are 'uniquely fitted' to resolve issues relating to human rights,[6] (b) the belief that it is impossible for a citizen to choose an incompatible law within a constitution where the Human Rights Act has constitutional significance, or (c) the choice is incompatible with international obligations under the Convention. In the first case, the electorate accept the common argument that judges are better in rights issues than politicians and voters. In the second case, the electorate accept that they cannot both have the benefit of the rights protection pact represented by the Human Rights Act *and* use the formally open route to participate to promote non-compliance with the Act on specific issues. In the third case, freedom of choice cannot be restored by action solely within the domestic legal order, but requires either a repudiation or fundamental reconstitution of the Convention.

Participation, of course, is not something that can be legislated for, being the choices of participants in the political system from citizens to ministers. However, it will be clear that there needs to be a clear and common understanding as to what is or is not legitimate participation. The debates on a British Bill of Rights, whether or not leading to such a drastic reform, will be an opportunity to establish such clear understandings. This will not be an easy matter, as it will ultimately depend on how much the electorate want constitutional review to restrain politicians, a sentiment without which constitutional review would turn into a mere expert report. But without such a sentiment, constitutional review is surely built on sand, and rather undemocratic sand at that.

3 Chapters 3 'Republican freedom vs republican participation' and 4 'Expert deliberation'.
4 Chapter 4 'Polyarchy'.
5 Chapter 4 'The basics of democracy' and 'Dual-aspect nature of democracy'.
6 Chapter 4 'Select-group deliberation' above, in particular *Belmarsh* [39], [178], *RJR-MacDonald* [68]), and Clayton (2001: pp. 523–524; 2002: pp. 189–190), see also Chapter 4 ('The democratic audit') and in particular Beetham (1999: p. 9).

Enhancing quality of deliberation

The Human Rights Act should be applauded for (a) improving routes for contestation stimulating legislative remedies for injustices that might go without legislative solutions for want of Parliamentary time,[7] and (b) creating controversies around matters which have become accepted without significant continuing debate, such as prisoner voting.

However, we have seen that where constitutional review has stimulated controversy, such as in prisoner voting, it has not necessarily stimulated quality debate on the issue of prisoner voting. Absent a theory of legitimate breach, the debate stimulated by the Act and the Convention has focused on constitutional issues to the detriment of deliberation on the actual rights and wrongs of the issue at hand.[8]

Internationalisation

There is no complete solution within the Human Rights Act to the counter-majoritarian effect arising out of the ECHR, which sees the domestic requirements internationalised. The Human Rights Act implements 'Convention rights'. Any severance of that link is not a reform of the Act or a rebalancing of the Act, but the creation of a whole new system.

A possibility that may arise out of proposals for a 'British Bill of Rights' is to retain British membership of the Convention as a matter of international obligations, but to sever the domestic law link between UK constitutional review and the Convention. This would make it less clear if Convention-compliance was a reason for domestic human rights compliance. That would weaken the tendency of compliance with domestic human rights legislation to become a constitutional convention by withdrawing the only identifiable *legal* reason for legislators to feel an obligation to comply with judicial decisions.[9] However, it would also prevent the case law of the European Court acting as a restraint of and critique of domestic decisions, particularly insofar as the ECtHR has offered a culturally sensitive margin of appreciation. For example, were the United Kingdom Supreme Court to rule that the Human Rights Act requires the law to permit assisted suicide, but the ECtHR were to maintain the opposite position, then the authority of the UK Supreme Court would be somewhat weakened. It would not mean that the UK Supreme Court was wrong, it could justifiably say that as a domestic court it need not show the same broad margin of discretion as the Strasbourg Court must,[10] but opponents could identify grounds for non-compliance with

7 Chapter 6 'Behaviour within the constitution' and Chapter 7 'Improved contestation'.
8 Chapter 8 'Human rights decisions and the quality of deliberation'.
9 Chapter 8 'Legal obligation to comply'.
10 Chapter 7 'Structure of the Act' Chapter 8 'International legality' and Bellamy (2011: p. 97).

domestic decisions without undermining the Human Rights Act's core role of bringing Convention Rights home.

For this reason, where internationalisation is seen to overlap with Human Rights Act decisions, internationalisation will provide a reason underpinning a constitutional convention in favour of compliance; but it may also provide an argument to depart from decisions when the UK courts engage in a more intrusive approach to justification issues.

Lord Hoffmann (2009: [24]) argued that the ECtHR lacked legitimacy to develop the Convention as a 'living instrument', at least in the same way a national court had it.[11] The counter-intuitive result of creating a British Bill of Rights may be to increase the practical counter-majoritarian effect by increasing judicial activism due to losing the anchor of Strasbourg jurisprudence. Whereas the ECtHR is frequently (although not always) constrained by a sense of the limitations of an international court making law for the Council of Europe's 47 contracting states, British judges might feel a legitimate right to be activist.

Confronting the constitutive choice

As explained in Pettit's dual-aspect theory, there are two republican ways in which compliance with a system of constitutional review can be the steady rule: firstly, by a decision of the constituting people (i.e. the electorate as constituting power) that compliance should be a constitutional rule and secondly, by a pattern of participation by the constituted people (i.e. the people as exercising power through the constitution as constituted) which, whenever a particular question of compliance arises, favours compliance. The former represents the choice of the people as to how they should be governed; the latter, represents a choice as to how the people exercise self-government within the chosen system. Constitutionally, once the system is established, the former argument operates as a 'top-down' approach, where a governing document by way of (judicial) expert deliberation sets the rules on what can be achieved by way of (legislative) select group and popular participation; the latter is a 'bottom-up' approach, where at any point in time it is the opinion of electors that underpins compliance. The sovereignty of a constitution which is not freely open to change may start as a statement of popular sovereignty, but thereafter power may vest in the elite that interprets the constitution.

If compliance comes through popular participatory choices, then compliance is like the putative pre-1940 US constitutional convention against a President standing for a third term:[12] there is a question as to whether such a step is wise, but it is for public opinion to decide whether to accept a change from the usual practice.

11 Chapter 9 'Illegitimate decisions'.
12 Chapter 8 'Atrophication and constitutional review' and Dyer (1943).

If the argument in favour of compliance rests on the importance of maintaining the reliability of the Human Rights Act (or any future British Bill of Rights) as a rights protection pact ('the structural argument'), then the electorate should consider defining or restating the constitutional position. In a representative democracy, popular control is mediated through elected representatives. Such representatives are subject to the inhibitory control of the electorate in terms of supporting legislation during their term of office, and in terms of what policies they feel can be offered to the electorate.[13] If established parties and their elites are inhibited from violating the Act by a general assumption that non-compliance will lead to the electorate exacting political costs, even if the non-compliant law appeared popular, then such a belief will make politicians reluctant to take seriously calls for non-compliant legislation. Politicians come to make assumptions as to the popularity of particular policies and their salience in voting intentions; and those assumptions may mean that the inhibitions that ordinarily restrain politicians from enacting non-compliant legislation may arise even when public opinion has settled in the opposite direction. Politicians may act on such assumptions for want of information assuring them that such wisdom does not apply in a particular case. Furthermore, the electorate may come to believe that politicians invariably treat non-compliance as illegitimate, in which case the participation costs of campaigning for non-compliant measures are increased, with the prospects of reward reduced. Cartelisation of politics may result, with non-compliant choices never offered by established parties and the entry costs for new parties appearing prohibitive.

Inhibitory control requires a common understanding between electorate and politicians.[14] Without that, in the human rights context, a strong public opinion in favour of non-compliance might be viewed as precisely the 'phrensy'[15] of public opinion that the Human Rights Act was created to control. Absent a clear constitutive decision as to the 'rules of the game', the question of what the electorate require from their representatives, and what the representatives believe is required from them, will be obscured; and with that obscurity, accountability becomes difficult.

If the choice to comply with the Human Rights Act appears to atrophy into a constitutional rule for compliance, then we have the problem noted in Chapter 8 that the reason for treating compliance as obligatory is unclear. It is possible to follow the example of the Government of Ontario in 1999, which named an Act so as to attribute responsibility of it purely to the courts, and then boycotted the relevant debate so as not to take responsibility for compliance.[16] The ability for elected representatives to plausibly represent to

13 Chapter 4 'Schumpeterian democracy critiqued'.

14 Chapter 3 'The framework approach' and 'The axioms' (second axiom), Chapter 9 'Legitimate breach'.

15 Chapter 4 'Schumpeterian democracy critiqued', quotation from Burke.

16 Chapter 5 'The linking of issues'.

their own electorates that a law is someone else's responsibility is inimical to the 'come-at-ability' that is at the heart of responsibility of Parliament to electors for legislation. There is an absence of information to judge consequences of non-compliance, which is particularly difficult for accountability when the risks (e.g. in international affairs) are considerable.[17]

The common good

Republican political theory requires that a state should track the worldview of the public itself. To apply this to constitutional review, the electorate should not participate so as to cause the worldview of the judiciary to be tracked instead.

Citizens should, in particular, not feel constrained from disagreeing with judicial decisions when those decisions address the common good. As was shown in Chapter 9 ('Back to republican basics'), the questions that a court must answer in respect of the proportionality test are perfectly capable of being answered by ordinary citizens as a matter of natural reasoning – the difference is that the answer given by constitutional review will derive from expert deliberation and be affected by principles of legal reasoning, most notably adherence to case-law precedent.

It is common in the literature for issues of the proper role of the judiciary under constitutional review to be addressed by way of 'judicial deference'. This is to say, the more willing the judiciary are to make a ruling on whether a law is proportionate, the further judicial power is taken into the field of legislation. The more restrained the judiciary are, the more democracy is upheld, is the theory.[18] The correct republican view is that where any group or body has the power to exercise alien control, it does not cease to dominate through self-restraint. It is only if the potentially dominating agent is subject to a 'disabling effect' under the control of the potentially dominated party (i.e. a power of counter-control) that domination is removed.[19] As we concluded in 'Confronting the constitutive decision' above, in a 'bottom-up' approach to determining the effect of constitutional review on legislative change, it is the participatory choices of the electorate that ought to be determinative.

These choices should be based on the electorate's views of the issue and not mediated through a filter of the legal rights and wrongs of the constitutional-review decision. Any view that the possibility of overriding constitutional review decisions is a 'safety valve', as Jean Chretien described

17 Chapter 8 'Internationalisation, statecraft and accountability' and 'Conclusion on internationalisation'.

18 Chapter 2 'Deference and the scope of counter-majoritarianism', Chapter 7 'Reconciliation and judicial deference'.

19 Chapter 3 'Republicanism and domination', 'The axioms' (third axiom), Chapter 7 'Reconciliation and judicial deference'.

the notwithstanding clause procedure for overriding judicial decisions under the Canadian Charter,[20] erects a hurdle of certainty and importance. The question should be one of whether the electors rouse themselves to form opinions and participate in opposition to a constitutional-review decision to assert their view of the common good. We may expect such cases to be rare, but the expectation of infrequency creates no rule as to how often this may happen.

To this end, citizens will be best placed to choose to press their own views on issues of the common good if judicial decisions admit the extent to which the answers derive from choices that can reasonably be taken differently. We noted earlier Lord Hoffmann's (2002: [8]) comment that judges in the highest court typically employ 'the usual polemic' to present the view that only one answer is possible, when the case could have decided in either direction.[21] We have seen that 'powerful rhetoric' may be used to reduce choice by misrepresenting the position.[22] This is the case when a publically respected and ostensibly objective arbiter such a judge presents a matter as obvious, when in fact the matter was either not obvious or the judge's firmness of conclusion was based on subjective factors.[23] This is clearest where judicial decisions are based on one or more of the elements of the proportionality test, which includes such issues as the efficacy of a measure, the possibility of alternatives, the relative importance of the goal sought and the harm done by the measure. In this, we must part company with Danny Nicol's dictum that the courts should act 'as ideological partisans who will lay down fearless challenges to legislators in defence of constitutional liberties'. The consequence of, as Nicol (2006b: p. 750) argues, 'human rights adjudication [being] an undertaking in which the "one correct answer" paradigm of law cannot credibly be maintained' is rather that judges must admit in their decision the existence of the other answers. Legislators and citizens wishing to depart from judicial decisions must in the course of public deliberation argue why the judges were wrong and why the usual compliance should not follow. Overstated judicial certainty will represent powerful rhetoric reducing the reality of choice, whereas judicial modesty will open the door to ordinary electors believing that on this subject their opinions on the common good and society's priorities are worthy, in a democracy, to stand alongside those of judges and other experts. To take a mundane example: experts can determine the health risks of boxing – they cannot determine the rights and wrongs of banning the sport.

20 Chapter 7 'Structural argument for duty of compliance' and Manfredi (2001: p. 184).
21 Chapter 8 'F and Thompson'.
22 Chapter 3 'The framework approach'.
23 Chapter 9 'Conclusion on the common good and proportionality'.

Summary of conclusions

The conclusions that we reach in this thesis are summarised as follows:

i. As between judges and legislators/ministers/administrators it is correct to see constitutional review as giving an invigilatory role to the judges. However, effective counter-control of that power is dependent on electoral support. Hypothesising a general support for the Human Rights Act, the electorate can be seen as invigilating the judicial power, as their support is necessary for legislators to be confident that they can exercise Parliament's legal power to override Human Rights Act decisions without political (electoral) costs. The electorate's power is no less dominating for being rarely used.[24] As a representative democracy, the British Constitution has been constituted to be attuned to the strong preferences of the electorate, and such a light-touch popular invigilatory power is in tune with the electorate's power in the British Constitution.[25]
ii. It is necessary for citizens to confront what they really require from constitutional review in terms of entrenchment and enforcement. If compliance with the Act is necessary for the Act's having the desired effect in restraining politicians and themselves ('the structural argument'),[26] then that should be recognised by a clear decision of constitutional effect.
iii. The present political debates about creating a British Bill of Rights or otherwise reforming the Human Rights Act provide an opportunity to confront the central issue of how the country wants constitutional review to work at the 'participatory' level. Issues of the significance of retaining Parliamentary Sovereignty, and the accountability of politicians for choosing to comply, have to date been at best glossed and often ignored. The electorate needs to know if 'the rules of the game' are that compliance must almost always follow a judicial decision,[27] and what those rules say about participating so as to seek non-compliance.
iv. The argument that the Human Rights Act is needed to fix faults in the British Constitution as regards executive power over Parliament (the 'elective dictatorship argument') should be understood for what it is: an opinion as to what action the constitutive power should take to achieve a particular result. Presenting it as a matter of constitutional maintenance, rather than constitutional reform, is to misrepresent the choice to be taken.

24 In particular, Chapter 3 'The four theorems' (second theorem), above.
25 Chapter 6 'Behaviour within the constitution' to 'Conclusion'.
26 Chapter 7 'Structural argument for duty of compliance'.
27 Chapter 7 'Structural argument for duty of compliance', see Greer and Slowe (2015: p. 383).

v. If the electorate does not wish for the Human Rights Act (or any future British Bill of Rights) to be treated as if it were strong-form constitutional review, then this should be clearly acknowledged in terms of the supremacy of public opinion.
vi. A reaffirmation by the electorate of the Human Rights Act would tell politicians that there will ordinarily be a political cost to overriding the Human Rights Act. It would reaffirm a constitutive commitment by the people to the 'rights' side of the elegant balance. Electors would be saying that they normally prefer legislators to be constrained by the deliberation of a judicial elite.
vii. However, such a reaffirmation that the Human Rights Act should continue in its present terms could also affirm that the electorate is open to participate so as to support the overriding of judicial decisions, asserting its view of the common good over the legalised equivalent reached by judges during expert deliberation. It would be an opportunity to affirm that the electorate saw no illegitimacy in pressing such views, and it could thus give the message that no politician should seek to avoid accountability by pretending that there was no choice.
viii. The internationalising effect of the Convention must be acknowledged. The position is as expounded prior to the enactment of the Communications Bill 2003: an adverse domestic decision may be reason to think again, but an adverse decision in Strasbourg would create an international obligation to comply.[28]
ix. If the Human Rights Act is retained in its present internationalised form, the government should see the ECtHR as a court of appeal insofar as it (not the UK courts) has ultimate authority on whether a domestic decision is underpinned by ECHR obligations. This is of fundamental importance to the question facing citizens as to whether to support the use of statutory override under the Human Rights Act. To this end, the government when choosing not to comply with domestic human rights decisions should see an application to Strasbourg as a test case, and pay the costs of bringing the case.
x. It is likely that any decision to *not* comply with Strasbourg decisions will represent a crisis for the United Kingdom's membership of the Convention.[29] It follows that decisions not to comply will be encumbered with, at the very least, a serious risk of leaving the Convention. In such circumstances, any wish to enact a particular law infringing the Convention would not be reliably compatible with a stronger desire to remain in the Convention. Outside of a wish to denounce the Convention, it would be impractical for a government to be accountable

28 Chapter 2 'European Convention interplay', Chapter 7 'Mechanism of compliance', Chapter 8 'The Communications Bill 2003'.
29 Chapter 8 'International legality' to 'Conclusion on internationalisation ...'.

as to how it negotiates Council of Europe diplomacy should forgiveness be sought for particular acts of incompatibility.[30] Hence, as long as Convention membership remains a priority for public opinion, the 'elegant balance' hypothesis will not apply insofar as the Human Rights Act serves to bring home rights claims which would be successful in Strasbourg.

xi. Despite the Human Rights Act being aimed at achieving a counter-majoritarian effect, the Act's existence and observance should be taken to be rooted in public opinion. If that is not the case, then the Act itself arises out of alien control by a political elite. If the structure of the Act is not to be an attempt at manipulation (itself an example of alien control) – outwardly maintaining Parliamentary legal sovereignty and popular political sovereignty, whilst in fact maintaining only a 'façade'[31] – then the Act's observance must rest on popular support. There needs to be a measure of faith that, whatever 'phrensies' of public opinion there might be, the normal position that faces politicians is that political costs will be exacted for non-compliance. However, there also needs to be recognition that issues may arise where 'highly ranked, intense, stable, and relatively broad preferences of the greater number [of citizens]'[32] will emerge supporting incompatible legislation, and that the political costs may be exacted not in support of the Human Rights Act but instead against legislators responsible for complying with the Act in defiance of public opinion.

xii. The elegant balance ultimately depends on ordinary citizens participating and believing that their view of the common good ought not to be withdrawn from public deliberation purely because of the results of constitutional review. This balance would be best advanced within the structure of the Human Rights Act if judges refrained from the 'usual polemic' of presenting their decisions on the common good as if they were the only possible answer, but admitted doubts and subjectivity, so that their decisions may become part of meaningful public deliberation.[33]

xiii. It must also be recognised that the availability of a meaningful 'elegant balance' is speculative. There is no information as to whether a theory of legitimate breach would lead to an existential crisis for the Act as a means of constitutional review.[34] It may be that in practice a theory of legitimate breach would only be compatible with meaningful constitutional review if the making of breaches were restricted by something other than the limited willingness of public opinion to participate for such ends. There would then be a constitutive decision to be made as to whether to

30 Ibid., in particular 'Internationalisation, statecraft and accountability'.
31 Chapter 2 'Aspiration to uphold democracy'.
32 Chapter 4 'Polyarchy'.
33 Chapter 9 'Conclusion on the common good and proportionality'.
34 Chapter 8 'Atrophication and constitutional review'.

rebalance the Act in favour of rights or democracy. However, to date, the Human Rights Act's experiment in the reconciliation between rights and democracy has been half-hearted, through an unwillingness to apply the logic of an unrestricted power of Parliamentary override. A theory of legitimate breach that is not circumscribed by issues of jurisprudential propriety of the decisions under scrutiny will be a first step to carrying through the experiment – even if the experiment might, in the long term, need to be resolved in favour of one or other side of the rights/democracy balance.

Bibliography

Part 1 – Judicial decisions

A v Secretary State for the Home Department [2004] UKHL 56; [2005] 2 AC 68
A v Secretary of State for the Home Department [2005] UKHL 71; [2006] 2 AC 221
Abu Qatada (Othman) v United Kingdom (2012) 55 EHRR 1
Al-Khawaja v United Kingdom (2009) 49 EHRR 1
Anchugov and Gladkov v Russia [2013] ECHR 638
Australian Capital Television Pty Ltd v Commonwealth of Australia (1992) 177 CLR 106
Barclay v Secretary of State for Justice [2008] EWCA Civ 1319; [2008] EWCA Civ 1319
Belfast City Council v Miss Behaving Ltd [2007] UKHL 19; [2007] 1 WLR 1420
Bellinger v Bellinger [2003] UKHL 21; [2003] 2 AC 467
Belmarsh: alternative name for *A v Secretary State for the Home Department* [2004] UKHL 56; [2005] 2 AC 68
Blood v Human Fertilisation and Embryology Authority [1997] 2 WLR 806
Blood and Tarbuck v Secretary of State for Health (unreported, 28 February 2003)
Bowers v Hardwick (1986) 478 US 186
Brown v Board of Education of Topeka (No.2) (1955) 394 US 294
Brown v Stott [2003] 1 AC 681
Buckley v Valeo (1976) 424 US 1
BVerfG, 2 BvE 2/08 ('*Lisbon Case*')
BVerfGE 39, 1 ('*Abortion in Germany Case*')
Costa v ENEL [1964] ECR 685
Cream Holdings Ltd v Banerjee [2003] EWCA Civ 103; [2003] Ch 650
Ellen Street Estates v Minister for Health [1934] 1 KB 590
Entick v Carrington (1765) 2 Wils. KB 275
Gafgen v Germany (2010) 52 EHRR 1
Ghaidan v Godin-Mendoza [2004] UKHL 30; [2004] 2 AC 557
Greens and MT v United Kingdom (2011) 53 EHRR 21
Hirst v United Kingdom (No. 2) (2006) 42 EHRR 41
Horncastle v United Kingdom [2014] ECHR 1394
Huang v Secretary of State for the Home Department [2007] UKHL 11; [2007] 2 AC 167
International Transport Roth Gmbh [2002] [2002] EWCA Civ 158; [2003] QB 728
Jackson v Attorney General [2005] UKHL 56; [2006] 1 AC 262

Lisbon Case, BVerfG, 2 BvE 2/08
M v H [1999] 2 SCR 3
Mathieson v Secretary of State for Work and Pensions [2015] UKSC 47; 2015 1 WLR 3250
McGinty v Western Australia (1996) 134 ALR 289
McHugh v United Kingdom [2015] ECHR 155
McIntosh v HM Advocate [2001] UKPC D 1; [2003] 1 AC 1078
McR's Application for Judicial Review [2002] NIQB 58
Nationwide News Pty Ltd v Wills (1992) 177 CLR 1
Nicklinson v United Kingdom [2015] ECHR 709
R (Bourgass) v Secretary of State for Justice [2015] UKSC 54
R (Carlile) v Home Secretary [2014] UKSC 60; [2014] 3 WLR 1404
R (Cart) v Upper Tribunal [2009] EWHC 3052 (Admin); [2010] 2 WLR 1012
R (Chester) v Secretary of State for Justice [2013] UKSC 63; [2014] 1 AC 271
R (Limbuela) v Secretary of State for the Home Department [2005] UKHL 66; [2006] 1 AC 396
R (Nicklinson and another) v Ministry of Justice [2014] UKSC 38; [2015] 3 AC 257
R (ProLife Alliance) v BBC [2003] UKHL 2; [2004] 1 AC 185
R v Horncastle [2009] UKSC 14; [2010] 2 AC 373
R v Oakes [1986] 1 SCR 103
R v Secretary of State for the Home Department, ex parte Simms [2000] 2 AC 115
R v Secretary of State for Transport, ex parte Factortame Ltd (No. 2) [1991] 1 AC 603
R v Special Commissioner, ex parte Morgan Grenfell & Co Ltd [2002] UKHL 21; [2003] 1 AC 563
R (on the application of F (by his litigation friend F)) and Thompson (FC) v Secretary of State for the Home Department [2010] UKSC 17; [2011] 1 AC 331
R *(on the application of Aguilar Quila) v Secretary of State for the Home Department [2011] UKSC 45; [2012] 1 AC 621*
Rendall v Blair (1890) 45 Ch. D 139
RJR-MacDonald Inc v Attorney General of Canada [1995] 3 SCR 199; 127 D.L.R. (4th) 1
Roe v Wade (1973) 410 U.S. 113
Saunders v United Kingdom (1997) 23 EHRR 313
Scoppola v Italy (No 3) (2013) 56 EHRR 19
Secretary of State for the Home Department v Rehman [2001] UKHL 47; [2003] 1 AC 153
SG v Secretary of State for Work and Pensions [2015] UKSC 16; [2015] 1 WLR 1449
Smith v Scott [2007] CSIH 9
Söyler v Turkey [2013] ECHR 821
Stockdale and Hansard (1840) 11 Adolphus and Ellis 253
Swann v Charlotte-Meklenburg (1970) 402 US 1
Thoburn v Sunderland City Council [2002] EWHC 195 (Admin); [2003] QB 151
Vauxhall Estates v Liverpool Corporation [1932] 1 KB 733
VGT v Switzerland (2002) 34 EHRR 4
Vriend v Alberta 1998 1 SCR 493; 156 D.L.R. (4th) 385
Washington v Davis (1976) 426 US 229

Part 2 – Books, articles, speeches, and newspaper articles

Ahmed, F., and Perry, A., (2014). 'Quasi-entrenchment of constitutional statutes', 74 *Cambridge Law Journal* 284

Allan, J., (2006). 'Thin Beats Fat Yet Again: Conceptions of Democracy', 25 *Law and Democracy* 533

Allan, T.R.S., (2000). 'Common Law Constitutionalism and Freedom of Speech', in Beatson, J. and Cripps, T. (eds), *Freedom of Expression and Freedom of Information Essays in Honour of Sir David Williams*, Oxford: Clarendon Press

Allan, T.R.S., (2006). 'Publication Review: Our Republican Constitution', *Public Law* 172

Allison, J.W.F., (2007). *The English Historical Constitution*, Cambridge: Cambridge University Press

Alterman, E., (1996). 'A Democratic Foreign Policy', 13 *World Policy Journal* 23

Amery, L.S., (1952). 'The Nature of British Parliamentary Government', in Craik Henderson, J.J. (ed.), *Parliament: a Survey*, London: George Allen & Unwin Ltd

Amery, L.S., (1964). *Thoughts on the Constitution*, London: Oxford University Press

Anson, W.A., (1909). *The Law and Custom of the Constitution, Vol. 1: Parliament*, Oxford: Clarendon Press

Arden, M., (2005). 'Human Rights in the Age of Terrorism', 121 *Law Quarterly Review* 604

Arden, M. (2010). 'Human Rights and Civil Wrongs: Tort Law under the Spotlight', *Public Law* 140

Arden, M., (2013). 'Proportionality: the way ahead', *Public Law* 498

Arora, N.D., and Awasthy, S.S., (2007). *Political Theory and Political Thought*, New Delhi: Har-Anand Publications

Bacharach, P. (1971), 'Introduction', in (ed. Bacharach, P.) *Political Elites in a Democracy*, New York: Atherton Press

Bagehot, W., (2007). *The English Constitution* (2nd Ed.), New York: Cosimo

Baker, J., (2013). 'The Unwritten Constitution of the United Kingdom', 15 *Ecclesiastical Law Journal* 4

Bamforth, N., and Craig, P., (2001). 'Constitutional analysis, constitutional principle and judicial review', *Public Law* 763

Barber, N.W., and Young, A.L., (2003). 'The Rise of Prospective Henry VIII Clauses and their Implication for Sovereignty', *Public Law* 112

Bates, E., (2010). *The Evolution of the European Convention on Human Rights*, Oxford: Oxford University Press

Bates, E., (2012). 'British Sovereignty and the European Court of Human Rights', 128 *Law Quarterly Review* 382

Beatson, J., (2010). 'Reforming an Unwritten Constitution', 126 *Law Quarterly Review* 48

Beatson, J., (2012). 'Legal Academics: Forgotten Players or Interlopers?', *Inner Temple Reader's Lecture Series*, 12 November 2012

Beetham, D., (1993). 'The Limits of Democratization', in Held, D. (ed.), *Prospects for Democracy: North, South, East and West*, Stanford, CA: Stanford University Press

Beetham, D., (1994). 'Key Principles and Indices for a Democratic Audit', Beetham, D., (ed.). *Defining and Measuring Democracy*, London: Sage

Beetham, D., (1999). *Democracy and Human Rights*, Cambridge: Polity Press

Bellamy, R., (2011). 'Political Constitutionalism and the Human Rights Act', 9 *International Journal of Constitutional Law* 86

Berlin, I., (1969). *Four Essays on Liberty*, Oxford: Oxford University Press
Bickel, A., (1962). *The Least Dangerous Branch: The Supreme Court at the Bar of Politics*, 2nd Ed, New Haven, CT: Yale University Press
Bingham, T., (2010). *The Rule of Law*, London: Penguin
Bjorge, E., (2011). 'Exceptionalism and internationalism in the Supreme Court: Horncastle and Cadder', *Public Law* 475
Blackman, O., (2004). 'War on the Law Lords: Clarke defies Decision on Belmarsh Inmates', *The Daily Mirror* (London), 17 December 2004 (www.highbeam.com/doc/1G1-126221823.html, last accessed 25 June 2015)
Blair, T., (2010). *A Journey: My Political Life*, Toronto: Alfred A Knopf
Bodnar, A., (2012). 'Poland: Strasbourg Court holds state liable for failure to provide adequate abortion services', *Public Law* 157
Bogdanor, V., (2009). *The New British Constitution*, Oxford: Hart Publishing
Bohman, J., (2007). 'Nondomination and Transnational Democracy', in Laborde, C. and Maynor, J. (eds), *Republicanism and Political Theory*, Oxford: Blackwell
Bowen, P., (2016). 'Does the renaissance of common law rights mean that the Human Rights Act is now unnecessary?', *Public Law* 361
Bratza, N., (2014). 'Living instrument or dead letter – the future of the European Convention on Human Rights', *European Human Rights Law Reports* 116
Briant, S., (2011). 'Dialogue, diplomacy and defiance: prisoners' voting rights at home and in Strasbourg', *European Human Rights Law Reports* 243
Butler, A., and James, D., (2005). '"We got the balance wrong"; Falconer admits anti-terror legislation broke the law', *Daily Post* (Liverpool) 4 February 2005 (www.highbeam.com/doc/1G1-128087463.html, last accessed 25 June 2015)
Butler, P., (2011). 'It take Two to Tango – Have They Learned Their Steps', Victoria University of Wellington Legal Research Paper No. 136
Carter, V., and O'Brien, D., (2000). 'Constitutional rights, legitimate expectation and the death penalty', *Public Law* 573
Chandrachud, C., (2014). 'Reconfiguring the discourse on political responses to declarations of incompatibility', *Public Law* 624
Choudry, S., and Herring, J., (2006). 'Domestic Violence and the Human Rights Act 1998: A New Means of Legal Intervention', *Public Law* 752
Clayton, R., (2001). 'Regaining a sense of proportion: the Human Rights Act and the proportionality principle', *European Human Rights Law Review* 504
Clayton, R., (2002). 'Developing principles of human rights', *European Human Rights Law Review* 175
Clayton, R., (2004). 'Judicial Deference and "Democratic Dialogue": The Legitimacy of Judicial Intervention Under the Human Rights Act 1998', *Public Law* 33
Cohen, F., (1935). 'Transcendental Nonsense and the Functional Approach', 35 *Columbia Law Review* 809
Colaresi, M., (2012). 'A Boom with Review: How Retrospective Oversight Increases the Foreign Policy Ability of Democracies', 56 *American Journal of Political Science* 671
Collins, P., (2014). 'Labour's had all the luck, but it's going to lose', *The Times*, 14 November 2014.
Colon-Rios, J., (2014). 'Five conceptions of constituent power', 130 *Law Quarterly Review* 306
Conservative Party (2015). 'The Conservative Party Manifesto 2015'
Cooke, R., (1988). 'Fundamentals', *New Zealand Law Journal* 158.

Cooke, R., (1999). 'Human Rights in Hong Kong', 29 *Victoria University of Wellington Law Review* 45

Cooke, R., (1999). 'The British embracement of human rights', *European Human Rights Law Review* 243

Council of Europe, (2012). 'Brighton Declaration' (www.echr.coe.int/Documents/2012_Brighton_FinalDeclaration_ENG.pdf, last accessed 25 September 2016)

Cowley, P., (1996). '"Crossing the floor": representative theory and practice in Britain', *Public Law* 214

Craig, P., (1997). 'Formal and Substantive Conceptions of the Rule of Law: an Analytical Framework', *Public Law* 467

Craig, P., (2014). 'Constitutionalising constitutional law: HS2' *Public Law* 373

Crawford, C., (2013). 'Dialogue and Declarations of Incompatibility under Section 4 of the Human Rights Act 1998', 25 *Denning Law Journal* 43

Dahl, R., and Lindblom, C., (1953). *Politics, Economics and Welfare*, New York: Harper and Brothers

Dahl, R., (1956). *A Preface to Democratic Theory*, Chicago, IL: University of Chicago Press

Dahl, R., (1966). 'Further Reflections on 'The Elitist Theory of Democracy', 60 *The American Political Science Review* 296

Dahl, R., (1971a). *Polyarchy: Participation and Opposition*, New Haven, CT: Yale University Press

Dahl, R., (1971b). 'Further Reflections on "The Elitist Theory of Democracy"', Bacharach, P. 'Introduction', in Bacharach, P. (ed.), *Political Elites in a Democracy*, New York: Atherton Press

Dahl, R., (1989). *Democracy and its Critics*, New Haven, CT: Yale University Press

Dahl, R., (2000). 'A Democratic Paradox?', 115 *Political Science Quarterly* 35

DCMS, (2002). *Political Advertising: Explanatory Note by DCMS*, 10 December 2002 (www.publications.parliament.uk/pa/jt200203/jtselect/jtrights/24/2413.htm, last accessed 25 May 2015)

Dejung, J., (2010). '"Switzerland must be a special democracy": Sociopolitical Compromise, Military Comradeship, and the Gender Order in 1930s and 1940s Switzerland', 82 *The Journal of Modern History* 101

Dicey, A.V., (1899). 'Will the Form of Parliamentary Government Be Permanent?', 13 *Harvard Law Review* 67

Dicey, A.V., (1982). *Introduction to the Study of the Law of the Constitution*, Indianapolis, IN: Liberty Fund

Dicey, A.V., (2008). *Law and Public Opinion in England in English during the Nineteenth Century*, Indianapolis, IN: Liberty Fund.

Dimopolous, A., (2015). 'Balancing disability protection against freedom of speech: should an offence of incitement to disability hatred be introduced?', *Public Law* 79

Dothan, S., (2016). 'A Virtual Wall of Shame: The New Way of Imposing Reputational Sanctions on Defiant States', *iCourts Working Paper Series*, No. 54

Douzinas, C., (2000). *The End of Human Rights – Critical Thought at the Turn of the Century*, Oxford: Hart Publishing

Downs, A., (1957). 'An Economic Theory of Political Action in a Democracy', 65 *Journal of Political Economy 135*

Dworkin, R., (1998). *Law's Empire*, Oxford: Hart Publishing

Dyer, B., (1943). 'Review: The Third-Term Tradition: Its Rise and Collapse in

American Politics by Charles W. Stein', 12 *Pacific History Review* 319

Dyzenhaus, D., (2015). 'What is a "Democratic Culture of Justification"?' in Hunt, Hooper, and Yowell, *Parliaments and Human Rights: Redressing the Democratic Deficit*, Hart: Oxford.

Edward, D., (2008). 'Foreword', 4 *Cambridge Student Law Review* xxi

Edwards, R.A., (2002). 'Judicial Deference Under the Human Rights Act', 65 *Modern Law Review* 859

Elgot, J., (2016). 'UK bill of rights will not be scrapped, says Liz Truss', *GuardianOnline*, 22 August 2016 (www.theguardian.com/law/2016/aug/22/uk-bill-of-rights-will-not-be-scrapped-says-liz-truss, last accessed 25 September 2016)

Elliott, M., (2004). 'United Kingdom: Parliamentary Sovereignty Under Pressure', 2 *International Journal of Constitutional Law* 545

Ely, J.H., (1980). *Democracy and Distrust: A Theory of Judicial Review*, Cambridge, MA: Harvard University Press

Ely, J.H., (1991). 'Another Such Victory: Constitutional Theory and Practice in a World Where Courts Are No Different from Legislatures', 77 *Virginia Law Review* 833

Epstein, R., (1988). 'Modern Republicanism. Or the Flight from Substance', *97 The Yale Law Journal* 1633

Ewing, K., (2004). 'The Futility of the Human Rights Act', *Public Law* 829

Ewing, K., and Tham, J-C., (2008). 'Continuing futility of the Human Rights Act', *Public Law* 668

Fallon, R.H., (1997). '"The Rule of Law" as a Concept in Constitutional Discourse', 97 *Columbia Law Review* 1

Feldman, D., (2002). 'Parliamentary scrutiny of legislation and human rights', *Public Law* 323

Feldman, D., (2015). 'Democracy, Law and Human Rights: Politics as Challenge and Opportunity', in Hunt, Hooper, and Yowell, (2015). *Parliaments and Human Rights: Redressing the Democratic Deficit*, Hart: Oxford.

Fenwick, H., (2012). 'The Human Rights Act or a British Bill of Rights: creating a down-grading recalibration of rights against the counter-terrorism backdrop?', *Public Law* 468

Finer, H., (1960). *The Major Governments of Western Europe*, Evanston, IL: Row, Peterson

Fordham, M., (2011). 'Do we need a UK Bill of Rights', *Evidence to the First Consultation on the British Bill of Rights*, 11 November 2011

Forst, D., (2013). 'The Execution of Judgments of the European Court of Human Rights: Limits and Ways Ahead', ICL-Journal ©Verlag Osterreich

Foster, S., and Leigh, G., (2016). 'Self-defence and the right to life; the use of lethal or potentially lethal force, UK domestic law, the common law and article 2 ECHR', *European Human Rights Law Review* 398

Frantz, L., (1963). 'Is the First Amendment Law? A Reply to Professor Mendelson', 51 *California Law Review* 729

Fredman, S., (2001). 'Scepticism under Scrutiny: Labour Law and Human Rights', in T. Campbell, K. Ewing and A. Tomkins (eds), *Sceptical Essays on Human Rights* Oxford: Oxford University Press

Fredman, S., (2013). 'From dialogue to deliberation: human rights adjudication and prisoners' rights to vote', *Public Law* 292

Friedman, L.M., (2009). 'Some thoughts about citizen lawyers', 50 *William & Mary Law Review* 1153

Friedman, D., (2016). 'A common law of human rights: history, humanity and dignity', *European Human Rights Law Review* 378

Fuller, L.L., (1969). *The Morality of Law*, (2nd. Ed), New Haven, CT: Yale University Press

Fuller, L.L., (1978). 'The Forms and Limits of Adjudication', 92 *Harvard Law Review* 353

Gallagher, T., (1983). *Portugal: A Twentieth Century Interpretation*, Manchester: Manchester University Press

Gardbaum, S., (2001). 'The New Commonwealth Model of Constitutionalism', 49 *The American Journal of Comparative Law* 707

Gearty, C., (2002). 'Reconciling Parliamentary democracy and human rights', 118 *Law Quarterly Review* 248

Gearty, C., (2006). *Can Human Rights Survive?*, Cambridge: Cambridge University Press

Geddis, A., (2011). 'Inter-institutional "rights dialogue" under the New Zealand Bill of Rights Act', in T. Campbell, K.D. Ewing and A. Tomkins (eds), *The Legal Protection of Human Rights: Sceptical Essays*, Oxford: Oxford University Press

Gilligan, A., (2008). 'It was not the Standard wot won it for Boris', *Independent Online*, 5 May 2008 (www.independent.co.uk/news/media/andrew-gilligan-it-was-not-the-standard-wot-won-it-for-boris-821013.html, last accessed 12 August 2015)

Gilmour, D., (1968). 'The Sovereignty of Parliament and the European Commission of Human Rights', *Public Law* 62

Ginsburg, T., and Versteeg, M., (2013). 'Why Do Countries Adopt Constitutional Review?', 30 *Journal of Law, Economics and Organization* 587

Gledhill, K., (2015). *Human Rights Act: The Mechanisms Compared*, Oxford: Hart Publishing

Goldsworth, J., (2000). 'Interpreting the Constitution in its second century', 24 *Melbourne. University Law Review* 677

Goldsworthy, J., (1999). *The Sovereignty of Parliament: History and Philosophy*, Oxford: Clarendon Press

Goodwin, J., (2012). 'The last defence of Wednesbury', *Public Law* 445

Greene, I., (1989). *The Charter of Rights*, Toronto: James Lorimer & Co

Greer, S., and Slowe, R., (2015). 'The Conservatives' proposals for a British Bill of Rights: mired in muddle, misconception and misrepresentation?', *European Human Rights Law Review* 372

Grieve, D., (2014). 'Why Human Rights should matter to Conservatives', *Speech, University College London*, 3 December 2014 (www.ucl.ac.uk/constitution-unit/constitution-unit-news/031214a, last accessed 23 June 2015)

Griffith, J.A.G., (1997). *The Politics of the Judiciary*, 5th Ed., London: Harper and Collins

Grubb, A., (1986). 'Review: Psychiatry, Human Rights and the Law by Martin Roth and Robert Bluglass; Abortion: Medical Progress and Social Implications by Ruth Porter; Maeve O'Connor', 45 *Cambridge Law Journal* 153

Hailsham, Lord, (1978). *The Dilemma of Democracy*, London: Collins

Hale, B., (2011). 'Beanstalk or Living Instrument? How tall can the ECHR grow?', *Barnard's Inn Reading*, 16 June 2011, (www.supremecourt.uk/docs/

speech_110616.pdf, last accessed 20 May 2015)
Hale, B., (2013). 'What's the point of human rights?', *Warwick Law Lecture 2013*, 8 November 2013 (www.supremecourt.uk/docs/speech-131128.pdf, last accessed 13 August 2015)
Hale, B., (2015). 'The Bryce Lecture 2015: The Supreme Court in the United Kingdom Constitution', *Somerville College Oxford*, 5 February 2015 (www.supremecourt.uk/docs/speech-150205.pdf, last accessed 11 June 2015)
Hardin, R., (2004). 'Representing Ignorance', in Frankel Paul, E., Miller Jr, F.D., and Paul, J. (eds), *Morality and Politics*, Cambridge: Press Syndicate of the University of Cambridge
Hare, I., (2006). 'Crosses, Crescents and Sacred Cows: Criminalising Incitement to Religious Hatred', *Public Law* 521
Harel, A., (2003). 'Rights-Based Judicial Review: A Democratic Justification', 22 *Law and Philosophy* 247
Hart, H.L.A., (1994). *The Concept of Law*, (2nd Ed), Oxford: Oxford University Press
HC Debate, (1998a). HC Deb, 16 February 1998, vol. 306, cc. 767–93
HC Debate, (1998b). HC Deb, 3 June 1998, vol. 313, cc. 415–37
HC Debate, (1998c). HC Deb, vol. 312, cc. 1295–1368
HC Debate, (2005). HC Deb 26 January 2005, vol. 430, col 305–323
HC Debate, (2011a). HC Deb, 10 February 2011, vol. 523, cc. 493–584
HC Debate, (2011b). HC Deb 16 February 2011, vol. 523, cc. 959–972
HC Debate, (2012). HC Deb 22 November 2012, vol. 553, cc. 745–761
Hickman, R., (2005). 'Constitutional dialogue, constitutional theories and the Human Rights Act 1998', *Public Law* 306
Hiebert, J., (2012). 'Governing under the Human Rights Act: the limitations of wishful thinking', *Public Law* 27
Hiebert, J., (2015), 'Legislative Rights Review: Addressing the Gap between Ideals and Constraints', in Hunt, Hooper, and Yowell, (2015). *Parliaments and Human Rights: Redressing the Democratic Deficit*, Hart: Oxford.
Hiebert, J.L., (2005a). 'Interpreting a Bill of Rights: the Importance of Legislative Rights Review', 35 *British Journal of Political Science* 235
Hiebert, J.L., (2005b). 'Rights-Vetting in New Zealand and Canada: Similar Idea, Different Outcomes', 3 *New Zealand Journal of Public and International Law* 63
Hiebert, J.L., (2006), 'Parliamentary Bills of Rights: An Alternative Model?', 69 *Modern Law Review 7*
Hiebert, J.L., (2013). 'The Human Rights Act: Ambiguity about Parliamentary Sovereignty', 14 *German Law Journal* 2253
Hilbink, L., (2008). 'Beyond Manichaeism: Assessing the New Constitutionalism' 40 *Comparative Politics* 227
Hill, C., (2003). 'What Is to Be Done? Foreign Policy as a Site for Political Action', 79 *International Affairs* 233
HL Debate, (2011). HL Deb, 16 Feb 2011, vol. 725, cc. 714–722
HL Debate, (1996). HL Deb, 23 May 1996, vol. 572, cc. 1025–76
HL Debate, (1997a). HL Deb, 3 November 1997, vol. 582, cc. 1227–312
HL Debate, (1997b). HL Deb, 18 November 1997, vol. 583, cc. 533–62
HL Debate, (1998). HL Deb, 5 February 1998, vol. 585, cc. 747–842
HL Debate, (2003a). HL Deb, 25 March 2003, vol. 646, cc. 655–790
HL Debate, (2003b). HL Deb, 18 December 2003, vol. 655, cc. 1287–1326

HL Debate, (2005). HL Deb, 22 February 2005, vol. 669, cc. 1102–16

HL Debate, (2012). HL Deb, 5 July 2012, vol. 738, cc. 875–891

Hodges, D., (2014). 'Time for the main parties to stand up to UKIP on immigration', *Daily Telegraph Online*, 24 November 2014 (www.telegraph.co.uk/news/politics/ukip/11249979/Time-for-the-main-parties-to-stand-up-to-Ukip-over-immigration.html, last accessed 29 May 2015)

Hoffmann, L., (2002). 'The COMBAR Lecture 2001: Separation of Powers', 7 *Judicial Review* 137

Hoffmann, L., (2009). 'The Universality of Human Rights', Judicial Studies Board Annual Lecture, London, 19 March 2009

Hogg, P.W, and Thornton, A.A., (1999). 'Reply to "Six Degrees of Dialogue"', 37 *Osgoode Hall Law Journal* 529

Hogg, P.W., and Bushell, A.A., (1997). 'The Charter Dialogue Between Courts and Legislatures (or Perhaps the Charter of Rights Isn't Such a Bad Thing After All)', 35 *Osgoode Hall Law Journal* 75

Home Office, (2012). *Statement by Home Secretary on Extradition of Gary McKinnon*, 16 October 2012 (www.gov.uk/government/news/theresa-may-statement-on-gary-mckinnon-extradition, last accessed 2 June 2015)

Honohan, I., (2009). 'Republican, Rights, and Constitutions: Is Judicial Review Compatible with Republican Self-Government?', in Besson, S. and Marti, J.L. (eds), *Legal Republicanism*, Oxford: Oxford University Press

Hope, D., (2011). 'Sovereignty in Question', *Paper presented at the W.G. Hart Workshop*, 28 June 2011 (www.supremecourt.gov.uk/docs/speech_110628.pdf, last accessed 30 August 2015)

Horne, A., and Walker, C., (2014). 'Lessons learned from political constitutionalism? Comparing the enactment of control orders and terrorism prevention and investigation measures by the UK Parliament', *Public Law* 267

House of Commons, (2012). *Explanatory Notes to Bills: House of Lords Reform Bill*, Introduced to House of Commons, 27 June 2012

Hudec, R.E., (2002). 'Free trade, sovereignty, democracy: the future of the World Trade Organization', 1 *World Trade Review* 211

Hunt, M., (2015). 'Introduction', in Hunt, Hooper, and Yowell, *Parliaments and Human Rights: Redressing the Democratic Deficit*, Hart: Oxford

Hunt, M., Hooper, H., and P. Yowell, P., (2012). 'Parliaments and Human Rights: Redressing the democratic deficit', *Arts and Humanities Research Council Public Policy Series No. 5*

Hunt, M., Hooper, H., and Yowell, P., (eds), (2015). *Parliaments and Human Rights: Redressing the Democratic Deficit*, Hart: Oxford

Ip, J., (2013). 'Sunset clauses and counterterrorism legislation', *Public Law* 74

Irvine, D., (2003). 'The impact of the Human Rights Act: Parliament, the courts and the executive', *Public Law* 308

Irvine, D., (2012). 'A British interpretation of Convention rights', *Public Law* 237

JCHR, (2011). 'Uncorrected transcript of oral evidence – human rights judgments', Joint Committee of Human Rights, 15 March 2011

JCHR, (2013). *Joint Committee on the Draft Prisoner Voting (Eligibility) Bill*, London: The Stationery Office

Jennings, W.I., (1938). *The Law and Constitution* (2nd Ed.), London: University of London Press

Jennings, W.I., (1941). 'The Rule of Law in Total War', 50 *Yale Law Journal* 365

Jennings, W.I., (1964). 'Limitations on a "sovereign" Parliament', 22 *Cambridge Law Journal* 177

Joseph, P.A., (2001). 'The demise of ultra vires – judicial review in the New Zealand Courts', *Public Law* 354

Jowell, J., (2003). 'Judicial deference servility, civility or institutional capacity?', *Public Law* 592

Jowell, J., (2004). 'The rule of law's long arm: uncommunicated decisions', *Public Law* 246

Jowell, J., (2006). 'Parliamentary sovereignty under the new constitutional hypothesis', *Public Law* 562

Kaltefleiter, W., (1970). 'The Impact of the Election of 1969 and the Formation of the New Government on the German Party System', 2 *Comparative Politics* 593

Katz, R.S., and Mair, P., (1995). 'Changing models of party organization and party democracy: the emergence of the cartel party', 1 *Party Politics* 5

Kavanagh, A., (2009). *Constitutional Review under the UK Human Rights Act*, Cambridge: Cambridge University Press

Kavanagh, A., (2015). 'The Joint Committee on Human Rights: A Hybrid Breed of Constitutional Watchdog', in Hunt, Hooper, and Yowell, *Parliaments and Human Rights: Redressing the Democratic Deficit*, Hart: Oxford

Keneally, T., (2008). *Schindler's Ark*, London: Hodder & Stoughton

King, A., (2007). *The British Constitution*, Oxford: Oxford University Press

Kinley, D., (2015). 'Filling the Democratic Deficit', in Hunt, Hooper, and Yowell, *Parliaments and Human Rights: Redressing the Democratic Deficit*, Hart: Oxford

Klug, F, and Wiliam, A., (2012). 'Response by Professor Francesca Klug and Amy Ruth Williams, London School of Economics', *Commission on a Bill of Rights: A Second Consultation*, September

Klug, F., (2001). 'The Human Rights Act – a "third way" or a "third wave" Bill of Rights', *European Human Rights Law Review* 361

Klug, F., (2006). *Oral evidence: Taken before the Constitutional Affairs and Home Affairs Committees*, 31 October 2006 (www.publications.parliament.uk/pa/cm200506/cmselect/cmconst/1703/6103101.htm, last accessed 17 July 2015)

Klug, F., and Stamer, K., (2005). 'Standing back from the Human Rights Act: how effective is it five years on?', *Public Law* 716

Klug, K., (2007). 'A bill of rights: do we need one or do we already have one?', *Public Law* 701

Knecht, T., and Weatherford, M.S., (2006). 'Public Opinion and Foreign Policy: The Stages of Presidential Decision Making', 50 *International Studies Quarterly* 705

Knight, C.J.S., (2009). 'Bi-polar sovereignty: restated', 68 *Cambridge Law Journal* 361

Knight, C.J.S., (2011). 'Striking Down Legislation under Bi-Polar Sovereignty', *Public Law* 90

Kramer, M., (2008). 'Liberty and Domination', in Laborde, C. and Maynor, J. (eds), *Republicanism and Political Theory*, Oxford: Blackwell

Kyritsis, D., (2012). 'Constitutional Review in Representative Democracy', 32 *Oxford Journal of Legal Studies* 297

Laborde, C. and Maynor, J., (eds), (2008). *Republicanism and Political Theory*, Oxford: Blackwell

Laborde, C. and Maynor, J., (2008). 'The Republican Contribution to Contemporary Political Theory', in Laborde, C. and Maynor, J. (eds),

Republicanism and Political Theory, Oxford: Blackwell
Laski, H.J., (1919). 'The Responsibility of the State in England', 32 *Harvard Law Review* 447
Laski, H.J., (1921). 'Foundations of Sovereignty', in Laski, H.J., *The Foundations of Sovereignty: and Other Essays*, New York: Harcourt Brace & Company
Laski, H.J., (1951). *Reflections on the Constitution* Manchester: Manchester University Press
Laws, J., (1995). 'Law and Democracy', *Public Law* 72
Laws, J., (1998). 'The Limitations of Human Rights', *Public Law* 254
Laws, J., (2012). 'The good constitution', 71 *Cambridge Law Journal* 567
Le Sueur, A., (2011). 'Response from Professor Andrew Le Sueur', *Evidence to the First Consultation on the British Bill of Rights*, 11 November
Lester, A., (1988). 'The art of the possible – interpreting statutes under the Human Rights Act', *European Human Rights Law Review* 665
Lester, A., (2005). 'The utility of the Human Rights Act: a reply to Keith Ewing', *Public Law* 249
Levant, E., (2007). 'Judicial Accountability', *Canadian Lawyer*, 1 June
Liberty, (2011). 'Human Rights or Citizens' Privileges?', Liberty
Lindblom, C., (1977). *Politics and Markets – The World's Political and Economic System*, New York: Basic Books
Lloyd, A., (2006). 'The Judges and the Executive – have the Goalposts been Moved?', 18 *Denning Law Journal* 79
Loveland, I., (2000). 'Public law, political theory and legal theory – a reply to Professor Craig's paper', *Public Law* 205
Loveland, I., (2007). 'Public Protest in Parliament Square', *European Human Rights Law Reports* 252
Low, S., (1920). *The Governance of England*, New York: G.P. Putnam's & Sons
Lynch, A., (2007). 'Exceptionalism, politics and liberty: a response to Professor Tushnet from the Antipodes', 3 *International Journal of Law in Context* 305
Magna Carta, (1215). British Library Translation (www.bl.uk/magna-carta/articles/magna-carta-english-translation, last accessed 30 May 2015)
Mair, P., (2013). *Ruling the Void*, London: Verso
Malkani, B., (2011). 'Human Rights Treaties in the English Legal System', *Public Law* 554
Manfredi, C.P., (2001). *Judicial Power and the Charter; Canada and the Paradox of Liberal Constitutionalism*, (2nd ed.), Don Mills: Oxford University Press
Manfredi, C.P., and Kelly, J.B., (1999). 'Six Degrees of Dialogue: A Response to Hogg and Bushell', 37 *Osgoode Hall Law Journal* 513.
Mansbridge, J., (1999). 'Everyday Talk in the Deliberative System', in Macedo, S. (ed.), *Deliberative Politics – Essays on Democracy and Disagreement*, Oxford: Oxford University Press
Marti, J.L., (2009). 'The Republican Democratization of Criminal Law and Justice', in Besson, S. and Marti, J.L. (eds), *Legal Republicanism*, Oxford: Oxford University Press
Masterman, R., (2009). 'Interpretations, declarations and dialogue: rights protection under the Human Rights Act and Victorian Charter of Human Rights and Responsibilities', *Public Law* 112
Masterman, R., (2011). *Separation of Powers in the Contemporary Constitution*, Cambridge: Cambridge University Press

Maynor, J., (2003). *Republicanism in the Modern World*, Cambridge: Polity Press

Mba, O., (2009). 'Positive obligations under the African Charter on Human and Peoples' Rights: the duty of the Nigerian Government to enact a Freedom of Information Act', 35 *Commonwealth Law Bulletin* 215

McLachlin, B., (2006). 'Judicial Accountability', *Law and Parliament Conference in Ottawa*, 2 November 2006 (www.scc-csc.gc.ca/aboutcourt/judges/speeches/index_e.asp (last accessed 4 September 2007, since deleted; reproduced (http://content.yudu.com/Library/A14643/RelevanIssueNo12007/resources/8.htm, last accessed 13 August 2015)

Michelman, F., (1988). 'Law's Republic', 97 *The Yale Law Journal* 1493

Michelman, F., and Sullivan, K., (1986). 'The Supreme Court, the 1985 Term', 100 *Harvard Law Review* 1

Mill, J.S., (1998). *On Liberty and Other Essays*, Oxford: Oxford University Press

Miller, D., (1995). 'Citizenship and Pluralism', 43 *Political Studies* 432

Miller, V., (2011). 'European Court of Human Rights rulings: are there options for the governments?', House of Commons Library, 18 April 2011 (http://researchbriefings.files.parliament.uk/documents/SN05941/SN05941.pdf, last accessed 2 October 2016).

Morton, F.L., and Knopff, R., (2000). *The Charter Revolution and the Court Party*, Orchard Park: Broadview Press

Mulholland, H., (2006). 'Cameron "muddled" on human rights', *Guardian Online*, 26 June 2006, (www.theguardian.com/politics/2006/jun/26/immigration policy.constitution, last accessed 22 May 2015)

Mullin, C., (2009). *A View from the Foothills: The Diaries of Chris Mullin*, London: Profile Books.

Munday, R., (1996). '*Cum Tacent Clamant*: Drawing proper inferences from a defendant's failure to testify', 55 *Cambridge Law Journal* 32.

Neuberger, D., (2015a). ''Judge not lest you be judged': judging judicial decision-making', *F.A. Mann Lecture*, 29 January 2015 (www.supremecourt.uk/docs/speech-150129.pdf, last accessed 24 June 2015)

Neuberger, D., (2015b). 'Magna Carta: The Bible of the English Constitution or a disgrace to the English nation?', Guildford Cathedral, 18 June 2015 (www.supremecourt.uk/docs/speech-150618.pdf, last accessed 23 July 2015)

Nicol, D., (2006a). 'Professor Tomkins' House of Mavericks', *Public Law* 467

Nicol, D., (2006b). 'Law and Politics after the Human Rights Act' *Public Law* 722

Nicol, D., (2010). *The Constitutional Protection of Capitalism*, Oxford: Hart Publishing

Nicolson, H., (1939). *Diplomacy*, London: Harcourt Brace

Nicolson, H., (1946). *The Congress of Vienna, A Study in Allied Unity: 1812–1822*, London: Harcourt Brace

Nussbaum, M., (2005). 'Beyond social contract: capabilities and social justice', in Brock, G. and Brighouse H. (eds), *The Political Philosophy of Cosmopolitanism*, Cambridge: Cambridge University Press

O'Neill, A., (2002). 'Fundamental rights and the constitutional supremacy of Community law in the United Kingdom after devolution and the Human Rights Act', *Public Law* 724

Ontario Deb, (1999). Ontario Legislative Assembly, 27 October 1999 (www.ontla.on.ca/house-proceedings/transcripts/files_html/1999-10-27_L005B.htm, last accessed 2 July 2015)

Otte, T.G., (2001). 'Nicolson', in Berridge, G.G., Keens-Soper, M. and Otte, T.G. (eds), *Diplomatic Theory from Machiavelli to Kissinger*, New York: Palgrove

Paine, T., (1791). *Definition of a Constitution*, London: J. Debrett

Palmer, S., (2008). 'Publication Review: Future of human rights in the United Kingdom: essays on law and practice', 57 *Cambridge Law Journal* 408

Parekh, B. (2000). *The Future of Multi-Ethnic Britain: The Parekh Report*, London: Profile Books

Parris, M., (2013). 'The Tory views you won't hear on television', *The Times*, 30 March 2013

Parris, M., (2015). 'Labour knows its heart. Tony Blair doesn't', *The Times*, 25 July 2015, p. 21

Pedain, A., (2003). 'The human rights dimension of the Diane Pretty case', 62 *Cambridge Law Journal* 181

Pelizzo, R., (2003). 'Cartel Parties and Cartel Party Systems', PhD dissertation, John Hopkins University, Baltimore, MD.

Pettit, P., (1997). *Republicanism: A Theory of Freedom and Government*, Oxford: Oxford University Press

Pettit, P., (2001–02). 'Is Criminal Justice Politically Feasible?' 5 *Buffalo Criminal Law Review* 427

Pettit, P., (2004). 'Depoliticizing Democracy', 17 *Ratio Juris* 52

Pettit, P., (2008). 'Republican Freedom: Three Axioms, Four Theorems', in Laborde, C. and Maynor, J. (eds), *Republicanism and Political Theory*, Oxford: Blackwell

Pettit, P., (2009). 'Law and Liberty', in Besson, S. and Marti, J.L. (eds), *Legal Republicanism*, Oxford: Oxford University Press

Pettit, P., (2012). *On the People's Terms: A Republican Theory and Model of Democracy*, Cambridge: Cambridge University Press

Phillips, N., (2010). 'The art of the possible: statutory interpretation and human rights', *First Alexander Weedon Lecture*, 22 April 2010

Pinto-Duschinsky, M., (2011). *Bringing Rights Back Home: Making human rights compatible with parliamentary democracy in the UK*, London: Policy Exchange

Pitt, W., (1801). 'Resignation letter: Mr Pitt to the King' in Costin, W.C. and Watson, J.S. (1964), *The Law and Working of the Constitution: Documents 1660–1914*, London: Adam & Charles Black

Popkin, S.L., (1991). *The Reasoning Voter: Communication and Persuasion in Presidential Campaigns*, Chicago, IL: University of Chicago Press

Popkin, S.L., (1995). 'Information Shortcuts and the Reasoning Voter', in Grofman, B. (ed.), *Information Participation, and Choice: An Economic Theory of Democracy in Perspective*, Ann Arbour, MI: Michigan University Press

Prebble, P., (2005). 'Constitutional Statutes and Implied Repeal: The Thoburn Decision and the Consequences for New Zealand', 36 *Victoria University of Wellington Law Review* 291

Ripsmann, N.M., (2004/2005). 'The Politics of Deception Forging Peace Treaties in the Face of Domestic Opposition', *International Journal* 189

Rivers, J., (2014). 'The presumption of proportionality', 77 *Modern Law Review* 409

Rivers, J., (2006). 'Proportionality and Variable Intensity of Review', 65 *Cambridge Law Journal* 174

Roach, K., (2001). 'Constitutional and Common Law Dialogues between the Supreme Court and Canadian Legislatures', 80 *Canadian Bar Review* 481

Robinson, W.I., (1996). 'Globalisation: nine theses on our epoch', 38 *Race & Class* 2
Rousseau, J-J., (1988). *The Social Contract*, (tr. Cole, G.D.H.), New York: Prometheus Books
Rycroft, T., (2008). 'The Rationality of the Conservative Party's Proposal for a British Bill of Rights', 1 *UCL Human Rights Review* 51
Sales, P., (2009). 'A comparison of the principle of legality and section 3 of the Human Rights Act 1998', 125 *Law Quarterly Review* 598
Sales, P., (2012). 'Strasbourg jurisprudence and the Human Rights Act: a response to Lord Irvine', *Public Law* 253
Sand, I-J., (2007). 'From National Sovereignty to International Global Cooperation: The Changing Context and Challenges of Constitutional Law in a Global Society', 52 *Scandinavian Studies in Law* 273
Schauer, F., (1999). 'Talking as a Decision Procedure', in Macedo, S. (ed.), *Deliberative Politics – Essays on Democracy and Disagreement*, Oxford: Oxford University Press, pp. 17–27.
Schumpeter, J., (2011). *Capitalism, Socialism and Democracy*, Mansfield Centre, CT: Martino Publishing
Scott Baker, Sir, (2011). The Rt Hon Scott Baker, *A Review of the United Kingdom's Extradition Arrangements*, 30 September
Sedley, S., (1995). 'Human Rights: A Twenty-First Century Agenda' *Public Law* 386
Sedley, S., (2015). *Lions under the Throne: Essays on the History of English Public Law*, Cambridge: Cambridge University Press
Sellars, M.N.S, (2003). *Republican Legal Theory: The History, Constitution and Purposes of Law in a Free State*, New York: Palgrave Macmillan
Singh, R., (1997). *Future of human rights in the United Kingdom: Essays on Law and Practice*, Oxford: Hart Publishing
Sinnott-Armstrong, W., (2003). 'Weak and Strong Judicial Review', 22 *Law and Philosophy* 381
Skinner, Q., (1969). 'Meaning and Understanding in the History of Ideas', 8 *History and Theory* 3
Skinner, Q., (2008). 'Freedom as the Absence of Arbitrary Power', in Laborde, C. and Maynor, J. (eds), *Republicanism and Political Theory*, Oxford: Blackwell
Southerden, T., (2014). 'Dysfunctional dialogue: lawyers, politicians and immigrants' rights to private and family life', *European Human Rights Law Reports* 252
Starmer, K, (2007). 'Setting the record straight: human rights in an era of international terrorism', *European Human Rights Law Review* 123
Starmer, K., (2015). 'The arguments against the Human Rights Act are coming. They will be false', *Guardian Online*, 13 May 2015 (www.theguardian.com/commentisfree/2015/may/13/arguments-human-rights-act-michael-gove-repeal-myth-busting, last accessed 18 May 2015)
Stephenson, M., (2008). 'The Price of Public Action: Constitutional Doctrine and the Judicial Manipulation of Legislative Enactment Costs' 118 *Yale Law Journal* 2
Steyn, J., (2002). 'Human Rights: the legacy of Mrs Roosevelt', *Public Law* 473
Steyn, J., (2005a). 'Deference: a tangled story', *Public Law* 346
Steyn, J., (2005b). '2000–2005: Laying the foundations of human rights law in the United Kingdom', *European Human Rights Law Review* 349
Steyn, J., (2006). 'Democracy, the rule of law, and the role of the judges', *European Human Rights Law Review* 243

Steyn, J., (2009). 'Civil Liberties in Modern Britain', *Public Law* 228
Sumption, J, (2013). 'The Limits of Law', *27th Sultan Aslan Shah Lecture*, 20 November
Sumption, J, (2015). 'Magna Carta and the Déclaration des Droits de l'Homme et du Citoyen', *Opening Address at the Franco-British Council Conference*, 11 June
Sunstein, C., (1988). 'Beyond the Republican Revival', 97 *Yale Law Journal* 1539
Sunstein, C., (2005). *Laws of Fear: Beyond the Precautionary Principle*, Cambridge: Cambridge University Press
Swinford, S., (2015). 'Prisoners may be given the vote because of human rights climbdown, Tory adviser warns', *Daily Telegraph Online*, 1 June 2015 (www.telegraph.co.uk/news/politics/david-cameron/11644188/Prisoners-may-be-given-vote-because-of-human-rights-climbdown-Tory-adviser-warns.html, last accessed 25 June 2015)
Taylor, C., (1999). 'Conditions for an Unforced Consensus on Human Rights', in Belgrade Circle (ed.), *The Politics of Human Rights*, London: Verso
Taylor, M.M., (1995). 'When Are Juridically Autonomous Agencies Responsive to Elected Officials? A Simulation Based on the Costa Rican Case', 57 *Journal of Politics* 1070
Tham, J-C., (2010). 'Parliamentary Deliberation and the National Security Executive: The Case of Control Orders', *Public Law* 79
Thayer, J.B., (1893). 'The Origin and Scope of the American Doctrine of Constitutional Law', 7 *Harvard Law Review* 129
Tierney, S., (2013). 'Whose Political Constitution? Citizens and Referendums', 14 *German Law Journal* 2185
Tomkins, A., (2005). *Our Republican Constitution*, Oxford: Hart Publishing
Tomkins, A., (2007). 'Professor Tomkins' House of Mavericks: a reply', *Public Law* 33
Tomlinson, H., (2003). 'Privacy and expression: Convention rights and interim injunctions', *European Human Rights Law Review* 37
Toynbee, P., (2015). 'MPs should be brave – and finally give us the right to die', *Guardian Online*, 8 September 2015 (www.theguardian.com/commentisfree/2015/sep/08/mps-brave-vote-right-to-die, last accessed 10 September 2015)
Trakman, L.E., Cole-Hamilton, W., and Gratien, S., (1998). 'R v Oakes 1986–1997 Back to the Drawing Board', 36 *Osgoode Hall Law Journal* 83
Tushnet, M. (2003a). 'Forms of Judicial Review as Expressions of Constitutional Patriotism', 22 *Law and Philosophy* 353
Tushnet, M., (2003b). 'Alternative Forms of Judicial Review', 101 *Michigan Law Review* 2781
Tushnet, M., (2007). 'Review: "The Constitution of Law: Legality in a Time of Emergency" by David Dyzenhaus', *Public Law* 604
Udehn, L., (2003). *The Limits of Public Choice*, New York: Routledge
UNHCR, (2015). 'Your Human Rights – What are Human Rights', UNHCR Website, (www.ohchr.org/en/issues/pages/whatarehumanrights.aspx last accessed 25 June 2015)
Van Bueren, G., (2002). 'Including the excluded: the case for an economic, social and cultural Human Rights Act', *Public Law* 456
Van der Rijt, J.W., (2012). 'Non-domination and Dignity', 25 *Library of Ethics and Applied Philosophy* 117
Vermeule, A., (2012). 'The Atrophy of Constitutional Powers' 32 *Oxford Journal of Legal Studies* 421

Walker, N., (2014). 'Our Constitutional Unsettlement' *Public Law* 529

Waldron, J., (2004). 'Compared to what? Judicial activism and New Zealand's Parliament', *New Zealand Law Journal* 441

Waldron, J., (2006). 'The Core of the Case against Judicial Review'. 115 *Yale Law Journal* 1346

Waldron, J., (2009). 'Judges as Moral Reasoners', 7 *International Journal of Constitutional Law* 2

Weill, R., (2003). 'Dicey was not Diceyan', 62 *Cambridge Law Journal* 474

Weyland, I., (2002). 'The Application of Kelsen's Theory of the Legal System to European Community Law: The Supremacy Puzzle Resolved', 21 *Law and Philosophy* 1

White Paper, (2011). *Rights Brought Home: The Human Rights Bill*, October 1997, CM3782

Wiecek, W., (2001). 'Felix Frankfurter, Incorporation, and the Willie Francis Case', 26 *Journal of Supreme Court History* 53, (http://supremecourthistory.org/pub_journal_samples_01.html, last accessed 25 June 2015)

Wilkinson, M., (2016). 'Human Rights Act will be scrapped in favour of British Bill of Rights, Liz Truss pledges', *Daily Telegraph Online*, 22 August 2016 (www.telegraph.co.uk/news/2016/08/22/new-british-bill-of-rights-will-not-be-scrapped-insists-liz-trus/, last accessed 25 September 2016)

Williams, I., (2006). 'Dr Bonham's Case and "Void" Statutes', 27 *Journal of Legal History* 111

Woolf, H., (1995). 'Droit Public – English Style', *Public Law* 57

Wray, H., (2013). 'Greater than the sum of their parts: UK Supreme Court decisions on family migration', *Public Law* 838

Yap, P-J., (2012). 'Defending Dialogue', *Public Law* 527

Yap, P-J., (2013). 'Dialogue and subconstitutional doctrines in common law Asia' *Public Law* 779

Young, A., (2009). *Parliamentary Sovereignty and the Human Rights Act*, Oxford: Hart Publishing

Young, A., (2011). 'Is dialogue working under the Human Rights Act 1998?', *Public Law* 773

Young, E.A., (2002). 'Protecting Member State Autonomy in the European Union: Some Cautionary Tales from American Federalism' 77 *New York University Law Review* 1612

Young, I.M., (1990). *Justice and the Politics of Difference*, Princeton, NJ: Princeton University Press

Yowell, P., (2015). 'The Impact of the Joint Committee on Human Rights on Legislative Deliberation', in Hunt, Hooper, and Yowell. *Parliaments and Human Rights: Redressing the Democratic Deficit*, Hart: Oxford.

Zaillian, S. (1990). *Schindler's List, First Revision of Screenplay*, (www.pages.drexel.edu/~ina22/splaylib/Screenplay-Schindlers_List.htm, last accessed 30 July 2015)

Index